The Inside Story Of The

HARDING TRAGEDY

by Harry M. Daugherty
U.S. Attorney-General, 1921–1924

In collaboration with Thomas Dixon

Originally published in 1932

Reissued by Western Islands
with an Introduction by William P. Fall

WESTERN ISLANDS

BOSTON   LOS ANGELES

THE INSIDE STORY OF THE HARDING TRAGEDY

A Western Islands reissue of a book long out of print, which retains great historical interest and value as a contribution to better understanding of conspiratorial forces currently operating within the government.

Except for correction of obvious typographical and editorial errors, this reprint version is faithful to the text of the original edition, and to the style of the writer.

Library of Congress Catalog Card Number: 75-27054
ISBN: 088279-118-4

"AFTER many years of experience at first hand with the universal and inexplicable quirk in human nature, by which honest and truthful men become obscene liars the moment the name of a public man is mentioned; after running down, as a newspaper man, an infinite number of circumstantial slanders told 'on unimpeachable authority,' and never finding one such story to be true, I have adopted an invariable rule for myself in all such cases. Whenever I hear any scandalous story whatever about a *public man* I instantly say, without any inquiry whatever, 'That is false,' and dismiss it from my mind. It may happen, once in a hundred times (though it never has yet), that I am mistaken and the story is true; but the chances are so much against it as not to be worth taking."

CHARLES WILLIS THOMPSON
In *Presidents I've Known*

IN THE preparation of this volume I have carefully read more than two thousand autographed letters, important telegrams, documents, secret service reports, and signed affidavits.

Every fact has been verified by authentic records which are now in my possession and open to inspection.

It is surely time that some measure of the truth should be told about President Harding and his life.

This book will certainly discredit three scurrilous attacks, entitled *Revelry, The President's Daughter,* and *The Strange Death of President Harding.*

Mr. Daugherty's story is an astounding one. A big, objective, colorful record of the storm through which he passed. Truth stranger than fiction is its substance. It will be a revelation to the American people.

THOMAS DIXON

New York
January 20, 1932

Contents

Appendix Contents

List of Illustrations

Publisher's Introduction

There was one scene in a well-known war novel that was particularly memorable. Its setting was Normandy Beach on the morning of the frightful invasion. A somewhat elderly French couple were depicted sitting in their beachside home, seemingly unaware of — or at least not visibly disturbed by — the heavy artillery fire raining down on all sides as they calmly finished breakfast.

What was so moving about that scene was its dramatic portrayal of the human being's ostrich-like ability to escape painful reality. It could be easily imagined that those two people had begun years earlier when the first threats of war appeared to shut out such unpleasantness from their otherwise serene life. Perhaps, too, they had continued doing so in increasingly greater degree as the horror steadily advanced on them. Now World War II was raging in full fury, unnoticed, only a breath away.

Such a situation seems incredible; yet there are millions of people today in the shrinking free world who, much like that not-so-imaginary French couple, for years have been growing ever more complacently oblivious to their own oncoming destruction. This gruesome prospect is no mere figment of imagination. On the contrary, it is a reality threatening terror on a far greater scale than any actual invasion. And the fall and enslavement of one country after another under the cruel boot of Communism is its visible proof.

Modern-day Communism is a barbaric tyranny that has come to rule over billions of pitiful human beings not by popular demand or conquering armies, but by *conspiracy*. It is, in fact, the product of the most powerful, most ambitious, and most ruthless Conspiracy ever known in history. So it is alarming that western nations, while watching the mass prison of Communism spread, have ignored ample clear warnings that the *same* end was being contrived for them by the *same* determined force. Worse yet, even as those unheeded warnings slipped out of memory, new conspiratorial strands were being spun into the intricate "web of subversion." Consequently, such attempts as have been made to unravel this entangling plot, and to expose its deadly network, for the most part have been hopelessly frustrated.

If the Conspiracy is to be stopped — as indeed can be done — it first must be widely recognized and thoroughly understood. The guiding policy of Western Islands, therefore, has been to help awaken the public to its presence and purpose, by publishing informative, authoritative works that treat important aspects of this menace. *The Inside Story Of The Harding Tragedy* is another such book.

This firsthand account would be fascinating enough just for the little-known truth it brings to light about the extremely vicious campaign to discredit members of President Harding's Cabinet. Even more interesting to readers today is its disclosure that this smear, aimed primarily at Attorney-General Harry M. Daugherty, was engineered by the Conspiracy essentially because of Daugherty's opposition to Communist machinations in America. Significantly, it was the first of many such large-scale campaigns in this country directed against individuals who threatened to expose some part of the Conspiracy's operations. Other victims to follow in later years included Elizabeth Bentley, Whittaker Chambers, Defense Secretary James V. Forrestal, the Danish diplomat Povl Bang-Jensen, and Senator Joseph McCarthy, among many others.

But the most important aspect of *The Inside Story Of The Harding Tragedy* is its authoritative testimony that this conspiratorial consortium already had established tremendous power in the United States, at high levels, by the time Warren G. Harding entered the White House in 1921. Greater power, perhaps, than even its knowledgeable author realized. And so, to help put the Harding tragedy into clearer perspective, we will present this shocking story against the still more shocking background of the era preceding it – the Wilson years.

To do this, however, at least some scant outline of the Master Conspiracy itself will first be necessary for a better understanding of its operations in the early decades of the Twentieth Century.

Attorney-General Daugherty almost certainly never fully perceived the elaborate nature of the cabal behind the attempts to destroy him. What he saw, understandably, was a Moscow-directed plot to overthrow governments of the world – including the United States – by revolutionary force. Actually, however, the Conspiracy already had existed for more than a hundred years when its murderous agents seized control of the Russian Revolution. We cannot here go into its complex but well-documented history further than to say that it was composed not of more or less common revolutionary thugs, but rather, in most instances, of men with established position and wealth, seeking to amass enormously greater power. Very simply, their bold plan from the outset was to create a "New World Order" – a term still flaunted in the vocabulary of world planners – in which the *Insiders* of this elite criminal corps would exercise absolute rule over the collective masses of all the people on the entire planet.

The general scheme for achieving that end — and it has been followed with much consistency — was a perfected "pincer" strategy of "pressure from above and pressure from below"; that is, gradually and systematically to trap whole national populations between the forces of Communist revolution at the bottom and tremendously expanded governmental power at the top. Both jaws of the pincer, of course, would be under the *Insiders'* complete control. Likewise, for use on the international level, a very similar formula had been devised for consolidating their control of the world, long before the public heard of the League of Nations plan. And this, as will be seen, played a major role in Wilson's designs.

It is important to note that throughout most of the first century of the Conspiracy's existence, its agents were subtly but steadily building their numbers as well as their influence in key positions all over Europe and America. More visible, all this while, were the activities of the bottom jaw of the pincer, evidenced by the growing presence of revolutionary forces throughout the Nineteenth Century. Toward the end of the century, however, a new drive was inaugurated to capture the mainstream of academic and political thought by bolder tactics.

Through an organization of their own creation called the Fabian Society, *Insiders* in England attempted to dress Socialism in a cap and gown, making it appear more respectable — even attractive — to the intellectual elite. And the ploy worked. Ostensibly stripped of its barbaric militancy — though remaining essentially the same deceitful doctrine preached by Marxist Communists — Socialism, with all its phony humanitarian appeals, suddenly became a prestigious fashion, one that spread rapidly through higher social levels and soon dominated political trends.

The Fabian contagion then promptly swept into the

United States. The timing was perfect. The country then was beginning to suffer from the normal, temporary dislocations that frequently accompany major shifts towards industrialization, and in this mild state of economic confusion, Americans were more susceptible than usual to the Socialist disease. And quite a few of those who were infected with the poisonous doctrine of the Fabian epidemic were men of established prominence, or destined to become so. Two such figures were Woodrow Wilson and Edward Mandell House.

Enter The Orator

Given the names Thomas Woodrow at birth, Wilson came from Scottish and Scots-Irish lineage, which over many generations had included numerous scholars, theologians, and ministers. In fact, his father was a dynamic Presbyterian minister, and his maternal uncle, Dr. James Woodrow, was a science professor of controversial notoriety at Columbia Theological Seminary. Both men profoundly influenced the future President. In the close-knit atmosphere of his home, Wilson was so steeped in family traditions — to a point approaching snobbish ancestral pride — that he esteemed almost everything bearing a British label as superior. And that definitely included himself.

As a boy he was enraptured by the legendary fame of British statesmen and, after their example, was determined "to have a lofty position" himself one day. That high aspiration, by the time Wilson entered college, gelled into a firm resolution to become a great political orator. For this role he practiced diligently in seclusion, by reciting famous speeches of historical political leaders — mostly British, of course. "The object of oratory," Wilson wrote as a sophomore at Princeton, "is . . . the control of others' minds by a strange personal influence and power."

Both his exaggerated concept of British superiority in virtually all things and his yearnings for personal power increased with age. Nor were the two traits unrelated, as at first they may seem to have been. One biography of Woodrow Wilson notes: "The political system which appealed most to him was the British, and the main reason for the preference was that in the House of Commons, great leadership was a function of great oratory and debating skill. In the United States, on the other hand, the committee system in Congress tended to reduce the importance of discussion on the floor." This explains why, as a student and later as a teacher, he gravitated to school debating societies, and in each instance promptly converted the group into a mock "House of Commons," writing its constitution and installing himself as "prime minister." After the first such experience he wrote to his fiancée of his success and commented: "I have a sense of power in dealing with men collectively which I do not always feel in dealing with them singly."

This is quite revealing about the ego of a college student, particularly one so certain of his destiny "to do immortal work" as a statesman that he prepared cards identifying himself as "Senator from Virginia." (He also experimented at length with various signatures to find one high-sounding enough to be worthy of his anticipated future importance. As a result he decided to drop the "Thomas" from his name.)

Woodrow Wilson graduated from Princeton in 1879 more confident than brilliant. Seeing law as his key to the political gate leading to greatness, and being undaunted by his less than impressive scholastic achievements in college, he promptly enrolled in the law school at the University of Virginia. He received his degree in 1882 and, together with a partner, opened a law office in Atlanta. This endeavor lasted only about a year, with "the potentially great firm of Renick and Wilson doing very little but hoping very much . . . ." More accurately, the counselor was a total failure at the profession of the law. Wilson explained it differently, of course: "I can never be happy unless I am enabled to lead an intellectual life . . . but hereabouts culture is very little esteemed . . . ." So he left "uncultured" Atlanta in 1883 to join the intellectuals at The Johns Hopkins University.

Now we are not attempting to narrate the life story of Woodrow Wilson, but simply to illustrate some of the background and disposition that governed his aspirations as politician and President. And this point in time marks a most important development in his career.

Even though the Fabian Society then was still in its formative stages, the Conspiracy, as noted earlier, long had been active in penetrating key positions of power and influence. For many years, *Insiders* in England had played a leading role in quietly promoting Socialism in political and especially academic realms. Thus it is very likely that Wilson, having breathed deeply of the British intellectual winds all his life, by this time had already inhaled enough toxic fumes of Socialist doctrine to have muddled his political thinking.

In any event, there is no question about his exposure to it at Johns Hopkins. Under the tutelage of Dr. Herbert B. Adams — among others — Wilson's distaste for the American congressional system was greatly augmented. So much so, in fact, that he was inspired to publish that attitude in a book entitled *Congressional Government*, which received wide acclaim and attracted favorable attention from academic *Insiders*. One of these was Prof. Richard T. Ely, a Johns Hopkins faculty member who was recognized as a leading academic Socialist of the day. Ely organized in this country an arm of the Fabian Society called the American Economics Association, which held its founding meeting on September 9, 1885. Historian Rose L. Martin observes: "Minutes of this historic meeting show that the Socialist-minded element at once captured a majority of the Association's elective offices." Notably, Woodrow Wilson was named to its council.

This apparently was the starting point of Wilson's lasting fraternity with Socialists and Conspirators. One member of the Fabian Society acknowledged that "the future secret weapon of strategy would be the university professor." And so the *Insiders*, seeing in the ambitious Dr. Wilson a promising supporter of their schemes, eagerly promoted him up the ladder of an academic career.

A few years, several university positions, and another book later, he was at the Philadelphia University Extension, while also holding a full-time position at Princeton. He headed a circle of Socialists and political reformers, which bowed to British academe as a sort of mecca and attended summer seminars at Fabian-infested Oxford. Included in the group were Prof. Richard T. Ely, Prof. Henry C. Adams, Dr. Albert Shaw, Lincoln Steffens, and William Bayard Hale.

It was, by the way, the "Christian Socialist" William Bayard Hale who, as was revealed in a Senate investigation, held a contract from the outset of World War I until 1918 as a secret agent of the German Foreign Office, at a salary of $15,000 a year. It was also Hale who became President Wilson's "trusted friend" and confidential emissary, and it was Hale who compiled Wilson's book, *The New Freedom*, based on his 1912 campaign speeches. The book denounced capitalism and peddled Socialism disguised as a democratic concept. Significantly, it predicted that "we are just upon the threshold of a time when the systematic life of this country will be sustained, or at least supplemented, at every point by government activity."

The Champion Of Democracy

Wilson's Fabian friendships obviously had much to do with his appointment as president of Princeton University in 1902. And in that position he was able to ingratiate himself still further with the intellectually elite Socialist crowd. His impositions of radically new systems at Princeton, modelled after those being used in English universities, and his writing of yet another book highly critical of our congressional system, helped to make him the most widely publicized university president in the country in the first decade of the century. It was actually this controversial notoriety that brought about Wilson's first realistic opportunity for achieving the political power he had long desired.

Alexander and Juliette George explain the circumstances: "George Harvey, editor of *Harper's Weekly* . . . and a close associate of both political bosses and industrialists, was one of the first to advocate that Wilson be groomed for high political leadership. At a dinner in Wilson's honor in February, 1906, Harvey publicly speculated about Wilson's becoming President of the United States. Newspapers throughout the country quoted Harvey. Many commented favorably on the idea. From that time forth, Harvey energetically championed Wilson's political career."

Harvey's first effort in Wilson's political behalf was to organize the formidable resources of big bankers and industrialists behind Wilson's successful bid to win the New Jersey governorship in 1910. This victory in reality was tantamount to winning a Presidential primary.* Once elected to the governorship of New Jersey, Wilson never broke stride in his campaign race, except to bounce from the springs of New Jersey's well-cushioned gubernatorial chair directly into the national running.

Ellery Queen would be hard put to devise a thicker plot than this one. Harvey was an agent for finance baron J.P. Morgan, who happened to control *Harper's Weekly*. (And who had been educated in England where most conspiratorial roads of this period led — and was tied in no small way to the English Rothschild empire.) Morgan was foremost

---

*Wilson had confided in a private letter: "*My friends* tell me that if I will enter the contest and can be nominated and elected Governor of New Jersey, I stand a very good chance of being the next President of the United States." (Emphasis added)

among the key trust figures who manipulated economic booms and busts as a means of vastly increasing their already great wealth and power. Besides grooming Democrat Wilson for the White House through George Harvey from 1906 on, Morgan also guided and financed Theodore Roosevelt in his third-term bid as a Progressive against both Wilson and the incumbent President Taft.

What we had, then, in 1912, was a Presidential race in which two of the three entries were the property of the wealthy trusts, with J.P. Morgan holding the corporate title to both. The most obvious purpose, of course, was to defeat William H. Taft, and it became evident that Roosevelt was being used only to split the Republicans and thus assure Wilson's victory.

But the plot continued to thicken. Wilson, who had often been touted as — believe it or not — a "conservative" university president, suddenly was inspired by Harvey to establish a more "progressive" image. Immediately after his inauguration as Governor in 1911 he began pressing what the Georges describe as "The sort of legislation which would bring him to the public's attention as an outstanding liberal reformer." What this means is that both of the Morgan-owned and Morgan-financed contenders — Wilson the authentic candidate and Roosevelt the decoy — had campaigned as deadly foes of the very *Insider* trust forces that were running their campaigns. As the Hoboken *Observer* noted: "There is no denial of the fact that Dr. Wilson was induced to enter the race by a combination of the very elements which the Progressives are fighting and that these elements have assumed charge of his candidacy . . . . ." Why would Conspirators deliberately invite opposition from their own hand-picked candidates? Let's examine the situation more closely.

Wilson biographer Arthur S. Link commented in typical Fabian parlance on the public mood of the era: "The [*Presidential*] election of 1912 marked the culmination of more than twenty years of popular revolt against the state of affairs that seemed to guarantee perpetuated political and economic control to a privileged few . . . ." Of course, by "privileged few" he meant the money trusts. In other words, the tried and proven pincer strategy was being skillfully employed once again. Wealthy and powerful *Insiders* had deliberately engendered bitter public animosity toward themselves, as living "proof" of capitalistic "decadence," by means of the economic crises they periodically created. Thus, industry — the symbol of free enterprise — which had continued to raise the standard of living in this country despite the criminal abuses of these ruthless few, suffered as a whole the contempt of a deceived public. And in their confusion, the American people were turned more and more leftward by the radical rantings of so-called "progressives" and "liberal reformers," who insisted that government regulation was the only way such economic injustices could be cured. Needless to say, government regulation and control was precisely what *Insiders* like J.P. Morgan wanted.

But overtones of another, and in many ways more mournful, dirge were echoed in Link's reflective sentiments. The "popular revolt" against a vague image of "perpetuated political control" marked the beginning of a transition which Fabians called "giving the people more voice in government." What it really meant was the gradual conversion of the American government from a *republic* into a *democracy*. While the distinction between these two forms of government is too little appreciated today, the difference is tremendous.

Republican government, by far the highest form ever devised by men, is government "of law and not of men." Democracy is, on the other hand, correctly speaking, simply mob rule by the sheer weight of malleable majority whim. The Conspiracy had very strong reasons for wanting to establish a democracy in the United States. G.K. Chesterton summed them up rather effectively in a single sentence: "You must have a democracy in order to have a revolution." And a Twentieth Century historian (the Duke of Northumberland, in his 1931 booklet, *The History of World Revolution*), said the same thing, more completely: "The adoption of Democracy . . . is fatal to good government, to liberty, to law and order, to respect for authority, and to religion, and must produce chaos from which a *new world tyranny* will arise." (emphasis added)

Woodrow Wilson, however, had reasons all his own for his personal affinity with democracy. They go back to his worship of British government, in which a prime minister of dynamic oratorical skill can wield tremendous power; to his view of "the object of oratory" as being "the control of others' minds"; to his own practical rhetorical skill; and to that "sense of power in dealing with men collectively," from which he derived immense satisfaction. So it was only natural that he would want to replace America's republican form of constitutional government with a democratic state. The first steps in that direction were accomplished under his Administration when the direct election of Senators and women's suffrage became law, broadly expanding the base and power of the popular electorate. With those two hurdles passed, he was well on his way toward destroying the United States Constitution — a job which he continued by appointing a Socialist, his close friend and advisor Louis Brandeis, to the Supreme Court.

It is interesting to note that "liberal reformer" Wilson — probably more than any other American politician in history — audaciously represented his every grab for more and more personal power as being in accord with "the will of the people." In fact, he frequently scolded Congress, when it was slow to act on his proposals, for not obeying "the will of the people." Yet, according to close associates — including Colonel House — and even by his own admission, the champion of democracy seldom read either correspondence or newspapers and had no patience with others — except House — who tried to offer him their views. ("Wilson," House explained, "loved humanity, but he didn't like people.") So he generally was poorly informed of, and had little regard for, the real "will of the people." He was far more concerned with having the people conform their will to his.

No better illustration of this arrogant attitude is needed than his dragging the United States into a war in which the American people, almost to a man, wanted no part.

In other words, Wilson, like most would-be rulers, really considered himself the best judge of what was for the people's good. Moreover, he intended to impose it on them whether they liked it or not. And this is precisely the attitude that was present in every instance, and on every occasion, when he thunderously evoked the high-sounding name of democracy.

Thus, by establishing the basis for an American democracy, first in principle and then in practice, Woodrow Wilson delivered one of the subtlest and most destructive single blows ever struck against the masterpiece of government left to us by our Founding Fathers. In so doing, he was consciously clearing the way for a gradual conversion of the Presidency into a dictatorship by demagoguery, and the Congress into a cabinet. Later, under Franklin D. Roosevelt, the process was given a new impetus that has continued undiminished until the present day.

But Wilson might never have succeeded in his ruinous, self-gratifying designs without the skill, cunning, and perception of another man even more ambitious than himself.

The President That House Built

Wilson was at once pompous, unscrupulous, vain, hypocritical, arrogant, sanctimonious, and extremely zealous. But for some reason he lacked self-assurance — a weakness that gave rise to an unpredictable temperament. That, and his unusually distrustful nature, must have made him a somewhat difficult subject for his conspiratorial managers. Fortunately for them, Edward Mandell House was a master at handling such personalities. And he was able to meet the challenge of Wilson's temperament brilliantly.

Skillful manipulation of political affairs and officials, in fact, was Colonel House's forte. In that capacity, he very likely was without equal in modern history — save possibly for Henry Kissinger today.

"My recollection of Ed House . . . is that he always played the part of a quiet peacemaker," a former college chum reminisced. "Whenever there was a disturbance Ed would silently appear, and in a few minutes — you wouldn't know exactly how it happened — the trouble would be all over." But "Ed" in his later years didn't mind admitting what actually did happen: "I used to like to set boys at each other to see what they would do and then try to bring them around." He explained at another time, "It was a joy to play such pranks and appear to be an innocent bystander."

Alexander and Juliette George, the two eminent psychologists who studied the lives and careers of House and Wilson, say that these nasty little games House played made him "feel superior." For "he could then sit back and contemplate with quiet amusement, an amusement tinged with contempt. To 'control' people, to be able, while himself seemingly calm and unruffled, to turn their emotions on and off at will, gratified him enormously." Note that he differed only in method from Wilson, who likewise wanted "to control others' minds."

The Georges add: "It gave him [*House*] pleasure in those early days, as it did later, to be in possession of special knowledge or power and then toy with those ostensibly in control of the matter. To have his own competence suddenly and dazzlingly revealed without the least show of bravado or self-advertisement afforded him great satisfaction." George S. Viereck confirms their observation about House, the political operator. "His powerful mind," he says, "utilized others. It pleased him to play with human beings, to direct their moves as if they were kings or pawns in a game of chess. A master psychologist, he turned their emotions on and off like a faucet." As to why he chose to manipulate others in politics, rather than to seek office himself, House explained: "I prefer the vicarious thrill that comes to me through others."

Over a ten-year period, in his "urge for mastery" (as author Alan Stang describes it), House was able to "elect" four Texas governors by his powerful but unobtrusive sideline quarterbacking. For this he received the purely honorary title of "Colonel," by which he was called the rest of his life. Yet he soon found state politics too boring, too small-time, and offering too little challenge to his genius. All this while, he wrote, "I had never for a moment overlooked the national situation, and that was where my real interest lay." In scanning the national scene for prospective marionettes, the Princeton University president did not escape his trained eye. Says historian Rose Martin: "From Sidney Mezes — the brother-in-law whom House elevated by political leverage to the presidency of the University of Texas — and from other professional friends, House heard about the battle waged by Dr. Wilson at Princeton in the interests of academic 'liberalism.' " The Colonel, you see, kept cozy company with educational mandarins from British Fabian intellectual society.

For House himself was an anglophile. His father, Thomas W. House, came to Texas from England and — reportedly as a Rothschild agent — amassed a fortune during the Civil War by blockade-running with his own fleet of ships. Edward Mandell House had been schooled in England for several years as a boy and visited the British Isles regularly during both his youth and his adult life.

No doubt it was in this environment of close ties with England that his contempt for the American Constitution was nurtured. According to biographer A.D.H. Smith, House believed that "the Constitution, product of eighteenth-century minds and a quasi-classical, medieval conception of republics, was thoroughly outdated; that the country would be better off if the Constitution could be scrapped and rewritten." It is no wonder, then, that democracy's champion, Woodrow Wilson, also a bitter critic of America's Constitution, kindled a gleam in the Colonel's eye — and vice versa.

So when perennial Democratic candidate William Jennings Bryan finally fell from power, the two anti-constitutionalists, House and Wilson, got together at the Colonel's apartment in New York, in November, 1911. It was love at first sight. The hope that House confided to E.S. Martin of *Life* magazine, "to have someone [*to*] carry out our views as nearly as we can influence him to do so," had been completely fulfilled. His evaluation of his meeting with the pro tempore governor was as follows: "We had a perfectly bully time . . . . It is just such a chance as I have always wanted, for never before have I found both the man and the opportunity." And: "It was remarkable. We found ourselves in agreement upon prac-tically every one of the issues of the day. I never met a man whose thoughts ran so identically with mine . . . . He seems too good to be true." The feeling was mutual. Wilson said: "House is my second personality; he is my second self. His thoughts and mine are one."

And what were these remarkably identical thoughts? They are enumerated somewhat cryptically in a novel called *Philip Dru: Administrator*, which House published anonymously in 1912. The revelations in that "story of tomorrow," in fact, bear so heavily on events in the Wilson Administration that a brief synopsis of it is very much in order.

* * *

Philip Dru is a brilliant young idealist, who graduates from

West Point in 1920 with a burning concern about social justice. He sees America being "debased by the power of wealth under the thin guise of constitutional protection of property," and he observes that this condition has "existed largely by the grace of exploitation — exploitation of men, women, and children." Our compassionate hero is seized with the idea of establishing a "new order of things" to remedy all that scandalous "selfishness." In this "new order," we learn, "the strong will help the weak, the rich will share with the poor, and it will not be called charity, but it will be known as justice." Every man and woman will perform "his duty, not as he sees it, but as society sees it."

After the author has carefully conditioned the reader with plenty of moral-sounding euphemisms, he openly acknowledges that Dru's "new order" of forced "altruism" is really "Socialism as dreamed of by Karl Marx" — that is, "a comprehensive system of state ownership and . . . the leveling of wealth."

The problem is the "defective" American constitution. In its existing form, it unfortunately prevents the establishment of the "much-to-be-desired" Socialist state. And "to have it righted, a century of public education would . . . [be] necessary." But fortune and the gods of social justice are on Dru's side. Ironically, a "mighty conspiracy," involving the President, a Senator, and a "high priest of finance" — a "conspiracy to control the government" — is exposed. The people are infuriated to the point of rebellion. Fearless Philip courageously leads them in an armed revolution against their capitalist oppressors — as humanely as possible, of course, in keeping with the "International Peace Society's" guidelines. The proletarians are victorious. And because "they recognized the fact that Dru dominated the situation, and that a master mind had at last arisen in the Republic," they now naturally turn to this great humanitarian to bring about order and social justice.

Dru sees his responsibility and unselfishly devotes himself to the noble task of "reform" by "assuming the power of a dictator, distasteful as it was to him, and, as he felt it might also be, to the people." For "such a radical step was necessary, in order to quickly purge the government of those abuses that had arisen, and give to it the form and purpose for which they had fought, *i.e.,* "Socialism as dreamed of by Karl Marx." Thus, after scuttling the old constitution, the reluctant dictator follows Marx's prescribed program as outlined in the *Communist Manifesto.* He imposes "a graduated income tax exempting no income whatsoever"; "an inheritance tax"; government control of credit by a new banking law "affording a flexible currency"; government control of industry, with "state and federal officials having jurisdiction on the premises" of all businesses; and nationalization of "certain of the public service corporations." Moreover, his central government takes "upon itself some of the functions heretofore exclusively within the jurisdiction of the States." And in the end, having established the sublime happiness of a Marxist paradise in America, he sails for other lands — presumably to repeat his self-sacrificing performance so as to consolidate a universal New World Order.

* * *

Concerning *Philip Dru: Administrator*, G.S. Vireck wrote that its author, Colonel House, "admits that it formulates his ethical and political faith." Furthermore, "he sees himself in his hero. Philip Dru is what he himself would like to have been. Every act in his career, every letter, every word of advice that passed from him to Woodrow Wilson was consistent with the ideas enunciated by Philip Dru." And there is this comment contained in a letter from House to Mrs. F.L. Higginson in 1915, when he was still concealing his authorship: "I am sending you the book of which I spoke . . . . It was written by a man I know . . . . My friend — whose name is not to be mentioned — told me . . . that Philip

Dru was all that he himself would like to be but was not."*

So Philip Dru, the "master mind" who became a Marxian Socialist dictator of America, was really Colonel House himself — "which," as Alan Stang observes, "would make him, would it not, a Marxian Socialist."

Woodrow Wilson, as we have seen, said that, with regard to "the common cause," his thoughts and House's were "one." The views he expressed in the October 8, 1917 issue of *New York Call* confirm this. Society, Wilson stated, "stood ready to attempt nothing less than a radical reconstruction, which only frank and honest counsels and the forces of generous cooperation can hold back from becoming a revolution. We are in a temper to reconstruct economic society, as we were once in a temper to reconstruct political society, and political society may itself undergo a radical modification in the process . . . ." It becomes clear from his words that this radical reconstruction would necessitate the elimination of our constitutional safeguard of checks and balances against tyranny: "Government is not a machine, but a living thing . . . . No living thing can have its organs offset against each other, as checks, and live." All of which was just Wilson's quaint way of saying that he too was a would-be Socialist dictator.

The truth about the political marriage of these two power-seekers, of course, is that the Colonel ran the administrative household from the outset, always being careful never to let the President realize who really was the dominant partner. As House frankly admitted, "He [*Wilson*] does not realize that there is but little of importance that

---

*Incidentally, there is no question but that Franklin D. Roosevelt was among the many who received copies of the book from House. F.D.R. was Assistant Secretary of the Navy under Wilson, and his mother, Sara Delano Roosevelt, was a long-time close friend of the Colonel. Roosevelt adopted and followed the Dru script in his Administration — including the "fireside chats" — even more completely than Wilson. Significantly, after his victory at the 1932 Chicago convention, Roosevelt went directly to Massachusetts to confer with House.

goes to him, either directly or indirectly, that I have not either passed upon beforehand or at least know about."* How was House able to manage his own personal President so effectively? He simply appealed to Wilson's vanity. As House once boasted to Charles Seymour, all that was necessary to manipulate the President was to suggest that the particular course of action advised would assure him of great historical fame. The Colonel simply poured out the intoxicants that sustained Wilson's fame-drunkenness.

This is what Clémenceau meant when he observed that Edward Mandell House was "the window through which light came to Wilson." As Viereck put it, Wilson merely provided the oratorical eloquence for the Colonel's ideas. He said it gave House "an impish pleasure to remain in the background while pulling his wires." All of which — and more — House himself cryptically admitted to in the person of his character Senator Selwyn, the top conspirator who resided at "Mandell House" in the Dru novel.

Colonel House, however, did more through Wilson's oratorical eloquence than just pay lip service to the Conspiracy's New World Order. Much more.

Marxians In Deed

The Founding Fathers viewed the power to legislate as the most dangerous of the routine powers of government. For that reason, they purposely diffused such power by investing it entirely in the two disparate houses of Congress, and by further subjecting it to the checks — but only the checks — of both the Executive and the Judiciary branches. And there it remained for over a hundred years.

But Woodrow Wilson changed all that. On April 7, 1913 —

---

*Even before the inauguration, for example, while Wilson was off vacationing in Bermuda — a favorite retreat of the anglophilic elite — Colonel House was busy hand-picking a Cabinet for him.

one month after his inauguration – he called a special session of Congress, which then sat continuously at his insistence for more than a year and a half, becoming the longest session in American history. In effect, he installed himself on that date as Supreme Legislator as well as Chief Executive. These combined powers provided the first vestiges of a dictatorship in this country. For through the sheer length of that exhausting session, and through his relentless bullying by threats and intimidation, he was able to wear down all congressional resistance to his self-imposed authority. As a result, *The New Republic* in later years was prompted to comment: "The private individual of Congress is dead . . . . The congressional committees have become less the moulders of legislation than recipients who . . . interpret the executive will; and we have seen recalcitrant members interviewed on policy by the President himself." The fact is that Wilson even had a special telephone installed so he personally could apply pressure to individual members of the Senate.

It was by these coercive tactics that Wilson managed to enact legislation so destructive to the Constitution, and so advantageous to the Conspiracy, that the American people – and the world – have been reeling from the blows ever since. Moreover, those laws invariably conformed to some step in the program laid down by Marx in the *Communist Manifesto* and reiterated by House in *Philip Dru: Administrator*. In Viereck's words, "Out of this book [*Philip Dru*] have come the directives which revolutionized our lives. The Wilson Administration transferred the Colonel's ideas from the pages of fiction to the pages of history . . . ." And Interior Secretary Franklin K. Lane attested: "All that book has said should be comes about." Let's look at some examples.

The Georges note: "The first major issue Wilson wished the special session to consider was revision of the tariff in the direction of reducing protection to American business." The direct attack on free enterprise was immediately obvious in the message Wilson personally delivered to Congress on April 8, 1913. But by the time his "tariff reform" was enacted as the Underwood Tariff Act, the now confiscatory inheritance and graduated personal income taxes had already been established. Marx, please remember, had called for "abolition of all right of inheritance" and "a heavy progressive or graduated income tax."

Also Marxian-inspired were the Clayton Antitrust Act and the Federal Trade Commission, which the Wilson Administration gave us. The result was that the federal government acquired so much arbitrary and contradictory authority in the regulation of private business that one disgusted F.T.C. Commissioner, Lowell Mason, referred to himself as "an administrator of two antitrust laws diametrically opposed to each other," and described such authority as "the modern tyranny of the total state." The unconstitutional federal control of private enterprise through a multiplicity of regulatory agencies has since grown into a tyranny of awesome proportions.

And there were, of course, the direct election of Senators and the granting of the vote to women, which, as mentioned, immensely contributed to Wilson's establishment of a political democracy. That accomplishment being highly conducive to the "much-to-be-desired" Socialist dictatorship which he and House yearned for, Wilson was able to move steadily forward during the war years, with rapacious determination, to complete his grab for absolute rule before his second term expired. The *New York Times* called it "unrestricted power to the President," but the Georges spoke of it more plainly: "When the United States entered World War I, President Wilson openly sought that dictatorial power which his critics suspected he had coveted all along." A.S. Link said that Wilson "virtually bludgeoned" members of Congress to give him such power — to such an extent that several Senators were quoted as saying, "We might as well abdicate." In this manner he instituted measures giving him sweeping control over almost every aspect of American life. Even the *Encyclopedia Americana* concedes that Wilson "established an economic dictatorship under Bernard M. Baruch of the War Industries Board." Furthermore, he virtually nationalized the railroad and shipping industries. He raised income taxes to as high as *seventy-seven* percent on the highest incomes. And he established food controls, price controls, fuel controls, military conscription, suppression of free speech, and many more tyrannical conditions recommended or inspired by Karl Marx. Strangely enough, the *Encyclopaedia Britannica* almost quotes Philip Dru when it says these acts "were distasteful but essential." Essential, we presume, "to make the world safe for democracy."

But of all the domestic "reforms" imposed by the Wilson Administration, seemingly none was more urgent to the Conspiracy's immediate plans than the currency and banking measures. The whole sinister story behind these interrelated measures, while illuminating, is too long for this discussion. But much of it can be projected from a few selected facts.

There is, for example, the fact that the "flexible currency" and central banking schemes both had their basis in one of Marx's prescriptions: "Centralization of credit in the hands of the State by means of a national bank with State capital and an exclusive monopoly." The Federal Reserve System, which Link called Wilson's "crowning achievement" is just such a central bank, fashioned after the Bank of England, with the exclusive power of creating money literally out of nothing to lend to the government, and collecting enormous interest on its loans. Of course such "flexible currency," which has no backing in precious metal, is totally inflationary, is therefore ruinous to the economy, and in short is nothing but legalized theft on a grand scale. Moreover, as Congressman Charles A. Lindbergh, Sr., warned: "This act establishes the most gigantic trust on earth . . . . When the President signs this act, the invisible government by the money power, proven to exist by the Money Trust investigation, will be legalized . . . . The new law will create inflation whenever the trusts want inflation . . . ."

So important were these measures that Colonel House devoted more of his personal attention to their passage than to any other domestic legislation. Shortly after Wilson's inauguration, the Colonel attended a private dinner to confer on the currency and banking issues with representatives of the "inner group of those reigning in Wall Street" — the very ones whose power the "reform" measures were supposed to check. Viereck summed up the outcome of the meeting: "The Schiffs, the Warburgs, the Kahns, the Rockefellers, the Morgans put their faith in House. When the Federal Reserve legislation at last assumed definite shape, House was the intermediary between the White House and the financiers."

We understand why when we see that the Federal Reserve was the same scheme that had failed in earlier years when it was introduced as the Aldrich Bill. Senator Nelson Aldrich was related by marriage to the Rockefellers (he was the maternal grandfather and namesake of un-elected Vice President Rockefeller), and was closely associated in this central banking scheme with Paul Warburg, a partner in the banking firm of Kuhn, Loeb and Company. The Aldrich Bill, in fact, had been formulated with the guiding expertise of agents of the finance barons.

Wilson had once naively opposed the Aldrich Bill for that reason, but according to Viereck, Colonel House "induced . . . a change of heart" in him. Thereafter, he backed the scheme with all the power of his office. When the measures finally were passed, it was House who personally selected the men appointed to the first Federal Reserve Board. They included Paul Warburg.

Wilson's Foreign Policy: A New World Order

Woodrow Wilson himself, for all his colossal ambition, was not farsighted enough to have sought after world rule. At one time he would have been perfectly content merely to become the first "benevolent" dictator of the United States. Probably never having been on the inside of the Conspiracy — or at best, having penetrated only to some peripheral realm of patronizing acceptance — he apparently didn't realize for some time that the Conspiracy's goal was not simply to socialize or communize the separate nations of the globe, but to establish absolute dominion over them collectively. It was Colonel House who showed him the vision of his own immortal greatness as a world liberator.

Unlike Wilson, House very definitely was an *Insider*. As evidenced in *Philip Dru: Administrator*, he not only was fully cognizant of the Conspiracy's plan for a New World Order, but he knew precisely how it was to be achieved.* Primary among his conspiratorial functions, it would seem, was the job of guiding the pious pedagogue in the White House into playing out one of the key roles in this sordid drama.

When problems boiled up in the politically unsettled Latin American nations, Wilson needed little provocation from the Colonel to attempt to impose his lofty idealism on their peoples. He was unsuccessful. But as a result of his reckless meddling, and of House's devious scheming, conditions were ripened for the rise of Communist intrigue in Mexico and other countries to our south. More important, however, these

---

*Both the war and the League of Nations figured in the plot of this book, written in 1911. In fact, the book is so "prophetic" that a prototype of the Watergate scenario is found in the chapter entitled "The Exultant Conspirators." Which proves once again that there is really nothing new under the Conspiratorial sun.

actions disastrously put an end to the United States Government's sound and long-standing policy of minding its own political business. Thereafter, Colonel House had no difficulty in nurturing Wilson's belief that he was destined by God to democratize the whole human race. And as "luck" would have it, the war in Europe erupted at just about the same time.

History books thoroughly treat many of the factors considered to be the general causes for the outbreak of World War I. In this discussion, however, we are concerned with only one factor, and one which is totally overlooked by most historians. That is the fact that agents of the Master Conspiracy long since had spread throughout Europe and could be found exercising tremendous power over the affairs of governments on both sides of the war. The extent to which they were involved in precipitating this spectacular conflict, we believe, can be surmised from Karl Marx's observation that a general war in Europe would provide the ideal opportunity for bringing Socialism to power. In light of this, it seems unlikely to have been through sheer coincidence that thirty nations were teetering on the brink of active hostilities among themselves all at the same time.

The truth is that the war was intended to serve primarily as the means of driving the major nations into a world-government trap. In other words, it was another variation of the pincer strategy. For by deliberately sustaining all the suffering and destruction of this massive conflict for five long years — which certainly was no easy accomplishment with Germany almost begging for a settlement, as she began to do after only two years — the peoples of every country involved were conditioned to accept almost any terms that would restore peace. Especially terms that promised eternal peace as well as "democracy" — as it was commonly *mis*understood — for all the world.

And of course it was Woodrow Wilson — inspired,

encouraged, and guided every step of the way by E.M. House — who emerged in the midst of the holocaust as the great spiritual leader and champion of "democracy" who would deliver all nations into the millennium by way of the League of Nations. That he clearly knew that in this role he was serving the Conspiracy's plans for his own gain could be easily proved, if space permitted the use of the abundance of illustrations that are available. Among these is the fact that every one of the numerous biographies we have examined repeatedly refers to Wilson's ambition to establish a "new world order" — the very term that has been reiterated by *Insiders*, from the time of the founding of the Master Conspiracy in 1776 down to the present day, as their ultimate objective. But there is too little space left to record more than a few such illustrations as they occur in the rest of this brief assessment of Wilson's foreign policy.

In the early years of the war, the President devoted much of his attention to domestic matters, leaving the bulk of foreign meddling to Colonel House's sinister scheming. From the outset, however, Wilson attempted to impose himself as a wise and father-like mediator between the belligerent powers. And both men all this time were doing everything possible to perpetuate the destructive conflict long enough for Wilson to drag the United States into it at the proper moment, even while going through elaborate but hypocritical motions of trying to bring about a settlement. All of which, of course, was essential to enable him to ride triumphantly across a shattered and war-weary Europe, proclaiming himself as the great peacemaker and founder of a New World Order under the League of Nations.

Altogether this three-part scheme was no easy juggling feat for Wilson and House. In the first place, there was the problem of maintaining a pose of neutrality before the American people, who adamantly wanted nothing to do with the war. It would take time to maneuver the United States carefully into a foreign conflict in which we had absolutely no business, without ruining the whole plot. And to do that, Wilson first would have to be reelected.

Another problem was containing the eagerness of England, which, by deliberate acts far more provocative than Germany's *retaliatory* submarine warfare, was trying to goad America into the war prematurely. England's behavior was so outrageous, in fact, that Wilson was almost tempted to declare war on the British Empire. The touchy situation was relieved by the House-Grey Memorandum, which pledged American intervention on the side of the Allies if Germany would not come promptly to the peace table. This agreement was approved by Wilson eight months *before* the 1916 election. (Bear in mind that his audacious campaign slogan that year was: "He kept us out of war!")

The House-Grey agreement led to the third problem briefly mentioned earlier. This was that war-weary Germany was much too eager to surrender. And that would have spoiled everything. Not only would it have upset the Conspiracy's scheme of a League of Nations as a physical foundation for a one-world empire. It also would have foiled another of its three principal purposes in contriving the First World War: the complete destruction of the German nation. The Conspiracy at one time had been centered in Germany, where it had hoped to establish through revolution a Communist beachhead for all of Europe. Not only did the plan fail, but Germany by the turn of the century, with her advanced technology and industry, rapidly was becoming a model of free enterprise.

If the Germans had been allowed to surrender at this point in the war, it would have been by negotiated peace terms, which necessarily would have allowed far less than complete emasculation of their industrial economy. But the problem was held in abeyance, largely by the cunning of Colonel

House and the diplomatic foot-dragging of Sir Edward Grey, long enough for a remedy to be secured. That remedy was the collapse of Russia, which momentarily freed Germany on the eastern front, and thus gave her renewed vigor for sustaining her war effort.

The fall of the Russian regime marked the first step toward achievement of the Conspiracy's third major objective in World War I — the long-awaited establishment of its first Communist base. Wilson and House again figured mightily in this cause. For the same powerful *Insiders* who had "put their faith in House" and their enormous campaign support behind Wilson were also financing the two murdering thugs who seized control of the Russian Revolution — Lenin, who with Warburg help was returned to Russia with an estimated five million dollars, and Trotsky, who left New York with some twenty million dollars of Wall Street backing, according to Jacob Schiff's grandson.

So it was not surprising that, when Trotksy and his entourage of almost three hundred revolutionaries were detained en route to Russia by the Canadian government, President Wilson promptly intervened through House and Grey to obtain the Communists' release. Nor is it surprising that a good friend and supporter of Wilson's, Charles R. Crane, helped to organize both the Kerensky Revolution and the Bolshevik Revolution. The President's liaison with Crane at the time was another crony from Wilson's circle of Socialists at the Philadelphia University Extension, the Communist Lincoln Steffens. And it is also no surprise that Colonel House cabled the President from Paris, telling him it was "exceedingly important" that newspaper reports unfavorable to the Communist Revolution "should be suppressed." Nor should we be surprised that Wilson acted on this advice; that he further ordered no interference with the Revolution; and that he immediately initiated the first "bridge-building" program of trade with the Communists in order to sustain them economically in power.

Finally there is the matter of Wilson's great Peace Plan — or rather, the Peace Plan that was reputed to be his. Actually, there was nothing in either the Fourteen Points or the League of Nations that was his own, except for some thunderous verbiage. The Fourteen Points were originally written in England years earlier by the arch Fabian Conspirator, Sidney Webb. Colonel House secretly assembled a committee in New York to tailor the Webb plan for use at the Paris Peace Conference. The committee, dubbed The Inquiry, included House's brother-in-law Sidney Mezes, Fabian Socialist Walter Lippmann, Socialist Norman Thomas, and other like-minded radicals, mostly from academic society.

As for the League of Nations idea, Ray Stannard Baker, Wilson's official biographer, wrote that "practically nothing — not a single idea — in the Covenant of the League was original with the President." Baker should have known. Not only was he press chief at the Paris Conference, but he had also been assigned by Colonel House to "report fully for the information of the President and the State Department on the state of radical opinion and organization, especially the attitude of labor in England . . . ." On that mission, he sought out and was welcomed by the British Labour Party, which was owned and operated by the Fabian Society. Historian Rose Martin records: "As Sidney Webb's honored guest, Baker was present at the fateful conference of June, 1918, when the British Labour Party was formally constituted under Fabian Socialist control and adopted Webb's blueprint for chaos, *Labour and the New Social Order*, as its platform." Baker thus was in an ideal position to learn about the Fabian concept of an international government, and to enlighten Wilson and House as to the Labour Party's plans for bringing it into being. Not to be outdone at his own game, House simply redrafted the Fabian version and introduced it through Wilson as the League of Nations. The President, now swollen with self-importance, claimed it as his own and presented the masterpiece to the world for adulation and acceptance.

But Woodrow Wilson's megalomania was his undoing. His passion for personal power had come to exceed and conflict with the Master Conspiracy's strategy of patient gradualism. As Colonel House wrote in his diary, "The President has nearly destroyed all the work I have done in Europe." Wilson had become so blinded by his own sense of power that he felt he could simply order the Senate to ratify "his" League of Nations unaltered in even the slightest detail. The League failed. And thereafter, so did Wilson. But he had never been more than a highly useful yet expendable tool.

The Conspiracy, on the other hand, survived the temporary and relatively minor setback that Wilson had dealt to its plans. Allowing a little time to cool the American public's indignation over Wilson's dictatorially imposed "idealism," the *Insiders* were soon back on course and running full steam ahead.

As for Colonel House himself, his personal dreams were fulfilled. He was able to boast in 1938: "During the last fifteen years I have been close to the center of things, although few people suspect it. No important foreigner has come to America without talking to me." In other words, he was back in power right after President Harding's death. A few years later, he "elected" another Wilson — one by the name of Roosevelt. "I was close to the movement that nominated Roosevelt . . . . He has given me a free hand in advising Hull [*the Secretary of State*]. All the Ambassadors have reported to me frequently." And we can see the fingerprints of House's "free hand" in the repeat performance of Roosevelt's dictatorial Presidency, World War II, and the United Nations.

But in those years immediately following Wilson's collapse of power, the Conspiracy faced an urgent danger. The American public's thinking, in the wake of the Wilson dictatorship, was flowing swiftly and strongly back toward normalcy and away from Socialist currents. With a loyally American President like Warren Gamaliel Harding and a staunchly anti-Communist Attorney General like Harry M. Daugherty helping to guide that thinking, something had to be done — and it was done. The following pages relate this tragic story.

William P. Fall

April 9, 1975

The Inside Story of the
HARDING TRAGEDY

CHAPTER I

By Way of Introduction

FOR three important reasons I have been silent until now.

The desire to see President Hoover, who owed his position to Warren G. Harding, dedicate for the Nation the Memorial built at Marion, Ohio.

A feeling that I ought not to discuss Albert B. Fall, or his case, until it had been finally disposed of by the courts.

And a personal reluctance to enter the field of political and historical controversy.

Mr. Hoover dedicated the monument on June 16, 1931, Albert B. Fall's case has been settled by his imprisonment, and the flood of scurrilous books continues to flow.

I feel, at last, that I must speak, telling for the first time the true story of the nomination and election of Warren G. Harding, the important struggles and achievements of his administration, and his tragic death.

I am, perhaps, the only living man who knows the facts.

The story will be told, not in justification or defense of my own life, or in apology for his, but as a duty to the American people.

It is the glory of our Republic that in all its history no dishonest or disreputable man has ever been President of the United States.

That Warren Harding's name should have been dragged through the mire since his death by a pack of wolves and jackals is an accident of the passions of a tragic era of Reconstruction, a period of temporary insanity which followed the World War.

It is a passing phase.

Harding's place in history is secure.

When the last obscene literary scavenger has uttered his dying howl, the figure of one of the knightliest, gentlest, truest men who ever lived in the White House will emerge from the din of slander and take his rightful place in the hearts of our people.

The American, deep down, loves fair play.

For a time he may listen to the clamor of fools and chuckle over vicious slander. But in the end he demands the truth.

In this hour, close to the events, it is inevitable that our people should for the moment forget that Harding appointed more than fifty thousand men and women to public office, among them many of the greatest minds of the Nation. But three of them, holding important positions, proved false to their trusts in a time of abnormal conditions following war.

We remember only these three.

Harding was most sadly betrayed by many who profited by his generosity and remained silent while jackals howled. It will certainly ever remain a disgrace to American politics that the beautiful tomb built by our people to Warren Harding's memory stood undedicated for years.

As a Trustee of the Memorial Association I was seated directly behind President Hoover on the platform the day he spoke at the dedication exercises, and heard the following curious sentences fall from his lips amid a painful silence:

And we came also to know that here was a man whose soul was

being seared by a great disillusionment. We saw him gradually weaken not only from physical exhaustion but from mental anxiety. Warren Harding had a dim realization that he had been betrayed by a few of the men whom he had trusted, by men whom he had believed were his devoted friends. It was later proved in the courts of the land that these men had betrayed not alone the friendship and trust of their stanch and loyal friend but they had betrayed their country. That was the tragedy of the life of Warren Harding.

About this speech Governor Patterson of Tennessee has expressed my feelings exactly:

The President's address struck the one discordant note in the solemn and impressive ceremonies. It was wholly uncalled for and inappropriate. It served no good purpose whatever.

Mr. Hoover, of course, did not apply his words to me. His attack on Harding's betrayers carried the qualifying clause that their guilt was "later proved in the courts of the land." No charge against me was ever proven in any court, and Mr. Hoover knew this.

Certainly my relations with President Harding could have contributed in no way, to either his collapse or his disillusionment.

The day before he left Washington on his trip to Alaska he called on me to help him clear his desk. For three hours we worked together disposing of accumulated business.

When we finished, he asked me to draw for him a new will. This I did and signed it as one of the witnesses. It was my last personal service to him. We discussed his trip and he again expressed disappointment that I was not to accompany him. From the beginning he had urged me to go, but finally concluded that, inasmuch as most members of his Cabinet would be away, it was advisable that I remain in or near Washington. We arranged, however, that I should meet him in Seattle and continue with him on the rest of the trip.

Surely these incidents prove the continuance to the last of the cordial, confidential relations of over a quarter of a century's duration.

Mr. Hoover's statement was misapplied by thoughtless people. It struck me as unfortunate from every point of view. And I was not surprised to read Senator Thomas Walsh's caustic comments the following day:

> Was Mr. Hoover's information, that the President had a dim realization that he, and the country as well, had been betrayed, acquired before or after the death of Harding?
> If after, who was his informant? And if before, why did Mr. Hoover remain inactive, being one of the Constitutional advisers of the President?

Incidentally it will be my duty in the course of this book to answer the Senator's questions.

I lay no claim to infallibility or sainthood. As a humble member of the Methodist Church, I sometimes fall from grace, ask the Lord to forgive, and try again. I can only promise always to speak from the fullness of personal experience and deep conviction.

I confess that I am, and always have been, a practical politician, though not a professional one. As I understand it, practical politicians created this Republic and make its continued existence possible. Fizzling pinwheels of so-called reform and progress, as a rule, splutter for a brief moment in history and go out in darkness. For this reason I've never affiliated myself with so-called "progressives." And thereby hangs a tale that I will also tell.

In fifty years of political activity naturally I have made enemies. Some of them remain.

In Ohio, rival leaders in the Republican Party have always fought each other with more ferocity than they fight Democrats.

I was offered positions on the bench by two Presidents and

United States Attorney-General, 1921-1924.

The Harding Memorial

President Hoover Dedicating the Harding Memorial

"Warren Harding had a dim realization that he had been betrayed by a few of the men whom he had trusted."

refused them, having grown to love the battles on the floor of a convention. I became a political leader instead of an officeholder — from choice.

In this I was a true son of Ohio, the battleground of the Nation.

I frankly confess to a leadership in the so-called "Ohio Gang" for about forty years.

On the lips of rival politicians the term "Ohio Gang" is an epithet. I wear its badge as a mark of honor:

For a hundred years the dominant group of politicians from my State have been the ablest strategists in America. They have nominated and elected eight Ohio men to the Presidency out of a total of thirty-one who have served since the foundation of the Republic. Virginia alone can count as many.

There's a reason for this power.

Ohio was the first great pioneer State created after the formation of the original Union. It was peopled by the best blood of New England, New York, Pennsylvania and Virginia. My grandfather moved from Richmond, Virginia, into Ohio about 1802.

When the State was twelve years old her "Gang" in the War of 1812 numbered a division of six thousand well-armed men, the largest army from any northern state.

Her "Gang" of '61-'65 numbered 350,000 soldiers of the Union. And she furnished every commanding general of first rank. Edwin M. Stanton of Ohio was the greatest Secretary of War who ever held office. And under his direction Generals McDowell, McClellan, McPherson, Sheridan, Sherman, and Grant — all Ohio men — led the North to victory and saved the Union.

In spite of the wealth and greater number of people in New York, Ohio is still *the* pivotal State of the Nation. Neither Democratic nor Republican, it contains an immense mass of independent voters. It is the battleground of the

Republic where contending forces from North, South, East and West first clash.

Ohio, therefore, has always been the training ground of political athletes.

And here have developed the most compact and powerful political machines, made necessary by our system of party government. They must face daily the menace of the independent voter. They must not only be strong, loyal, and efficient; they must also be honest or they can't survive.

Here the free-thinking, pioneer brain was raised by culture to the highest efficiency.

Our Rockefeller group revolutionized American trade and industry by substituting the principle of cooperation for cut-throat competition.

Our inventors, led by Edison and Brush, relighted the world and reunited its peoples in the new universal language of the motion picture.

The Wrights of Dayton, Ohio, created modern aviation, and blazed new pathways of travel and commerce through the skies.

The Anti-Saloon League of Westerville, Ohio, destroyed the saloon, and enacted the Eighteenth Amendment.

If the political strategists of Ohio who led in nominating Harding for the Presidency are criminals, our system of government is a crime.

Our enemies have spoken, early and late, and often. But there are two sides to every question. I am going to tell now the truth, and *nothing but the truth.*

CHAPTER II

How and Why Harding Was Selected

WE LIVE in a hard-boiled age. No man in this country is ever called to the Presidency by the clamor of millions. No man is so great in our democratic society that his name excites the masses. All Presidents are made by organization. Our system of party government makes this inevitable.

And I believe in our system of government. I believe it a great advance on the old world methods of governing by a combination of factional groups.

Our candidates for the highest office in the gift of the people usually select themselves. Or a political leader sees in his favorite statesman a presidential possibility, grooms him quietly for the office, and springs him on the party at the right moment.

The idea that Presidents are made by a spontaneous outburst of public opinion is no longer believed except by a few amateur political writers.

The nearest approach to a spontaneous call in our history was the first nomination of Bryan which followed his eloquent outburst on the floor of the convention. We have since heard that this piece of fireworks was a carefully laid plan by his political manager, and that every sentence of Bryan's speech had been carefully rehearsed.

Certainly no convention since Bryan's day has dared to repeat this kind of performance. The explosion of emotion among the delegates that swept Mr. Bryan into the limelight wrecked his party and held it on the rocks for a generation.

No Democratic convention will ever again yield to

7

"spontaneity." The Republican Party has always had better judgment.

In the winter of 1914 when Senator Foraker of Ohio announced his candidacy for re-election, I was sure he could not win under the conditions that had developed.

It was Harding's chance to make good his own defeat for the Governorship of Ohio.

I wired him to come to Columbus and urged him to enter the Senatorial fight. At my suggestion he saw Foraker. They were friends and after Harding had announced his candidacy they parted friends.

He entered the contest and began to stump the State.

A few weeks later I met him on the street in Columbus, the picture of despair. He had just come from a mass meeting in the southern part of the State where he had made a great speech that was poorly reported. It was raining torrents. He wore an old raincoat, and from the crown of his magnificent head to the wet soles of his shoes, he was a bedraggled sight.

"What's the matter?" I asked.

"Harry, it's awful," he sighed.

"Awful — what's awful?"

"This stumping the country and howling for myself."

"Who else would you howl for? Foraker?"

"I'm discouraged — disgusted. I'm going home and go to bed."

"Yes, you will!" I laughed. "You're going to stick and win. I'll make you a bet — "

Harding's eyes sparkled and his face flushed. He loved to bet. He was always betting me a dollar or two on something.

"You must feel pretty sure!"

"So sure that I'll bet you two suits of clothes — choose your own tailor and the goods — that you'll carry Ohio in this primary."

He smiled and gave me his hand.

He was elected by a hundred thousand plurality.

And the day after the election he walked into my office smiling:

"Go to your tailor's and order the two suits of clothes."

"Nonsense!" I laughed. "I didn't make the bet to win the suits. I made it to cheer your drooping spirits. Forget it."

We often joked about this bet.

As the time drew near for the 1916 Presidential convention we wanted Harding to be known to the delegates.

Half of them would certainly return in 1920.

As Chairman, making the opening speech — and principal speech — he would make a deep impression.

We secured his election as presiding officer.

When he took the gavel, rapped for order and made his vigorous opening address, the hall buzzed with excited comments.

"What a voice!"

"What a man!"

"He's magnificent!"

"He looks like a President."

"He talks like a President."

"He's going to be one."

I was not surprised that he received a few enthusiastic votes — but advised him to pay no attention to them. He stood squarely for Hughes and frowned on all attempts to launch his own name.

Exactly the same thing had occurred with McKinley at Minneapolis in 1892. I had advised McKinley strongly against any demonstration in behalf of his name. Our delegates were pledged to Harrison.

But when the roll was called on the first ballot. Colonel Robert M. Nevin of Dayton cast the entire Ohio vote for McKinley. Nevin was Acting Chairman in the absence of McKinley, who was presiding over the convention.

McKinley challenged the vote of Ohio, asked that the

delegates be polled, and when it came to his name he announced his vote for Harrison, who won. And four years later McKinley was nominated at St. Louis.

A curious coincidence.

McKinley presided over the convention that named Harrison in 1892 and was elected President in 1896. Harding presided over the convention of 1916 and was elected President in 1920. And both men suppressed premature demonstrations in their own favor.

Every man in the convention went home with a vivid picture of the man Warren Harding in his imagination. At least four hundred of them would likely come back in 1920 to name the new leader. He was in great demand as a speaker for Hughes in 1916, and made enthusiastic friends.

My next move led to our first and only quarrel. A group of Republican state leaders, dominated by the saloon crowd of Cincinnati, had fought Harding tooth and nail for years. They had helped defeat him for the Governorship by a hundred thousand majority. They had done their best to defeat him for the nomination for the Senate.

Harding's method was always one of conciliation. He believed he could convert and win his enemies.

Accordingly in the approaching state convention he had made overtures, without my knowledge, to his foes, and promised to place one of them at the head of the state organization. When I heard of this agreement I asked him:

"You don't mean this?"

"Certainly," he replied. "I thought it wise and satisfactory to you."

"And you never breathed a word of it to me!"

"I felt sure of your approval. You think it a mistake?"

"It's suicide."

"In that case I might withdraw the offer."

"No. That would be worse, if you've promised them — have you?"

"Yes. I've promised."

"All right, keep your promise. No man can ever get anywhere in politics unless he keeps his promises."

"What will you do?" he asked.

"There's but one thing to do. Organize our forces — your real friends, of course — smash your enemies, and put the right men in control of the state machine. You can't trust the gang you've tried to make up with. They've betrayed you twice. They will betray you again.

"I think they'll play fair this time," he interrupted.

"Yes — you *would* think that!" I laughed. "You're too straight and genial and kind to believe in treachery. I've met traitors face to face. I've met them in battle many a dark night. They can't fool me with smiles and promises."

"What shall I do?" he asked with a trace of anxiety.

"Nothing. Just sit still and let your real friends do it."

He chuckled genially and made no comment as I continued:

"This time I've got to fight you. The first fight we've ever had. If you win it, all right. We're still friends. If I win — "

"It'll be all right," he broke in. "We're still friends!"

I told him that I would begin the fight by proposing two new planks in our platform — one for Prohibition and one for Woman Suffrage. That I would organize the committee on resolutions and take the chairmanship myself.

"You are not in earnest?" he asked.

"As much as I ever was in my life."

"You've cut out a big job for yourself," he remarked, "the Republican Party in no state convention has yet dared so radical a move."

"That's why I am going to do it. We will take the lead on two great issues that can no longer be ignored. I am not a teetotaler, any more than you, but the corner saloon is doomed. The booze gang of Cincinnati has been a disgrace to our party for years. They have antagonized practically every

county in the State. The saloon controls the Democratic
Party. Its hold on politics is going to be broken. It is a
disgrace to the Nation. It has had its day."

"And Woman Suffrage?" he asked.

"It's coming too! We'll make the issue ours and beat the
Democrats to it."

He shook his head doubtfully and repeated:

"You've cut out a big job for yourself."

"We'll make the grade."

I organized the Committee on Resolutions and took the
chairmanship, drew the platform and inserted both planks in
plain words that a child could understand.

The booze crowd from Cincinnati made a minority report.

I went on the rostrum and read the platform and presented
the majority report. It was received with cries of amazement
and round after round of applause.

John Campbell, probably the ablest man in the Cincinnati
delegation, presented the minority report opposing both
declarations.

To my surprise he turned to me and said:

"If agreeable to you we'll send these reports to a vote
without discussion."

I looked at him a moment wondering if he were so
confident of victory he thought discussion a waste of words.
As a matter of fact he was.

I answered with a touch of feeling:

"If the gentleman who presents the minority report cannot
justify it by argument, certainly I have no wish to detain the
convention. Let's vote."

Harding, as presiding officer of the convention, called the
question, and the majority report was adopted by a five
to one vote amid a roar of applause that shook the
building.

Our future President's slate for the state organization was
smashed and his real friends took control.

I knew that this convention and its platform had cleared the way for Harding's candidacy in 1920.

In the summer of 1919 I believed that his hour had struck and that he should at once enter the race, and that we should organize his forces.

I had a vague fear that Mrs. Harding would give me trouble. She and I had always been the best of friends. She trusted my judgment, as a rule, against Harding's on political issues. She knew that he was a man easily fooled by his enemies. I would have to cultivate her to carry out my plans for the advancement of her husband.

I went to Washington to see the Senator, and took pains to sound out Mrs. Harding.

At the breakfast table she said to me:

"I want to talk to you."

I didn't hint that I had come to talk to her, but remained after the Senator left for the Capitol. I knew that I was in for a struggle and must handle her with tact. Harding was very fond of her and held the profoundest respect for her judgment, which had been sharpened by five years of contact with public life in Washington as a Senator's wife.

We wanted to make Harding President if we could, but I was afraid of his wife's keen eyes and brilliant mind if he should falter in ambition to make the race. If she backed our candidate he would make the fight. If she opposed it, the issue would be doubtful.

She looked at me steadily for a moment:

"You are going to ask Warren to run for the Presidency — "

"The people of Ohio will demand it — " I broke in.

"You're the people of Ohio now. The others will call for him if you say so."

"And you don't wish your husband to aspire to the highest office within the gift of any nation of the world?"

"No," she answered. "We are happy in our home in

Washington. He likes the Senate. I like being a Senator's wife. There is no strain. No pressure. No nerve-racking anxieties. We have charming friends. Warren is making a fine record. He can stay here as long as he likes."

"And you have no desire to become the first lady of the land?"

"None. I've seen the inside of the White House. I have a vivid picture of President Wilson harried and beaten by the cares of office. The office is killing him as surely as if he had been stabbed at his desk." She paused again and looked at me. "I've a presentiment against this thing. Don't ask him to run."

I spent three days in Washington talking with the Senator and his friends. He received an invitation to make the principal address at the annual banquet of the Ohio Society in New York. I saw immediately an opportunity to test his strength in the event he decided to be a candidate. I urged him to accept, and he did. We discussed his speech.

On my return to Columbus I sent him a telegram making suggestions as to its purport, and particularly urging him to dwell on adherence to the Constitution and "America First."

I wrote him at length making additional suggestions. On receiving this letter he wired me to meet him in Washington. He had partly prepared the speech. We talked it over at length and he completed the address before I left.

The oration made a stir. It struck a keynote that was never changed throughout his campaign for the nomination, the deliberations of the National Convention, his speech of acceptance, and his campaign for election. He made "America First" the outstanding issue of the campaign.

I toured the country in his interest, without any feeling against others. I was interested in Ohio, in Harding, in the Republican Party.

I paid my own expenses and when friends of the Senator

in Marion offered me contributions, I refused to accept them and advised that everybody engaged in the enterprise finance himself.

I suggested to Harding that before he tried to reach a decision it would be a good idea for him to make several speeches in Ohio, and we arranged to meet after he had done this.

When the last speech had been made he telephoned me from Marion and came to my house about eight o'clock the next evening. We went up to my library and talked for six hours.

I reviewed the whole situation with care.

It finally came down to three issues. He feared to sacrifice his solid position in the Senate for a chimera. Did he have a real chance? And was he fitted for the position?

"What would you do in my place?" he asked at last.

"I'd go into the big circus."

"And maybe lose the Senate?"

"You'll know in time to file your paper as a candidate for the Senate — if you can't win the nomination for the Presidency."

"And you think I have a fighting chance?"

"I think you have the best chance."

"How do you figure it?" he asked.

"On this line," I answered. "Neither one of the leading candidates can win. General Wood is backed by a powerful group of rich men who wish a military man in the White House. They are nervous over the social disorders following the World War. They are nervous over the growing demands of Labor. They wish to entrench themselves behind the invincible force of the bayonet and the machine gun. The scheme won't work. The people are sick of war. The boys who saw it in France have begun to tell tales out of school. They hate war to a man. They'll not vote for a General. The women will vote in the next election. It would be suicide on that account to name a General. The Republican Convention will not do it."

"Money's a powerful force in our primaries!" Harding sighed.

"That's so too. But there's not enough money in the world to buy the nomination for a man who wears epaulets in 1920."

"Lowden's a power to be reckoned with," Harding suggested.

"Sure. The best man on the list, too. I like him. He'd make a fine President. But he'll never have the prize of the nomination."

"Why?"

"He's too rich."

"Nonsense."

"Besides, he married Pullman's daughter. No party will name a railroad magnate for the office of President."

"Why, he's a farmer."

"Yes, but he married into the railroads. He'll never win. He and Wood will fight each other to a finish and deadlock the Convention."

"Then Johnson may slip in."

"Never. They'll say he defeated Hughes in California, and the real Republicans will not forgive him."

"Come down to brass tacks," Harding ordered. "Am I a big enough man for the race?"

"Don't make me laugh! The day of giants in the Presidential Chair is passed. Our so-called Great Presidents were all made by the conditions of war under which they administered the office. Greatness in the Presidential Chair is largely an illusion of the people."

I stopped, walked to a window and looked out on a swaying tree top, turned and continued:

"In spite of everything I still believe that our everyday garden variety of man is the best citizen of any republic of the world to-day. And that his love for his country, for his neighbors and government, is the prime force that makes our Nation great."

I stopped short and watched the struggle registering in the mobile lines of his face.

He held a dogged silence. He had the gift of silence, and used it often.

"Besides," I went on, "what is greatness? Who knows? I hold with the American poetess who said:

" 'The truest greatness lies in being kind.' "

Harding looked at me a moment through dimmed eyes and slowly replied:

"You know me better than any man in the world. Your opinion inspires me."

"Remember now and always I'm not presuming to decide this question. It's up to you. Between you and your God. But if you decide to run I believe we can win the nomination."

"You think so?"

"There'll be a desperate fight, but if we begin our organization in time you can win."

He shook his head slowly:

"I wish I could see it as clearly as you do."

"To my mind," I went on, "you are the man of the hour. They must name a candidate who can carry Ohio. This year, of all years, our state will be the battleground. But one man has been elected President in half a century without the vote of Ohio. The national leaders know this. They must carry Ohio. Governor Cox is a formidable candidate for the Democratic nomination. You are the man who can beat him. That fact will be a big thing in your favor. The Nation, I tell you, is sick of war. You're a man of peace, human, friendly, genial and popular. When General Wood and Lowden and Johnson have worn each other to a frazzle in the Convention we'll swing the delegates to you at the right moment."

"It may not work."

"Don't worry," I assured. "We'll take no chances. Our organization will be a perfect machine. It will begin to function from the day you make your decision."

He held his silence for a long while, and slowly rose:

"It's up to me to make the decision, of course. All right. I'll make the race."

"Good."

I walked back with him to the Malcom Jennings home, at which he was stopping. The families were life-long friends.

On the way I said to him:

"You should not ask me to manage your campaign."

"Why?"

"For one thing, Bob Wolfe, who owns two Columbus papers, is my mortal enemy. He has spent thousands of dollars trying to ruin me. Through his newspaper associations he will get a national hearing and they may make this grudge against me a hue and cry."

Harding made no reply except to ask me what time he could meet me at my office in the morning.

CHAPTER III

The Savage Fight in the Primaries

ON MY return home I faced the thing squarely and saw that I must manage his campaign.

He could not trust the crowd that Wolfe would certainly gather about him. In fact, Wolfe, although professing to run Republican papers, was in reality backing his fellow Democrat, James M. Cox. Ostensibly his papers were supporting General Wood.

It was my job, I realized. And I made up my mind to make the sacrifices necessary.

I was no amateur at the task which I faced. I had helped nominate McKinley twice, helped make Roosevelt President, managed Taft's last campaign in Ohio and led his cause in the tumultuous convention in 1912 that split the Republican Party, and helped to heal its wounds in the nomination of Hughes in 1916.

For more than a quarter of a century I had played a responsible role in every National Republican Convention and knew the job to which I had set my hand. John Sherman was my first mentor. McKinley had been my friend. I had wrestled with Foraker, fought Mark Hanna, and then helped send him to the United States Senate, the biggest man Ohio had produced in politics in half a century. I had grappled with Roosevelt, and as chairman of the campaign committee had defeated his forces in Ohio.

I had thousands of stalwart friends who would follow if I called them.

Harding entered my office at nine o'clock.

"Senator, did you have a good night's sleep?" I asked.

19

"No, I didn't sleep much."

"Well, I've thought it over," I said, "and realize that there will be an ugly contest in Ohio between your supporters and the crowd dominated by the Wolfes who have never been really friendly to you. In spite of the handicap of their hatred of me I'll have to offer you my services as your campaign manager."

He arose from his chair, walked over to me and said:

"I appreciate this more than you'll ever know, and that's what I wanted to talk over with you this morning. I couldn't get along without you. You must take the big responsibility. I will be the candidate and do my part, I trust you to do the rest. You can do it, if it can be done. This is a great relief to me."

I faced him squarely and said:

"If you are nominated and elected you must not ask me to take any public office in your administration. I am through with politics after this and purpose to give my attention to business. I have been away from home a great deal and I must settle down and settle up. I will render you any quiet service I can but will not accept public office. I am going to fight for you because I believe that you are the one man with a chance to win who can lead this country out of the passions of war and reconstruction into normal life."

"When do we begin the campaign?" he laughed.

"Right now. This is the biggest fight I've ever engaged in and it stirs me. Political wiseacres despise your chances. We'll hand them the surprise of their lives. We'll leave nothing to chance, study the field of battle, count our foes, determine their resources, measure ours against theirs, and in the first grip ask no quarter and give none."

He smiled and settled in his chair. As I've said, he had a genius for silence. He was a good listener.

"The first thing we're going to need is the thing we have least of — money. Our enemies are well supplied. We've got to hustle for the bare necessities. We'll not sell out to any man, set of men, or group of politicians. Are we agreed on that?"

"Agreed."

"All right. We need *some* money to-day. We'll need a lot in thirty days. The first contribution will be from a woman in Columbus — a Suffragist — you remember our first fight?"

"I'll never forget it."

"Good. Bread cast on the water now comes back. We'll see that the people of the United States hear of this first campaign gift. What will your home town of Marion do?"

"Forty or fifty thousand in twenty-four hours," was the prompt reply.

"Fine. That will make us a going concern with no strings tied to us."

"You can count on my home town every day in the year for all they're worth," Harding added with pride.

"No man could have a better endorsement. Now for an estimate of strength and weakness. And then a reckoning of our enemies. As I see it, our strength lies in your personality, your position in a great pivotal State, and the bitter antagonism of the three leading candidates, Wood, Lowden, and Johnson."

"I'm afraid you're overestimating the personal equation in me."

"I'm not!" I broke in sharply. "And I want you to get that idea out of your head. He who doubts and hesitates is lost. You're not a man of overbearing, selfish ambition. That's one of your best points. We'll play it, too, for all it's worth. But you must be poised and courageous. You must have backbone. You must believe in yourself or nobody else will. Don't think that anybody in this nation is clamoring for Wood, Lowden, or Johnson. The clamor is all manufactured."

"And you propose to manufacture a little?" he laughed.

"Exactly. I propose to manufacture a great deal of enthusiasm. Not brazenly or offensively, but quietly."

I stopped short and fixed him with a steady look.

"Now get this straight. You have come into the kingdom for such a time as this. You're man of the people. You're a typical average American. You're a Lincoln type who grew out of Ohio soil. Don't claim anything else or try to be anything else. You rose from a little ink-smeared printer's devil in a country town to the United States Senate. You made a solid, strong, clean record. From a humble home of poverty and honesty you have come to be a national leader exactly as Lincoln did. By your personal appeal. You're a great orator. The American people love their orators. You are the best balanced man I know in public life to-day. You can win the love of the Nation as you've won mine.

"You're a patient and thoughtful man, kindly and considerate . . . . America's gift to the progress of humanity.

"You are a great healer. In the split of our party in Ohio in the Roosevelt-Taft tragedy of 1912 you took sides, fought for Taft and stood your ground. But you did it so skillfully, so kindly, so courageously that you made few enemies. So in 1914 you were chosen to reunite the party and redeem the state. You did it, carrying Ohio by a 110,000 majority. You're called on now to heal the wounds of the nation and restore its normal life. You are the surest man to carry Ohio. We must carry Ohio to win. You don't have to argue that question this year with any delegate who has any common sense. If you are nominated you'll sweep the country."

"You really believe that?" he broke in.

"Sure."

His handsome face glowed for a moment before he spoke.

"All right. You've inspired me again — how about the enemy?"

"They're strong. There's no mistake about that. But I've an idea they're *too* strong. They've so much money to put into this campaign, it may be their undoing. Every grafter and loud-mouthed political moron in Ohio will rush to General Wood's standard at the first bugle call. They'll take his money and give as little as they can to get away with it. Unless I miss my guess they will raise a national scandal that may explode at the convention. John T. King of the National Committee has become Wood's manager. He's an able man. We'll not underestimate him. Johnson will cut no ice in Ohio. Lowden will not fight us in the primaries, because you will be a candidate."

"How do you know that?"

"I know because I know Lowden. He's a big, game square-shooter. I'm going to see him and have a talk with him. Wood's the man we must beat in our primaries. It will be a piece of unheard-of cheek if his manager invades Ohio against our own man. But I hear they're going to do it. And it means a knock-down and drag-out fight. You are ready to make it?"

"Certainly I'll make it," was the quick answer.

For all his suavity and kindliness, Harding came of a race of pioneer fighting men and he knew how to use his fists when put to the test.

"I've worked out our plans pretty thoroughly," I went on. "We'll open headquarters in Columbus, Washington, New York, and Indianapolis."

"Indianapolis?" he interrupted in surprise.

"There is a law in Indiana that delegates elected to a convention by a clear majority must vote for their candidate until he releases them. We can split Indiana's vote, prevent Wood from getting a majority, and release his delegates in time to vote for you. Senator New will be with us."

"I see."

"We'll open in Chicago, of course, before the Convention."

"You'll need some money for that purpose."

"We'll get it. St. Louis is important to our cause, but I'll work it from Chicago. I'm going to dig into the border Western States for second choice. Ringling is a friend of mine and he's in business with Jake Hamon of Oklahoma. Through Ringling I'll reach Hamon and mass our forces for second choice around him and Cole of St. Louis."

"I've lots of friends in the Senate," Harding observed.

I smiled.

"Sure, I had them in mind when I said that you're a great orator. A lot of them can't make a speech. If you throw a few hints, these fellows will ask you to help them out in their campaign for reëlection. They'll bite at the bait. Not one of them regards you as a serious candidate. Not one of them would lift his little finger to put you in the White House, but all of them will use your magnificent voice and commanding figure on the platform to win votes. Accept every invitation they give you. I'll see to it that you get a lot of them. Wherever you speak you'll win men who will be delegates at the national convention. Get to work now on some big speeches. We'll start you off in Ohio and Indiana."

Harding left me full of enthusiasm.

I perfected a pioneer organization and set to work.

We planned a nation-wide canvass of the delegates to the convention. Harding's work as presiding officer of the Hughes nominating assembly stood us now in good stead. We secured a list of every delegate and began to ply them with our literature.

We got up a biographical pamphlet, well written and beautifully printed and illustrated. The only thing lacking was a good photograph of Mrs. Harding. I asked Harding again and again to send me one. He tried and couldn't get it. His wife refused and stood her ground. It was the last day before the booklet must go to press. I had just come home, but hurried back to Washington to get the photograph.

I went to Harding's house for breakfast, sat down and talked to Mrs. Harding about it. She still refused. She didn't have a picture except on old one. I asked her to let me see it. As a joke she brought out the only picture she actually had — a very old one taken when she was a young woman — riding a bicycle. It was a funny-looking thing. I held on to the photo as we sat down and talked in a friendly way. She was still determined, and I said:

"Well, if you will not have a picture taken I will use this one." And I put it in my pocket.

She was amazed.

"You wouldn't use that thing, would you?"

"I will," I answered. "Unless you give us a better one. We cannot finish the booklet without a picture of you. It's ready to go to press, and I'll take this picture home and use it unless you have another one made immediately."

She tried to laugh it off as a joke but the joke didn't go with me, and when I grimly rose she consented to have her picture taken that day and have the Senator send it to me.

When I recall the vicious lies told of her overbearing ambitions, of her cold schemes to make her husband President and her attempts to dominate him and dictate the policies of his administration, I feel like murdering her slanderers.

She never once begged her husband to enter the race. She opposed it from the beginning. She was happy and content in his love and their ideal home life. She feared the tragic struggle in which he was entering with a dread that was pathetic.

But on the day she was forced into that photographer's chair she gave up the struggle and helped me in every way she could. Always with a wistful look in her eyes in which I saw mirrored the home dream that she would know no more.

I have never known two people better adapted to each other than Harding and his wife. I was, perhaps, their most intimate friend for thirty years. I never knew of a real quarrel between them about anything. I never heard her express a word of suspicion or jealousy about another woman. And we were at all times on terms of comradeship that would have made such talk inevitable had there been occasion for it. We laughed and joked with each other in the friendliest way, and I always enjoyed her keen sense of humor and her ready wit.

Little did she dream of the insane caricatures of her character that unscrupulous scribblers would make after her death!

In the middle of the campaign for the delegates of Ohio a sensation was suddenly sprung on us by the resignation of John King as General Wood's manager. The announcement was immediately followed by the appointment of Colonel Cooper Proctor of Cincinnati.

To me this news was ominous. Not because Colonel Proctor was a dangerous man. On the contrary he was a very mild-mannered, respectable millionaire of benevolent activities. I understood the real reason he was appointed from the moment I heard of it. He was a prominent Ohio citizen. This was a blow at Harding. And he would be a mere figurehead through whom more money would be poured into General Wood's coffers, while men behind the scenes would use this money in the deadliest possible way.

The thing developed with remarkable rapidity. From estimates our people carefully made we knew that Wood's managers were now distributing a fund of at least two millions in our state. The like of it had never before been known in the history of the country.

I knew that Harding's appeal to the Labor men of Ohio was a strong one. His newspaper had the unique distinction of never having reduced a single man's wages in the thirty-five years he had owned the plant. He had never discharged a man.

But the crisis was too acute for sentimental appeals to the poor laboring man against the rich. Something had to be done and done quickly or we were going to be swamped in a flood of gold. Not that it was the plan or purpose of Wood's managers to buy individual voters. That was long ago out of date.

They reached the leaders and molders of public opinion by the semi-legitimate use of advertising space in newspapers, the control of billboards, the hiring of every available hall in the state, and the retention of an army of paid orators.

I met the situation by a carefully guarded movement in Washington. I got the right man to pour into Senator Borah's ear the truth about this vast expenditure of money in a primary election and suggested that the foundations of the Republic were being destroyed by this method of making a President.

Borah made an eloquent speech and demanded an immediate investigation by a Senatorial committee, and got it.

I was summoned to appear and testify. I answered all questions with great caution and I made no bitter accusations against our opponents. In fact I refused to make any accusations whatever.

I gave a detailed account of our own expenditures, which at this time amounted to about $105,000. General Wood's managers were thoroughly cross-examined and acknowledged enough to load Borah with dynamite.

I was not foolish enough to believe that the Senatorial committee could get the full facts.

But I did believe that the investigation would put the fear of God into the hearts of the big interests who were making the enormous gifts to General Wood's cause.

The effect was excellent.

The flood of money stopped and we forged ahead. It was not stopped any too soon. When the primary was held, Harding came near being defeated. He carried the state by less than twenty thousand votes in a tremendous poll for the primary.

Still, he carried it, and won with a split delegation. I was a candidate for delegate-at-large, and my old friends, the booze ring of Cincinnati, counted me out by a few hundred votes. The delegation stood 39 for Harding and 9 for Wood.

Harding was shocked. He was in Louisville on speaking tour. I rushed to see him before he'd say something fatal.

When I met him at the station his face was a yard long.

"Well," he sighed, "it looks like we're done for."

"Yes, I knew you'd say that, and so I came to meet you."

"You still think we can win?"

"Certainly."

"With my campaign manager turned down and nine Wood men sent in against me?"

"Sure. That's nothing. I'll be there with my hand on the pulse of every man in the convention."

"Your Senatorial committee didn't do so much for us after all," he complained.

"More than you can see or dream at this early date."

"What do you mean?" he asked sharply.

"That Lowden's managers have an enormous campaign fund too. That the committee has set the hounds on a hot trail. They'll not give up the chase, with the results in Ohio."

"No?"

"No. I've planted a bomb under your rivals in that investigation. In the fierce heat of the fight in the Convention that bomb may explode — and if it does, there won't be a grease spot left of our leading opponents when the smoke clears."

Harding smiled grimly.

"That's a possibility, of course."

CHAPTER IV

The Skirmish Lines at Chicago

WE WERE going into the national convention at Chicago with a split delegation from Ohio. A serious handicap. And yet not fatal. Men had been nominated for the Presidency whose state delegates were split.

Sometimes the split meant a badge of honor for the candidate. It had been so with Grover Cleveland who won over the united opposition of the Tammany Democracy of New York City.

Governor Lowden, as well as Harding, was entering the convention with a split delegation. Seventeen delegates from Illinois, under the leadership of Mayor Thompson, were for either Senator Johnson or General Wood. For anyone, in fact, that they could nominate, except Lowden.

In Ohio, General Wood had nine delegates out of our forty-eight. Harding had thirty-nine. And I knew that we had at least one traitor in our thirty-nine who would betray us if he could, and try to lead others with him.

Rudolph Hynicka of Cincinnati, National Committeeman, had been elected a Harding delegate.

Immediately after the primaries I urged Harding to throttle Hynicka by putting him off the National Committee from our state. The Senator was insistent in his policy of conciliation. He still believed he could convert him. Hynicka was re-elected National Committeeman with Harding's approval.

I knew that Hynicka was whetting his knife to stab the Senator in the back but I couldn't budge Harding from the determination to "harmonize" Ohio at all hazards.

29

Knowing what Hynicka was going to do, I laid our plans to strangle him in the convention, and said nothing more to Harding about it.

We had six weeks in which to perfect our organization, and set ourselves to the task with tireless energy.

We made no effort, as a rule, to win the leaders, but rather the individual delegates. We made personal contact with three-fourths of the nine hundred eighty-four men and women who would make the nomination.

An exception to this rule was my approach to Jake Hamon of Oklahoma, a leader who controlled a large block of delegates, numbering over fifty.

My friend Ringling, of circus fame, Hamon's associate in business, was slow in making an appointment for me to meet Hamon.

I finally told him if he didn't bring Hamon to see me I'd slip into his circus enclosure some dark night and kill every elephant he had.

He brought Hamon to Washington and I made an engagement to breakfast with the famous big man from the West.

As we shook hands I sized him up as a real he-man with an appetite whetted by the great open spaces.

At breakfast, I asked my guest what he'd have.

"*Three* eggs and plenty of ham," he promptly ordered.

"*I'll* take three eggs and plenty of ham," I echoed firmly.

Hamon looked at me:

"You live among the tenderfeet but you know how to order a real breakfast."

I'd never eaten three eggs for breakfast before in my life. But I managed it.

Hamon spent the day with me and when he left I'd won him. He promised that if the time came that Harding had a chance of the nomination and Lowden could not win, he would support Harding.

I did not care at that time who his first choice was. Our whole plan of campaign was centered on second choice votes.

We invaded no state that had a candidate. We made no enemies among the delegates.

When the convention assembled we had, I believe, the most complete poll of delegates from first choice to fourth, and the most complete political organization ever set up for the nomination of a President.

Before the convention met, we transferred to Chicago the choice men of our organization from the several state headquarters, and consolidated our forces at the Congress Hotel, where we engaged sixty rooms, with an assembly room for which we paid seven hundred and fifty dollars a day.

To defray expenses we put up the money ourselves. Marion, Harding's town, and Columbus, my home town, raised most of it.

On the first floor we arranged, with movable partitions, a suite of offices, with five doors between my desk and the crowd.

Every Harding man in the throng that came in was instructed to smile, keep in good humor, and make no enemies. We recognized but one enemy — Mr. Rudolph Hynicka, National Committeeman, a delegate from Cincinnati solemnly pledged and elected to vote for Harding!

And we kept our eyes on Jake Hamon. He had more influence among the delegates than any other one man in the Convention.

I had promised to take breakfast with him at the La Salle Hotel, where he had headquarters, the morning I came into Chicago.

Two influential and active members of our organization who had been on the ground for several days met me at the train. They were for Lowden for second choice and were now convinced that he would be nominated. They came at the suggestion of Governor Lowden, who requested them to ask me to see him as soon as I reached Chicago.

I fenced a little:

"I've an engagement for breakfast with Hamon. I must see him first."

"It looks like Lowden," I was informed.

"It's too early yet to make predictions," I warned.

One of them touched my arm and spoke in low tones:

"I've a message from the Governor. He likes you. If you'll help him win — a place in his Cabinet is yours."

"I wouldn't take it if offered me," I frowned. "If Lowden wins I'll back Harding for a post if he wishes it. I want nothing for myself either from Governor Lowden or Senator Harding — "

I went to the La Salle to Mr. Hamon's rooms, where he was waiting. He insisted on my seeing Governor Lowden. I wanted to get to our headquarters, but on their insistence I agreed to see Lowden first.

Hamon called Lowden on the telephone and found that he was ill and the doctor would allow no one to see him.

Hamon asked that I have a talk with Emmerson, now Governor of Illinois, who was managing the Lowden campaign.

This I consented to do, and Mr. Emmerson came over.

I made my position clear:

"We'll do our best, Mr. Emmerson, to put Harding over. We know Governor Lowden has a large following. But we believe our man can win. He'll win on his merits. On his qualifications as a candidate. He can unite the Party and lead it to a great victory — "

"But you'll give Lowden a chance to land the nomination first?" Emmerson interrupted.

"That's exactly what I was going to tell you. General Wood must be beaten first. And Lowden's the man to beat him."

"Agreed. We'll form an alliance then to first beat Wood,

for we can't allow Harding's vote to be too small, but we'll loan you every vote we can until you pass Wood. The minute you do this, Wood is out of the race and all friendship on the floor of the Convention ceases between us — you understand that?"

"Certainly, you couldn't make a fairer proposition."

"And you know what that implies?"

"As clearly as if you'd put it in words."

We shook hands and I left with a feeling of elation. The game was set. The plan would work. I'd give Lowden his chance first. I'd give it freely and loyally — every vote we could spare without allowing Harding to slump on any ballot. He must slowly climb from the first.

When Lowden passed Wood there would be a bad hour for us. But I'd made my pledge and we would carry it out.

The agreement was confirmed by Governor Lowden.

Our main staff of workers numbered more than five hundred picked men. We had selected them carefully from our old headquarters in Columbus, Washington, New York, and Indianapolis. They had proven their loyalty and ability in the primary struggle. And there wasn't a traitor among them.

We put loyal Harding lookouts in *every hotel in town*, and got one or more of our representatives into the headquarters of every rival.

Our staff grew finally to two thousand men and women. They met every train, shook hands with the incoming delegates, and made engagements to see them.

We ordered a roll made of every delegate from every state, got their addresses and the number of each room they occupied.

George B. Christian of Marion, a life-long friend of Senator Harding, did valuable work. He had always been on the alert during the campaign, seeing that the right people met Harding in Washington. He later played an important rôle in the President's life as his private secretary.

We gave out no claims, made no statements to the press, and carefully concealed every move from the reporters.

I asked Harding to make no predictions or statements and gave Mrs. Harding a free hand in talking to anybody she pleased. I could trust absolutely her keen intuitions and her straightforward, honest thinking. She was a trained newspaper woman. She made friends with every reporter who talked to her. She disarmed criticism by her frank declaration that she only wished Harding's success because he wanted it. Personally she had always opposed his running.

We knew she would say this and she did. Her first interview with a reporter was an inspiration. She was exquisitely dressed in a way that gave the impression of severe black and white. Her manners were so pleasing, her affability so marked, the interviewer at once forgot about her clothes. She could talk indefinitely and never say a sharp or offensive word about a human being.

She extended her hand to her first reporter with a gracious smile:

"You know my husband ought to win this fight. He has a winning way about him that has always disarmed enmity. He can differ sharply with a man — but always without offending him — "

"I see you like him," the reporter laughed.

"Oh, I know you'll think I'm boasting," she apologized, "but I have only one fad. The only fad I've had for the last twenty-six years. And that is my husband. It's old-fashioned I know. But that is the way I feel about it."

Out of a clear sky the reporter shot a dangerous question:

"They say Hiram Johnson will bolt the convention if he is not nominated — do you think so?"

"Of course not," was the smiling answer. "I know Senator Johnson well. He's a fine fellow, though he does make a great noise at times. His bark is much worse than his bite. He's just trying to scare the delegates into voting for him."

"Think you'd like the White House?"

Her face clouded a moment and she firmly answered:

"I would not. We've a lovely home in Washington and many warm friends. Being a Senator's wife suits me. It's pleasanter, quieter, its problems never heartbreaking."

I enjoyed this interview. It was exactly the kind of talk expected of her. And it helped.

The situation developed as I had foreseen. It was anybody's fight. Wood and Lowden led, but no serious-minded man who knew politics believed that either could win. There were eighteen candidates.

There was no chance of a stampede for any man.

No body of men ever gathered in a political meeting with cooler judgment.

The usual coterie of United States Senators were interested observers. But they were all at sea, from Reed Smoot, the astute veteran, to Henry Cabot Lodge, the Puritan aristocrat.

The Lord had been good to us. Our plans were working with the sure, soft power of a big Packard motor.

I received, however, a dangerous call. William Hale Thompson, the Mayor of Chicago, who had split the Illinois delegation, made overtures for an alliance against his enemy. He hated Lowden with sullen fury. And he held twenty-one votes in the hollow of his hand against him.

I side-stepped him with swift tread.

"I'll tell you what I will do," I finally said. "I'll take off your hands the expensive rooms you've engaged at the Congress Hotel. I need them for my Women's Headquarters."

He accepted the offer and we parted friends, although I had not made him a single promise. He was a dangerous friend. I could not afford to have Harding mixed in his deadly feud. But with an eye on the election to follow I didn't antagonize him.

There was one thing I knew that Lowden couldn't guess. I was mortally certain that Borah would explode the bomb placed in his hands in the Senate committee's investigation of the money in the primaries.

He did as I had predicted to Harding.

The newspapers reported that at a big meeting of Johnson's supporters Borah had made a speech in which he denounced the corrupt use of money in our elections, told the story of the primaries and declared in substance he would bolt the convention, if either Wood or Lowden were named as its candidate.

The effect of this speech was tremendous. On the surface it was pooh-poohed as a mere articulation of wind by a Western orator.

Thoughtful men knew better. Johnson would poll over a hundred votes on the first ballot. He was a born revolutionist. Revolution was the breath of his nostrils, and Borah was voicing the grim determination of his chief. Johnson could split the Republican Party if he led a revolt with Borah as his prophet.

Will Hays was a skillful strategist. In his opening address as Chairman of the National Committee he uttered a sentence that was a trumpet call of alarm. But he worded it so skillfully that he brought the convention to its feet with a roar of applause that shook the rafters.

He said:

"This is a convention of such poise and careful thinking – from its decision there can be no bolt!"

The great mass of the delegates thundered their approval. The Johnson leaders remained silent. An ominous sign.

CHAPTER V

Harding's Nomination — Its Inside Story

WHEN THE convention assembled we had made personal contact with nearly every delegate. Our organization was working to perfection. Reports from our agents in each of the forty-eight state delegations gave us an accurate summary of the strength of each candidate.

When the first ballot was cast Friday morning, the actual record did not vary five per cent from our advices.

Lodge, as permanent chairman, opened the convention with a great speech, and set a high mark for the men who were to follow.

The speeches nominating Wood, Lowden, Johnson, Sproul, and Butler of Columbia University were standard political efforts, but roused no enthusiasm outside their own supporters.

The first ripple of genuine excitement was an unexpected one. It followed the speech of Nathan L. Miller of New York, who nominated Herbert C. Hoover. The noise and cheering, however, came from the well-packed galleries and not from the delegates. The chairman rapped in vain for order. With every smash of his gavel the din grew louder. It must have lasted a full quarter of an hour.

We had purposely held the nominating speech for Senator Harding back until toward the end. We had a reason — a big surprise for the 984 delegates packed on the floor of the Coliseum and their 30,000 guests. We had selected for Harding's nomination a man who could make a speech that would lift the tired delegates out of their seats — Governor Frank B. Willis of Ohio.

The heat was terrific. The crowd was tired.

The task before an orator was an appalling one, but when the far-reaching, sharp tones of his voice crashed over the crowd, an awed silence followed. He hadn't spoken five sentences before he caught the attention of every listener, and when he played his first trump card I saw that he had them.

Rising to his full height of over six feet he thundered:

"Every candidate before this convention is worthy of the honor, and the man nominated will be elected — no matter what his name!"

At this prophecy the delegates leaped to their feet and cheered.

His speech was the first sensation of the convention. It made a smashing impression. The members began to sit up and take notice. There wasn't a man among the leaders of the opposition who didn't recognize the fact that Willis had started something and that the man he had named was a force to be reckoned with.

Toward the conclusion of his speech, departing from the text, he paused a moment and in a low voice said:

"Boys and girls, come on now and give us your votes — to nominate Senator Harding."

An unexpected twist of the orator that created another burst of applause from delegates and gallery.

When the convention adjourned for the day Governor Willis's speech was the talk of the town. It was the high spot of the convention. We had scored our first victory and it was an important one. It afterwards helped send Willis into the Senate to succeed Harding, and he had won the honor fairly.

When the balloting began on Friday morning we were confident of success unless we had underestimated General Wood's strength.

On the first ballot Wood received 287 votes, Lowden 211, Johnson 133, Sproul 84, Nicholas Murray Butler 69, and Harding 65. The rest were scattered. Hoover got 5 1/2. On the next three ballots we continued to loan Lowden all the votes we could deliver.

At the end of the fourth ballot, which closed the day, Harding had but 61 votes and we had helped push Lowden up to 289, within 25 of tying General Wood. We estimated we had more than 200 votes to swing to Harding, if neither Wood nor Lowden was nominated, but we had no intention at that time to rush the game. Our purpose from the first was to pass Wood with Lowden, and then build Harding's vote from both until he won.

Friday night was a memorable one. We worked incessantly during the afternoon, at the Coliseum, around the hotels, and on the streets. It was a night of wild excitement. Everybody who could be induced to do so was talking in favor of Harding. The weather was hot, delegates and visitors were tired. Our organization had been instructed to meet the delegates after the adjournment for the day, and find out where they were located. Men were assigned to every group.

The Columbus Glee Club, a famous organization of singers numbering about 75 men, was on hand from the capital of Ohio. They visited the headquarters of every candidate, and serenaded him. They sang no Harding songs in the headquarters of other candidates. Every man was in full evening dress. Their good humor and fine singing captured the crowds.

A new set of Harding portraits were put out.

We made it a Harding night of good cheer and friendly gestures for every candidate.

Many conferences were held. We were told afterwards that Col. George Harvey met his friends in a smoke-fogged room in the Blackstone Hotel, decided on a candidate, and adjourned at 2 a.m. We paid no attention to these meetings, but sought out and gripped the hands of the delegates who were to vote. Every man pledged to Harding was busy urging that the deadlock be broken and the Senator nominated. We argued that neither Wood nor Lowden could be nominated, and Lowden would release his followers the next day.

My one fear was that there would be early treachery in the Ohio delegation. I believed that at least four delegates under the influence of Rudolph Hynicka might break from Harding, to whom they were pledged, and vote for Wood.

At midnight a meeting of the Ohio delegation was held. Senator Harding came from the meeting in high spirits. Our 39 men had pledged themselves anew to stand firm and support him to the end.

"The Cincinnati crowd, led by Hynicka, will betray you to-morrow," I warned. "But I've a plan to block their game. Go to bed and get some rest."

I quickly sent word to the delegates that there would be treachery in the Ohio delegation in the morning. The word traveled not only to the delegates but over the city, through the hotel lobbies.

At breakfast I told Harding it would happen. He still couldn't believe it.

The convention opened Saturday with a tension that was unmistakable. The great event was pending. The candidacy of eighteen men lay in the lap of the gods. There would be no adjournment over Sunday. Chicago was steaming. The heat was indescribable. The delegates were worn out.

The gavel of Chairman Henry Cabot Lodge sharply called the fifth day's session to order at 10:23 to take the fifth ballot. Bishop Nicholson of Chicago made the invocation. He asked God for delivery from pretense and hypocrisy and for His guidance in lending vision to the delegates.

"O God," he cried, "let every vote be cast with a deep sense of the responsibility that attaches to the man who casts it. May the man chosen to-day be worthy of the best traditions of our great Republic."

Every floor leader made his own interpretation of the prayer and sent his men flying to do his bidding, holy or unholy.

The balloting began. We threw the promised votes to Lowden, and when he passed Wood, a wave of wild excitement swept the floor. The poll stood Lowden 303, Wood 299, and Harding 78. While we had made good our pledge to Lowden and helped drive him ahead of Wood, we took pains to see to it that our man steadily gained. His votes had risen slowly from 61 to 78.

The traitors in the Ohio camp who had planned to stab Harding in the back were to pull it on this first ballot, but an accident happened. One of the crew tried to rob Hynicka of the role of chief traitor. He had heard during the night that Senator Harding had filed his papers as a candidate for the Senate in case he should miss the nomination, and he determined to spring a sensation on the convention and emerge a hero.

He jumped on a chair and shouted:

"Gentlemen, Senator Harding last night has refiled for the Senate — "

He had meant to add — "he is now out of this race!"

But a roar of the majority of our delegates in denial drowned his voice, and Ohio's vote was registered as usual, 9 for Wood and 39 for Harding.

We knew what was coming on the next ballot and again sent our couriers flying to each delegation with a whispered warning:

"Watch now for the attempted betrayal. Watch this ballot."

When the clerk called "Ohio" on the sixth ballot Hynicka promptly betrayed his chief. He cast four votes pledged to Harding for General Wood, and turned his head for an ovation from the General's followers.

He got the surprise of his life. From the galleries and

delegates of forty-eight states suddenly burst a storm of hisses, cat-calls, boos, and yells of derision.

"Traitors!"

"Treachery!"

"Rats!"

"Crawl back into your holes!"

The heat was terrific but the sweat on Hynicka's brow turned cold. He crumpled in his seat until the storm of derision had passed. Ohio's vote was recorded 35 for Harding and 13 for Wood.

But when the poll was announced Harding's total stood at 89, a gain of 11 votes in spite of his betrayal! The traitors gasped in surprise.

Their plot had failed. The sensation it created had made Harding stronger with the delegates.

If we had not carefully anticipated this treachery and turned it to our advantage, it might have put us out of the running. If we had not at all times had a support which we could use at any moment exactly as we wished, they might have beaten us with this betrayal.

We merely added 11 votes to Harding's total and the coup fell flat before the wave of hisses, yells, and cat-calls that rolled over the astonished traitors.

We made no effort on this ballot to draw men from Lowden's ranks. He had passed Wood on the previous ballot and we were free to fight now with every weapon at our command.

But the hour had not struck. We held our men steadily in line for Lowden for two more ballots and won his deepest gratitude.

The General's managers had shot ahead and Wood had tied Lowden on the next two ballots.

On the eighth we handed the Wood forces a surprise. We took a few of his votes. We also drew out four votes from Lowden and slipped them to Harding. The eighth ballot showed Lowden 307, Wood 299, and Harding 133 1/2.

The Wood camp was thrown into a panic. Lowden had again passed him, and Harding's name was on every lip. We had gained steadily and surely until we'd passed Johnson and stood within striking distance of leading the field.

On the next ballot we would lead it!

We sent our orders flying and began to marshal our votes for the first full record of Harding's strength. It had been carefully held back and guarded from the beginning.

The Coliseum was a mass of excited, perspiring humanity.

Hert of Kentucky, floor leader of the Lowden forces, made a motion that the convention take a recess until 4 p.m. The motion was seconded by a New York delegate.

We did not want a recess. We were moving swiftly to victory.

The chairman declared the motion adopted.

The Wood camp was thrown into another panic. Lowden had again passed him on the eighth ballot, and we had taken some of his votes.

A man on the rostrum called:

"The Ohio delegates have agreed to an adjournment."

"They have not!" cried Willis, whom we had rushed to the platform to protest.

I stood in front of Chairman Lodge and shouted:

"You can't beat this man by any such tactics! You ought to be ashamed of yourself! This is an outrage!"

Governor Myron T. Herrick, chairman of the Ohio delegation, was on the platform with Willis, protesting against the recess.

We made the best of the situation.

Lodge had suggested to Willis and Herrick that the recess might be beneficial to Harding. I did not think so. But the recess afforded us an opportunity to go to the delegations and urge them to put Harding over on the next ballot.

Lodge said to me before I left the hall: "We all want a

harmonious finish with a solid enthusiastic party. They are going to offer Johnson the Vice-Presidency and swing his stubborn followers over to Harding."

"Senator Johnson will insult your messengers," I warned. "They're on a fool's errand."

I visited the delegations during the recess.

Senator Penrose's headquarters were in the Congress Hotel. He called me on the long distance telephone from Philadelphia. Penrose asked:

"You think Harding will be nominated?"

"Beyond a question."

"I do not see myself how he can be defeated now if you have the organization I think you have. I am just about to issue a statement."

"Got it ready?" I asked.

"Yes. And the newspapers are waiting for me to give it out."

He read the statement to me and I had a stenographer take it down. It was a strong appeal for Harding. He was a great Republican, would make a splendid campaign, and would make a great President!

Instantly I knew that if this statement were given out in Philadelphia it would be carried in five minutes to Chicago, and a hostile press would have extras out and a copy on the seat of every delegate when he returned to the hall after the recess. There would be headlines:

"The Boss nominates Harding!" and the cry would be raised that it was a boss-controlled Convention.

I said to him:

"Now, Senator, when you are running things you don't let anyone interfere with you. I am in that position now. I don't want you to give out that statement in Philadelphia. I have it here and I'll give it out in conformity with my plans a little later."

"All right," he said, "maybe you are right. I'll do as you

suggest and you can give it out when you are ready."

I put it in my pocket and kept it there until after the convention had nominated Harding. Then I gave it to the press. It now could do no harm.

It was arranged for Lowden and Harding to meet. I went to the Lowden headquarters, but by the time I got there he had gone to the Convention to withdraw his name while he was yet in the lead.

Senator Harding was late in arriving. I met Emmerson, Governor Lowden's manager, and had a talk with him. I was afraid something might miscarry. But Mr. Emmerson said that we had played the game with them and they would play square with us.

The time was short. I sent word to Chairman Lodge that I would be late and not to call the convention to order until I could reach the Coliseum — that Senator Harding would be nominated on the next ballot. This was a courtesy to which we were entitled.

Lodge held the convention back until forty-six minutes after four o'clock. The delegates were getting restless.

Harding and I found Governor Lowden in the rooms of the National Committee in the Coliseum. He was very cordial to the Senator. He had made the announcement that his delegates were released and he was out of the contest. Although the ninth ballot had not yet been taken, he congratulated Harding on his nomination.

Johnson was deaf to all overtures and we got no support from him during the convention.

Our forces took their seats in the great hall full of fight, eager for the fray and confident of an early victory. A fresh supply of our banners, streamers, and portraits filled the Coliseum.

The atmosphere was charged with a hot electric current. The big event was pending and everybody knew it. Every street leading to the Coliseum was choked with a dense mass of wilting humanity who knew they couldn't get in but waited patiently for the news.

While the convention marked time we sent our men into the skylights of the arched ceiling and flooded the crowd with a storm of post cards bearing a handsome picture of Harding. They fell in endless waves for five minutes until a cheer broke from our enthusiastic ranks. At last three immense red, white, and blue flags came billowing down from the rafters and waved over the heads of the delegates.

A roar of excited cheers swept the crowd. They heard again Willis's proclamation of victory in November for the winner to-day.

At 4:46 Senator Lodge announced the taking of the ninth ballot. Connecticut swung to Harding; also three from Delaware. Florida leaped on the band wagon.

Wood's men were fighting desperately. Illinois and Indiana stood their ground.

W. J. Bailey of Kansas leaped upon a chair and roared above the din:

"Kansas casts her entire twenty votes for Harding!"

A delegate from Kansas took the state standard, raised it high in the air, with a picture of Harding on it, and started marching around the hall, followed by the entire delegation.

Kentucky cast her twenty-six votes for Harding. And pendemonium broke loose.

The Coliseum was in a furor. Police were hurled aside like children. Smoot and Lodge hammered their gavels in vain. When Ohio was called a hush fell over the sweltering mass. Every man except our delegates expected, of course, a solid vote at last from Harding's own State. And when the nine men still voted for Wood the most extraordinary thing happened that I ever witnessed in a national convention. Their vote was greeted with a sullen roar of indignation and surprise. Hoots, cat-calls, boos, yells, and hisses swept the delegates. From the gallery:

"Fools!"

"Cheap skates!"

"Poor losers!"

"Mule heads!"

I saw the nine Wood men go into a solemn conference with bowed heads. They wouldn't face that crowd again. I knew they, too, would vote for Harding on the next ballot. I felt sorry for them. They had made a sad show of themselves.

When the poll of the ninth ballot was called Harding led the field with 374 votes. He had taken 186 from Lowden and 50 from Wood.

It was all over but the shouting and that began in short order. Our men leaped to their feet and yelled themselves hoarse. They marched down the aisles with banners and streamers, and exhorted sinners to repent before it was too late.

"Come on, boys!"

"It's all over!"

"Climb on the bandwagon!"

"While the lamp holds out to burn, the vilest sinner may return!"

A fellow from another state yelled the last sentence into the ears of the nine Wood men in our delegation.

The galleries now caught fire from the volcano below and yelled themselves hoarse.

I looked into the boxes and caught sight of Mrs. Harding. I thought with a sudden gasp of fear of what might happen when her husband was nominated on the next ballot This last demonstration would be a zephyr in comparison. I knew that she suffered from a weak heart.

Harding had gone into this fight over her protest. If she should suddenly die in the wild scene that would follow his nomination, he would feel that he had killed her.

I sent a messenger to the manager of the Pennsylvania delegation and asked them to give us sixty votes for Harding on the next ballot.

And then I hurried up the stairs and found my way into Mrs. Harding's box.

She had removed her hat in the sweltering heat and sat humped forward in her chair, her arms tightly folded. In her right hand she gripped two enormous hat pins, in vogue at the time.

I drew a chair close beside her and she started at the touch of my hand on her arm.

A deep frown shadowed her face.

"It's terrible, isn't it?"

"What?"

"All this wild excitement. This yelling and bawling and cat-calling. I can't follow it — "

"I didn't think you would, but something's going to happen down there in a few minutes that may shock you if you don't look out — "

"What do you mean?" she asked sharply.

"I've come up here to ask you to keep cool."

"That's a good joke, I must say," she laughed. "It's a hundred and ten in this place and you advise me to keep cool!"

"You know what I mean. Something's going to happen on the next ballot and I want you to be prepared for it — "

"What?"

I leaned closer and whispered: "We have the votes. Your husband will be nominated on the next ballot — "

She gave a sudden start, fairly leaped from her chair. The movement drove both hat pins deep into my side.

I sprang back and felt the blood follow them. I had half expected to be assassinated by an enemy but I hadn't figured on being killed by one of my best friends at the moment of triumph.

I had come to save a woman's life and she had unwittingly murdered me!

I said nothing to disturb her but felt my head swimming as

the blood began to run down my leg and fill my shoe. For a moment I swayed, about to faint. I was smothering.

"The thing must have pierced a lung!" I muttered to myself.

Lodge called the tenth ballot and I moved unsteadily from the box.

I paused and smiled:

"Remember now, no excitement. Keep your head and laugh at the antics below — "

"I will," she promised.

I felt my way down to the floor of the Convention and listened to the roll call with a vague sense of detachment from the world.

When I walked I could hear the queer swish of the blood that filled my shoe. I felt my body sway, and caught a chair. I was smothering again.

I had no fear of the result of the ballot. The states were voting for Harding one by one as I knew they would. I sat down a moment to steady my nerves and managed to pull myself together as the clerk's voice boomed:

"Pennsylvania!"

I had counted the votes as recorded. Harding had 440. He only needed 52 more to give him the nomination. Off somewhere in space I heard a deep voice boom:

"Pennsylvania casts 60 votes for Warren G. Harding!"

He had won!

A cheer rose that shook the earth. The vast spaces of the Coliseum echoed with demoniac screams. Ambitions crumbled! And a new figure in history emerged from the din.

I tottered to my room, and examined myself. My lung had not been pierced. My smothering was only in imagination. My shoe was full of perspiration.

On the last poll Harding had received 692 1/5, Wood 156, Johnson 80 4/5, Lowden 11, and Hoover 9 1/2. A motion to make it unanimous was savagely opposed by Wisconsin, whose solid vote for LaFollette had been recorded on every ballot, accompanied by hisses.

In spite of the spectacle made by the protest vote of the LaFollette Wisconsin delegation, we faced the future with confidence.

CHAPTER VI

The Election and Its Boomerang

THE moment the heat and dust of the convention lifted one thing stood out with increasing clearness. Ohio was the pivotal state again. In half a century, only Grover Cleveland had been elected without her vote. The Democrats would move heaven and earth to carry the state.

Governor Cox was named by the Democrats two weeks later.

It was a unique situation — both nominees from the same state. Such a thing had not happened since Lincoln and Douglas. I was never surer of anything in my life than that Harding would carry Ohio. We had thousands of independent voters, and a tremendous reaction had set in among them against Wilson and the League of Nations. Cox was an echo of Wilson and the only way to strike at Wilson was to vote for Harding.

Ohio would give him a huge majority, and our state had always been a good barometer of the whole country.

I refused the national chairmanship, asked that it be given to Will Hays, and we organized an executive committee of five to stand behind the Chairman and help him in every way possible.

This committee of five, led by Mr. Hays, perfected the most powerful national political machine ever set up by any party in a presidential campaign.

The struggle rapidly developed into a tide for Harding. I had been in every campaign since 1892 and I had never seen anything like it.

We had to rub our eyes and ask if we were dreaming. Every

prediction we had made was coming true . . . and more.

When Harding swung from his front porch program to a circle of great states it was suggested to Mrs. Harding that she help him out with the women. He had never been a noisy supporter of Woman Suffrage and some of their leaders were not friendly to him.

In a quiet, efficient way Mrs. Harding worked wonders with the women of the West.

The *Minneapolis Tribune* was enthusiastic:

"If Senator Harding goes into the White House there will preside as its mistress a quiet, charming hostess with no social ambitions — a true 'First Lady' in the final sense of the word. With poise, sincerity, and an utter absence of sham. Who, it is safe to predict, will win all hearts and be more concerned over the little newsboys on the route receiving hot chocolate on cold nights than over the establishment of a new 'Four Hundred' that would owe its allegiance to her."

When bombarded by a question about the League of Nations, she smiled diplomatically and said:

"You know you really shouldn't ask me to talk politics. My husband will do that. I'm leaving it to him. And I'll back him on whatever he tells you."

Again she made a hit with the men and the women.

She was given a wonderful ovation when she stepped on the platform before the Senator was introduced. Throughout his speech she listened in rapt attention, her face showing plainly her joy in the enthusiastic reception he was receiving.

Wherever she went a swarm of photographers engulfed her. She had schooled herself to this, and won their friendship by quietly saying:

"All right. Come on, boys. I always take a frightful picture and I hate this. But I know you've got to do it."

Throughout the campaign Mrs. Harding was an enthusiastic and tireless worker. She took suggestions good-naturedly and executed them promptly.

As the campaign swept toward its conclusion something like a panic gripped the Democratic headquarters.

As the closing week approached a boomerang was sprung destined to have a sensational ending.

With no announcement from Democratic headquarters and no actual endorsement of the move by any man of standing in the opposition, a vicious and outrageous personal attack was made on Harding.

The nation was suddenly flooded with millions of scurrilous circulars of anonymous authorship declaring that the Hardings had in their family a trace of Negro blood.

Two hundred and fifty thousand of these circulars were discovered in the mails at San Francisco. The postage alone on this one shipment of letters amounted to five thousand dollars. The printing and mailing cost as much more.

President Wilson indignantly ordered the stuff destroyed, and the post offices refused to receive or handle the matter. Whereupon thousands of messengers were employed to distribute the circulars by hand, under cover of darkness.

The *New York Herald* carried a page story of denunciation of this canard. In an editorial, printed in display type at the head of the front page, Frank Munsey issued his proclamation:

"In the closing hours of the campaign a dastardly conspiracy is put on foot to steal the election through an insidious assertion that Warren G. Harding, Republican candidate for President of the United States, is of Negro ancestry.

"That this villainous undertaking has a thorough organization back of it with ample money to carry on the work is beyond question, though no Cox newspaper has dared to print the slander and no man of known standing has dared to utter it.

"William E. Chancellor, who has been expelled from a Professorship in Wooster College, Ohio (the same man who was expelled from the public schools of Washington for lying and incompetence), is quoted in this anonymous propaganda as authority for this defamation of the Harding family. His name alone comes to the surface in connection with this stealthy dagger-thrust in the back on the eve of the election.

"Hundreds of thousands of these cowardly circulars have been sent out through the mails, passed from hand to hand and slipped under doorways at night by an army of cowards of a well-organized conspiracy bent on throwing the election.

"In all our political history there is nothing comparable to this foul, eleventh hour attack on a Presidential Candidate, made without conscience or moral sense, solely for the purpose of defrauding the Republican Party of its impending victory. This is desperation carried to the verge of criminality."

An attempt to circulate these filthy circulars in the suburban trains running into Chicago resulted in fist fights that cleared each coach promptly of the intruders.

It was published that a Democratic official of Reading, Pennsylvania, Harvey L. Bausher, Clerk of the Court of Berks County, was arrested for criminal libel for circulating copies of this fictitious "family tree." He gave a thousand dollars bail and issued a statement on his release in which he is credited with saying:

"My arrest is an effort solely to stem the tide against Harding. I refuse to discuss the case further."

The Republican executive committee was thoroughly familiar with this ancient lie, which had its origin in a quarrel of children seventy-five years ago at the country schoolhouse which the Hardings attended. In a row between the children of the Applemans and the blue-eyed Hardings, vicious epithets were hurled, along with protruding tongues and gestures of contempt, in vogue among the young from time immemorial. This quarrel reached the heights of brutal tongue-lashing.

"Scum!"

"Trash!"

"Nigger!"

At this climax of insult a blue-eyed Harding punched the nose of a dark-eyed Appleman. When the story of the fight reached the Appleman home, the elders at first laughed at it, but it started a feud between the families that lasted for years.

The children of the Applemans kept it up. They had found an epithet that rankled and they used it again and more fights followed.

The discussion of the feud spread in the neighborhood. Unthinking people became involved in a foolish controversy. The Hardings, like all persons of strong individuality, had enemies who took up and spread a tale that they knew to be absolutely false.

At every election in which Harding was a candidate for office, from the beginning of his career in 1898 as a State Senator till his last campaign, this foolish lie was revived by the opposition in a whispering campaign. It cut no figure in the results in Ohio except possibly in his candidacy for Governor, because the people knew it was a silly falsehood.

No family in the State had a clearer or more honorable record than the Hardings, a blue-eyed stock from New England and Pennsylvania, of the finest pioneer blood, Anglo-Saxon, German, Scotch-Irish and Dutch.

Harding's great-grandfather, George Tryon Harding, eldest son of Amos and Phoebe Madison, was born in Pottstown, Luzerne County, Pennsylvania, June 15, 1790.

C. Alexander Harding, son of George Tryon, was born at Clifford, Pennsylvania, April 8, 1820.

The Wyoming, Pennsylvania, Historical Society, founded in 1858, has issued an official pamphlet of the Harding ancestry, complete from its European origin, covering two hundred years, to the present.

A ridiculous fake family tree always accompanied these circulars. It was printed on a cheap pulp paper about five by seven inches wide and bore the signature of no authority whatever.

This fake tree alleged that Warren Harding's grandfather was Amos Harding and his grandmother Mary Ann Dixon, a Negress.

The records of the Wyoming, Pennsylvania, Historical Society, covering a period of more than two hundred years, show that no such person as Mary Ann Dixon was ever married to a Harding. Senator Harding's grandfather was not Amos, but Charles Alexander Harding, whose wife was Mary Ann Crawford, of Scotch-Irish lineage.

The only Amos Harding among the Senator's ancestors was his great-great-grandfather, who married Phoebe Tripp. He was born in 1764 in Pennsylvania and died at Blooming Grove, Ohio, in 1839.

According to the fake family tree Amos Harding arose from the grave where he had moldered five years and begot a child by a woman who did not exist.

Senator Harding had agreed with our committee that this ancient lie was too contemptible for public notice. He had never stooped to deny it in all his political career and would not do so now.

On the last day of Harding's active campaign as we passed through Dayton, Ohio, the train was flooded with copies of the *Journal* carrying on its front page a screaming denial of this slander.

When Harding saw it he was wild with rage. He was a man slow to anger, and I had never seen him in such a fury. He had jumped immediately at the conclusion that I, as his campaign manager, had ordered this denial printed.

He came into my car, which was immediately in front of his, as the train was moving out of Dayton toward Cincinnati.

I was equally amazed and annoyed, and said to him:

"Senator, I gave everybody instructions to make no reference to this subject. I knew this was your desire, as it was mine."

He looked at me:

"Of course you didn't do it. I might have known that."

When the train arrived in Cincinnati I left his party and went to a different hotel and spent most of the evening talking over the long distance telephone. I called Will Hays, who was in New York, and many others over the country, and we discussed the situation.

During the evening Mr. E. B. McLean, owner of the *Cincinnati Enquirer,* the biggest and most influential Democratic newspaper in the Middle West, came in. He and Mrs. McLean were warm personal friends of the Hardings. His father, John R. McLean, had been a friend of mine. As a young man I did some cub reporting for the *Enquirer,* and later was Mr. McLean's attorney.

McLean was in a rage over the slander that had been so quietly and skillfully launched in the closing days of the campaign.

He drew from his pocket the proof sheet of a leading editorial denouncing the Democratic Party for this outrage, and swinging his paper squarely into the Republican column for Harding and Coolidge.

I read it with mixed feelings and handed it back to him. It was very drastic.

"You mustn't print that, Ned," I advised.

"Why not?"

"Many reasons. Among them, it would have broken your father's heart. Your father was one of the finest men I've ever known. But he was a dyed-in-the-wool Democrat. He built up a great piece of property in the *Enquirer* as a Democratic paper. That editorial would destroy in a day the work of his life."

"You think so?"

"I know so. Your father would turn over in his grave if he knew a Republican's name was printed at the head of your editorial column as your choice for President. Don't do it."

"But it's an outrage!"

"Don't worry," I assured. "It will turn out to be the worst boomerang in the history of American politics. Harding's election is as sure as if the votes were counted. You mustn't make this sacrifice and do this to your father's memory. It's not necessary. I figure that this canard will add a million votes to Harding's plurality."

"You feel sure of this?"

"As sure as that I'm living. Call your office and kill that editorial."

He did, and saved a great piece of newspaper property.

I left for Columbus on the three a.m. train. Harding was scheduled to make his closing campaign speech in the capital of Ohio.

As this meeting would be affected by the vicious story just published, I hurried to Columbus to confer with our organization and prepare for anything that might happen.

I met the Senator and his party at the train and took him and his wife to the hotel. There was no demonstration on the streets. A sullen atmosphere brooded over the city. He made no remark about it. Neither did I. Letters had been received threatening that we would both be shot that night.

After dinner we drove to Memorial Hall where the meeting was to be held.

Again we noticed the absence of any demonstration, although crowds of people lined the streets.

Probably ten thousand people were gathered outside the hall. The meeting was going on inside, with Senator Willis acting as chairman.

I had suggested to the local committee that, inasmuch as this was the Senator's last meeting, and in view of what might happen, I should preside.

Outside the hall a platform had been erected so that the Senator could address the crowd unable to gain admittance. On account of careless contruction part of the floor gave way and we both stood on the edge while speaking. I spoke briefly in introducing the speaker. Harding made a short address.

There was marked enthusiasm when he finished.

We went inside, Mrs. Harding, the Senator, and I. There was a great ovation when we reached the platform. Every inch of space in the vast hall was taken, including the aisles.

Senator Willis was speaking as we entered. He stopped and gave way to me as chairman.

I introduced Mrs. Harding. Time and again during the campaign the Wolfe newspapers, and others inspired by them, insinuated that my purpose had been to get control of the Ohio delegation at Chicago and deliver it to my second choice — a man more certain of the nomination than Harding.

I led Mrs. Harding to the edge of the platform and said:

"Ladies and gentlemen, permit me to present to you to-night my only second choice for the Presidency, Mrs. Warren G. Harding!"

While the crowd was cheering she turned to me:

"Harry, I could murder you for this. You never tell me what you are going to do."

But she took it good-naturedly, and while the crowd roared she smiled kindly and nodded her head in appreciation.

I spoke briefly, and introduced Senator Harding as the next President of the United states, closing with the words:

"No lip of libel nor tongue of slander can harm your cause, or you."

Every man in the audience knew what I meant and it was the only reference we ever made to the canard. The newspapers published it far and wide.

Harding made a great speech.

On the morning of the election we played golf at the Scioto Country Club of Columbus, and when the game was over started for Marion. The newspaper men were short of cars and I gave them mine while I rode with the Senator.

Late in the afternoon it rained quite heavily. The Senator had promised Mrs. Harding that we would be there in time for dinner, and his chauffeur was driving faster than usual. About ten miles out of Marion the car skidded, left the road, and barely missed a telegraph pole. Had we struck it every man in the car might have been killed. It was a narrow escape. Had the collision happened, the course of our national history certainly would have been materially changed.

Telephone and telegraph wires had been installed in the kitchen of the house next door to the Senator's home. It was used as an office and headquarters.

After dinner, Mr. and Mrs. Harding and I went there to receive the election returns. We had arranged to get reports of typical districts in several states so that we could strike an average of gains and losses. Will Hays was in our New York headquarters and we reported to each other at intervals over the long-distance wire.

Outside, the crowds were gathering in thousands and bulletins were issued frequently.

About ten-thirty I turned to Senator Harding:

"There is no doubt about the result. I am going over to Dr. Sawyer's to get some sleep."

Both the Senator and Mrs. Harding protested against my leaving and said I must spend the night at their house, as they had expected, but I insisted on getting away from the noise and the crowd.

"This will be the most exciting night Marion has ever experienced," I said in leaving. "You should be very happy. You are elected by the biggest majority any President has ever received. Nothing can change the result. Cox has been overwhelmingly defeated. It is certain, and I congratulate you. But before I go I want to say something you ought to know. Unless you have made promises, you will enter the White House one of the freest men ever elected President of the United States. I have not made a single promise to any man or interests for any position or favor."

He was deeply affected as he answered:

"I have made no promises except those contained in public speeches. You have conducted an unusual campaign, with hardships and abuse, and you will never know how much I appreciate it. Next to Mrs. Harding you are the best friend I have in the world."

She chipped in:

"Don't count me. You two old cronies take all the credit for everything done in this household."

Harding again urged me to stay, though he knew I was worn out and in need of rest.

As I reached the door I called:

"You are all happy over the result now, but considering the great responsibilities I don't feel so gay. But it's over, and God bless you."

CHAPTER VII

The Cabinet and Fall's Appointment

MY STAY at home was brief. The telephone rang day and night. My mail overwhelmed three secretaries.

"Chicago is calling you, sir."

"Indianapolis."

"Washington."

"Seattle."

"San Francisco."

"St. Louis."

"Marion."

"New York."

There was no rest. No time to work. No time to eat or sleep. I had always been a hound for work, but I had met my Waterloo.

I sent for Jess Smith.

Throughout the primary campaign he had acted as a buffer. He had a genius for detail. Energetic and genial, he was useful in making engagements, seeing people and looking after the endless things I had no time to attend to. During the convention in Chicago he was invaluable. He was noncommittal, careful and loyal.

My brother and I had helped to launch him in business in Washington Court House, Ohio, and had always treated him as a younger brother. He knew little about politics, never intruded himself, but was always available. He kept the expense accounts of the campaign and handled the contributions after I approved them. For it was our policy to accept no money from those who might be making contributions with ulterior purposes.

Smith was not a man of great mentality, but was always jolly, a good mixer and a faithful friend. He was head of the Elks in Ohio and had a large acquaintance among Elks over the country.

The Hardings knew him and liked him. He was popular with everyone who knew him.

After the nomination he went back to his business, a general store in his home town. I thought I would dispense with his services but found that I couldn't.

When I sent for him and explained the situation, he volunteered his services without compensation. He had grown to love the limelight in the campaign and had his picture taken several times standing beside Senator and Mrs. Harding. I don't think I ever saw a happier man than he was in answering my summons.

Little did I dream on that crisp November morning of the sinister stories an army of liars would tell of my relations with this simple, loyal friend.

I was not only receiving letters by the thousands, telegrams, and phone calls from every state in the Union, but callers also began pouring in on me from all points of the compass. It was a physical impossibility to see or talk to more than one in twenty of them.

Many I turned over to Jess, who entertained them and kept them in good humor in spite of denials on my part.

It became absolutely necessary to take Jess Smith with me wherever I went. The only other man in the country so harassed by callers was Harding.

It was generally believed that I was the closest man to him. And it was true.

But the idea that I could run him and his administration was a myth that seemed to grow with every denial.

A universal political slogan swept the country:

"See Daugherty."

And they came to see me. They came through good

weather and bad! They came in pairs, singly, and in crowds. And they demanded a hearing. Having called upon so many to help us in need, I felt they were entitled to a hearing. And they got it to the limit of my strength.

After I became Attorney-General they still came. They came in delegations from every state, from Alaska to Honolulu, on legitimate government business, and for appointments to offices in the Department of Justice. Interested, conscientious men also came to confer on policies and public questions that were pending.

Our party had been starved for eight years. The rank and file were place-hungry and anxious to secure appointments. They believed I could help them. I was willing to do what I could. To hear this great mass of people and their friends talk one would have thought I was the dispenser of all offices and had nothing to do but listen to their profound views on governmental policies, without suspecting their selfish interest. It was a task to break down any ten men.

Hundreds came to Columbus to employ me as their attorney. I could have made a million dollars a year, but I refused all offers. I had a good law business, all I could do. But now that I was supposed to be close to the next President, the opportunities increased a hundred fold. The railroads must have put on extra trains between New York and Columbus to carry the people who came to make offers of employment, to make suggestions regarding policies, and to ask for favors.

Many came out of a sincere desire to be of service to the new administration, lawyers I had known all over the country in the many years I practiced law. I perhaps knew more lawyers than any other man at that time, and probably had handled personally more law business in volume, involving more different questions, public and private, than any other man who had been Attorney-General of the United States.

It was necessary for me to assist the Republican Executive

Committee to close its accounts and help raise the money to carry at least the interest on its debts. Campaigns had grown increasingly expensive for a generation. Without spending a dollar in any illegitimate way our expenses had run into many millions. We owed over two millions. Hays knew how to spend money. And he got results.

I helped set his house in order, and answered Harding's call for a conference.

He was busy selecting his Cabinet. I had told him that unless he brought up the subject between us I would never discuss this matter with him.

He had set about the job with enthusiasm and a determination to give the country the strongest Cabinet it had known in half a century. There would be no figureheads and no "yes" men in his official family. This I knew for a certainty, because I knew Harding better than any other man alive.

I doubt if any President-elect ever gave as careful thought to the selection of his Cabinet. And no President in the long history of the Nation was more respected by the Cabinet he finally selected.

No President ever had more respect for his Cabinet. When a member differed from him he liked to be told of it at once. He always listened carefully to the dissenting opinion; and after hearing all sides and considering all phases he would make the decision and that settled it. He never sulked when a member disagreed with his views.

The qualities he looked for were loyalty, intelligence, ability, experience, courage, candor, honesty, and political sense; the ability to associate with each other in effective teamwork; the power to reason and listen to reason, and a willingness to stand the gaff of public criticism without weakening in an emergency. The men in his Cabinet must fit together, work together, and respect each other's work.

From the hour of his election wiseacres began, of course, to select his Cabinet for him — the men who thought he hadn't sense enough to do it for himself. Most of them were fools and were fooled.

The *New York World* especially was abusive and ugly during the entire campaign. A Democratic paper, of course, its stamp of approval couldn't be put on the President-elect in anything he did. After the election it started immediately to choose his Cabinet, discussing men who ought and ought not to be selected.

And a group of the "intellectuals" who generally proclaim that they know more than Almighty God announced at once that the men of Harding's Cabinet would comprise the quintessence of mediocrity.

In answer to this clamor I said to Harding:

"You are the President-elect of the United States. If I were in your place I'd select the men I like and believe in even if I had to take every one from the little state of Rhode Island. The Cabinet is your personal concern first and last."

"Fine," he laughed. "I'm just talking it over in an informal way. What do you think of Hughes as Secretary of State?"

"The best selection you could possibly make. The most important man in the Cabinet should be the biggest man but he should be a man who thinks and feels in sympathy with his chief. Not a William H. Seward who will despise his Abraham Lincoln.

"You and Hughes are men of the same breed. The religion you both profess is the most democratic of all denominations. You're a Trustee of the Trinity Baptist Church of Marion. Hughes is a Trustee of the Park Avenue Baptist Church of New York. Your temperaments are sympathetic He'll like you and you will like him.

"Considering his age, experience, training and general qualifications I believe that he is today the ablest man in the United States, or in the public service of any nation in the world."

Harding nodded genially.

"Just my idea of the man."

Recently I read with amazement A. B. Fall's statement in his series of articles published in a newspaper syndicate that Harding had offered to him first the position of Secretary of State, "the day after he was nominated at Chicago!" Harding never once mentioned such a thing to me. And if he had ever thought seriously of it, he would surely have talked it over in our frequent discussions of the Cabinet.

Such a thought never entered the President's mind unless he said it to Fall, his Senatorial desk mate, in a moment of fun or banter.

Charles Evans Hughes was the President-elect's first and only choice for Secretary of State.

"What do you think of Charlie Dawes for Secretary of the Treasury?" he suddenly asked me.

"Dawes," I repeated. "He's a great man. A man this country is going to hear from. A good second choice."

"He's a great banker."

"Granted. Dawes is also a born diplomat and a fearless leader. It would be a mistake to lock him up in the United States Treasury."

I paused and determined to make my first suggestion for a Cabinet officer. It turned out to be the only man I ever pressed for a position, except Sutherland for Attorney-General.

"The one man in the United States, in my opinion, for that position is Andrew W. Mellon of Pittsburgh."

"Mellon . . . Mellon," Harding muttered. "I don't know him."

"Well, I do," I assured. "I've met him, and in my opinion he is the ablest financier in America. He would doubtlessly deny it, but I believe he is the richest man in this country, richer than either Ford or Rockefeller. And he is the only man that the big interests, the Rockefellers and Morgans, will not bluff."

"And you think his great wealth a recommendation?" he broke in.

"I certainly do. A man who can quietly make the millions this modest-looking man has gathered is little short of a magician. If there is one thing he knows it's money. He will make for you the greatest Secretary of the Treasury since Alexander Hamilton and render the Nation an immense service, if you can get him."

"I'd like to talk to him."

"Send for him."

"You think he'd run over to Marion?"

"What a question! Any man in America would be honored by an invitation to see you."

"All right," he modestly smiled. "Suppose you get word to him that I would like to have a talk with him."

A wire was sent to Mr. Mellon and he came promptly.

When he got off the train he looked around and found no one there to meet him and no cabs waiting.

He walked about a mile to the Harding house, entered with the passing crowd of visitors and reporters and sat down in the hall.

Finally a newspaper man said to the usher:

"Great Scott, isn't that Andrew W. Mellon of Pittsburgh?"

"Dunno," the usher mumbled. "But if it is, his name's on the President's list for an appointment. I'll see."

He walked up to the quiet little man who sat patiently in a chair and asked:

"Are you Mr. Mellon of Pittsburgh?"

"Yes, but I can wait. Tell the Senator I am here at his bidding. I know he's busy."

"You're on his list, sir."

"Whenever he's ready I'm here. Tell him I'll take my turn."

The usher showed him into the room immediately.

Harding talked with him for an hour and when he came out he said to the reporters:

"Pay no attention to me, boys. I'm going out for a little walk. I'll be back in half an hour when the Senator is through with another caller and then I'm to lunch with him — that's all — good-by."

He strolled about town for half an hour, came back, lunched with Harding, and they had another conference.

Nothing was settled. But the President-elect liked him.

He started down the steps and an attendant said:

"A car will take you to the station, Mr. Mellon."

"Thank you. Don't bother. I'd rather stroll along and look at the town."

And without waiting for an answer the biggest financier of the modern world strolled carelessly along the streets toward the railway station for Pittsburgh.

When I saw the President-elect I asked him:

"Well, what did Uncle Andy say?"

"Said he didn't think he'd make a very good Secretary of the Treasury."

"Why?"

"Thought he'd be criticized because he owned interests in so many different enterprises over the country."

"He does too," I laughed. "Only Mellon and God know how varied those interests are. And what did you tell him?"

"I asked if he thought there'd be any real conflict between his duties and his interests," Harding laughed.

"He tried to smile and couldn't quite make it as he replied: 'I wouldn't let them conflict, of course, if I assumed such a duty. But honestly I don't believe I'd make a good Secretary of the Treasury.'"

They both agreed to think it over.

"Good!" I said. "You'll hear from Knox and Penrose."

And he did. Both Senators from Pennsylvania were elated

at the honor suggested for their state and began at once to press Mellon for the place.

Nothing was decided on the appointment for some time. And Mellon became the key to a dramatic and sensational struggle over the appointment of another member of the Cabinet.

A contest that made history.

It is all but universally believed that Fall and I were inseparable chums in the Harding administration. The press for the past ten years has constantly linked my name with his in a way that implied this.

"Fall and Daugherty."

"Daugherty and Fall."

These headlines have been run until the nation has about settled into the conviction that we two were the "Gold-Dust Twins" of the Harding régime.

Nothing could be farther from the facts.

When the President-elect first suggested to me the appointment of Fall as his Secretary of the Interior I did not oppose him for two important reasons.

Fall and Harding had been accidentally thrown into an intimate friendship by the assignment of seats in the Senate, a condition which placed them side by side for six years. Harding was the younger Senator, Fall the veteran. Naturally the newcomer consulted his seat-mate on many questions, especially Western matters, and early grew to admire the striking qualities of Fall's strong mind. He had been for a long time a distinguished Judge and was serving his second term in the Senate.

Fall was an able lawyer, an omnivorous reader, a student of law. And his personality was distinctly dominating, not to say domineering.

In almost every respect Harding and he were opposites: the younger man — suave, genial, friendly — a great mixer who was universally liked; the older man, stern, morose, cynical,

scornful of men and society. Men of such opposite temperaments are often drawn into strong friendship.

I made no effort to break their friendship. I could see at
the time no possible harm to Harding.

Fall had made a solid record as a Senator and lawmaker.
He had helped pass almost every law on the statute books
relating to the affairs of the Interior. He was, moreover, an
expert on the laws governing public lands, oil and mining.

The one thing which no human mind at this time could
have suspected was that the grim, austere man who sat beside
Harding in the Senate was dishonest. And to save my soul I
can't yet bring myself to believe that when he took, or
borrowed, the famous $100,000 from Doheny he realized it
was a bribe.

Another important reason why I did not oppose Fall's
selection for the Cabinet was that in this choice Harding was
again putting into practice his pet theory of converting,
reconciling, and harmonizing his opponents in the Party.

Fall was a typical Progressive, Harding a staunch Stalwart.
Fall had followed Roosevelt in smashing his party in 1912.
Harding had stood boldly by our traditions and fought for
Taft.

I always held, as a party leader, that the only way
to harmonize an enemy or a traitor inside the organization
was to throw him over the fence and put a loyal man in his
place.

I saw Harding use his pet theory on this distinguished
Progressive with forebodings. Yet I hesitated to antagonize
him over the matter.

Enough time has passed for us to discuss the Progressive
Movement with some degree of sanity and reason.

I repeat my political creed. I believe that the American
system of a responsible government by great parties is a
distinct advance in parliamentary democracy over the Kil-
kenny-cat groups in Europe.

Believing this, I believe in playing the game by the rules.

Looking back again and again over the twenty years that have passed since the Bull Moose capers of 1912, I have never yet been able to discover a single sound principle in the movement.

One thing caused the Bull Moose split: the overweening ambition of a single man to be the first American to serve a third term in the White House.

By all the rules of the game Taft was certainly entitled to the endorsement of his party and a renomination for his second term. He had proven himself an honest, capable President. He was in every way the same upright, distinguished public servant whom Roosevelt had nominated as his successor in 1908.

Every President in the history of the Republican Party who had successfully served a first term had been endorsed and given the nomination for the second.

What, then, under high heaven had happened to justify the attempt to murder Taft and throw his body to the dogs? But one thing could have happened. Roosevelt wanted a third term. To his dying day he lived this ambition with a deathless passion.

I know this because he made overtures to me for a reconciliation after our bitter fight in 1912, when he addressed a meeting in Columbus over which I presided.

I am saying nothing in detraction of Roosevelt as a great American. He was an outstanding national figure in his day His name will always shine as a man of genius and as a political leader. He was a shrewd politician. But in the launching of the Progressive Party he committed the one tragic blunder of his career — a blunder that, in my opinion, was an unpardonable sin, and which I am sure he regretted before his death.

Roosevelt, of course, attended the National Convention of 1912. He made a speech in which he charged that an attempt was being made to defeat him for the nomination by the adoption of the rules governing the Convention.

I was called upon and forced to make a speech in reply in front of our headquarters. Roosevelt was standing in the door listening. The excitement was intense. I spoke with sharp emphasis:

"The rules of this Convention," I commenced, looking the Colonel in the face, "were used by you to win the Vice-Presidency in the second McKinley campaign, and I was on the Committee on Rules when you were nominated for the Presidency in 1904. You were satisfied with those rules then. In the Convention of 1909, when you were leading in the nomination of President Taft, you were consulted about the same rules and used them. Eight years ago we were doing these same things *under* these rules *for* you. Four years ago we were doing these things *under* these same rules *with* you. Now we are doing these things under these same rules *to* you!"

Roosevelt turned quickly in anger and left the audience.

Elihu Root, his former Secretary of State, the strong man of his administration, and one of the great men of America, saw through his false position with merciless eyes and joined us in renominating Taft.

Roosevelt bolted and deserted the great party that had created him.

Fall and I could never have been chums in any political enterprise. And we never were. He had followed the sheep into the desert with Roosevelt, and I could never forget it.

I was always polite and personally friendly, but never could work with him politically any more than I could with any of the other men who had joined the utterly futile and fatal Bull Moose movement. And they were, of course, never friendly with me.

When Fall's appointment to the Cabinet was delayed by

Harding, the Westerner met the situation in characteristic fashion. Without saying anything to me about it he sent the following telegram to the President-elect and signed *my* name to it.

YOU UNDERSTAND OF COURSE FALL MUST RESIGN TO TAKE EFFECT NOT LATER THAN FOURTH AND GOVERNOR SHOULD APPOINT SUCCESSOR IMMEDIATELY STOP UNDERSTAND NEW MEXICO STATE COMMITTEE HAS BEEN CALLED TO ADVISE THE GOVERNOR ABOUT SUCCESSOR AND FALL HAS WIRED COULD NOT ATTEND STOP DO YOU NOT THINK ADVISABLE ANNOUNCE FALL'S APPOINTMENT AND ACCEPTANCE AT ONCE AS OF COURSE DISCUSSION WILL TAKE PLACE SANTA FE ON MEETING OF COMMITTEE AND FALL HAS INSTRUCTED GOVERNOR NOT TO GIVE PUBLICITY HIS APPOINTMENT UNTIL ANNOUNCED BY YOU STOP UNDER PRECEDENTS RESIGNATION CAN BE OFFERED IMMEDIATELY OR ON FUTURE DATE AND GOVERNOR BE NOTIFIED BY HIM OR RESIGNATION DIRECT TO GOVERNOR AND SENATE NOTIFIED BY HIM OR RESIGNATION OFFERED TO BOTH AT SAME TIME STOP I ADVISE YOUR IMMEDIATE ANNOUNCEMENT APPOINTMENT AND ACCEPTANCE UNLESS YOU HAVE REASONS

(signed)
HARRY M. DAUGHERTY

This message he had charged to his personal account.

The appointment was made and the mine laid for an explosion destined to shake the nation.

There was no question, however, about the popularity of Fall's selection. Harding received a flood of letters and telegrams of approval. Practically every Senator, Republican and Democrat, endorsed his appointment in one form or another.

And on the day of the inauguration an extraordinary scene in the Senate confirmed this popularity. In view of all that has happened since, I marvel as I recall it.

The new Cabinet was confirmed with record-breaking

promptness. Harding suddenly appeared in the Senate Chamber and, shattering all precedents, submitted in person the names of his chosen official family.

Among his reasons for adopting this plan was the importance of at once undertaking to establish the most cordial relations with the Senate. He wished no feuds with the upper chamber of Congress, and was particularly anxious to wipe out the memory of all conflict between the two branches of the government.

He was given a tumultuous welcome. The Senate was taken completely by surprise. They had just reassembled behind closed doors in executive session after attending the inaugural ceremonies on the East Front of the Capitol.

The new President ascended the rostrum in the Senate, and took a seat beside Vice-President Coolidge. He immediately rose, read the names of his chosen Cabinet, and made a brief address:

"Senators," he began in an even tone, "it is not necessary for me, as a former member of this body, to say that I am keenly mindful of its functions and responsibilities.

"I have chosen my Cabinet in accordance with my best judgment and my personal wishes. I trust it will meet with your speedy approval."

He left the Chamber amid a roar of lusty handclapping from Republicans and Democrats.

But the most sensational thing that happened in this precedent-breaking scene was the greeting of A. B. Fall's name with a spontaneous burst of applause from his fellow-members of the Senate.

He was seated at his desk in the Senate at the time. There is no other instance on record of a Senator receiving his appointment to the Cabinet in such fashion.

Amid tumultuous cheers from his colleagues Fall rose from his seat and tendered his resignation as a Senator. It was immediately accepted.

For a moment he found himself in the anomalous position of a private citizen intruding on the floor of the Chamber.

His colleagues hazed him in jovial fashion.

They crowded around in mock anger:

"Throw him out!"

"Get out!"

Senator Lodge, the Republican leader, finally came to his rescue with a novel suggestion:

"I move, Mr. President, that Senator A. B. Fall be immediately confirmed by the Senate as Secretary of the Interior without the usual formality of a reference to a Committee."

The motion was put and *unanimously* carried with another round of applause. Fall was the only member of a Cabinet thus confirmed by unanimous vote without a committee endorsement.

All the other nominations for the Cabinet, including Charles Evans Hughes, Secretary of State, ran the gauntlet of a committee report. All were immediately confirmed without a dissenting vote.

Little did any man in that joyous crowd of Senators foresee a tragedy in which Warren Harding would be betrayed by his trusted friend.

CHAPTER VIII

The Tragic Blunder of My Life

I PLUNGED into the rapids of politics after the election for the sole purpose of assisting in the settlement of the affairs and debts of the Party. Harding was embarrassed, and wanted all debts paid. And I was asked to give personal aid to the President-elect in a task that all but overwhelmed him.

The longer I was in the current the more irresistible it became, until I found myself helpless in the effort to retreat. Every time I went home and tried to pick up the thread of life and my practice, I was besieged by hordes of visitors and bombarded with letters and telegrams. The country believed, in spite of my protests, that I would have a great responsibility in the Harding administration, as I had managed his nomination and been prominent in his election.

Nothing was further from my desires. Yet nobody believed me when I said a thousand times I was going to retire from politics. And I'm afraid they will not believe the simple truth now when I repeat it.

I was tired of politics, mortally tired of its fierce feuds, its savage battles, its bitterness, its lies, its slanders, its foolish myths, and its devastating demands upon a man deep in the game.

Yet the amazing situation in which I found myself stunned me in every effort to withdraw. Whether I liked it or not, I found my position one of increasing demands and painful responsibility. It seemed that every man in the United States who wanted an office or had an ax to grind with the new administration persisted in coming or writing to me.

I told them I would not embarrass Harding in the exercise

of his duties. They wouldn't believe me. They waylaid me and repeated their pleas until I had to flee time and again.

It was assumed as a matter of course, by both my friends and enemies, that I would be given the post of Attorney-General in Harding's Cabinet.

I had made up my mind firmly from the day I accepted the management of his campaign to accept no office within his gift.

When I told people this they laughed. I was merely being facetious!

Harding's demands on me for conferences and advice became more frequent and insistent. He consulted me on his proposed appointments and the contemplated policies of his coming administration.

My first choice, when he proposed that I take the Attorney-Generalship, was Senator George Sutherland of Utah, now Justice of the Supreme Court of the United States.

"I hadn't thought of Sutherland as my Attorney-General," Harding replied. "He'll make a great Judge of the Supreme Court."

In spite of our understanding when I began his campaign, he finally urged me to accept the position.

I stoutly refused.

He urged the matter from every angle and pressed my acceptance.

"You've surely not forgotten our agreement," I said, "the day I took the job as your manager?"

"Was there an agreement?"

"Certainly."

"On your part an announcement, perhaps. I made no actual promises. You may recall my silence."

"Yes," I admitted. "You're great on the silences when you don't wish to commit yourself. But I meant it then and I mean it now. My answer is no."

Florence Kling Harding

"Her love for Harding was of the deep, eternal things of life, and he knew it."

Gen. Wood   *Gov. Lowden*

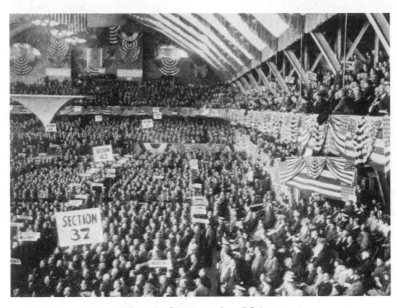

The Coliseum in Chicago

Lowden and Wood fight each other to a finish, deadlock the
Convention, opening the way for Harding.

"Absolutely?"

"Without reservation. I can't put it too strongly. Why do you persist in urging it?"

"Because I want you with me. I never needed your help and loyal friendship as I need them to-day."

"But why handicap your administration with my feuds and political enemies — especially with Bob Wolfe and his crowd?"

"Your enemies are mine," was his quick reply. "I've known you for thirty-five years. I know your standing as a lawyer. I don't need information from anybody about you."

"And you'll risk a corporation lawyer in the office of the Attorney-General?" I interrupted.

"I have no hope of finding another kind. Every lawyer in the United States capable of filling the office is a corporation lawyer. Hughes has been one all of his life. The silly talk of you representing 'interests' is childish twaddle. You know that as well as I."

"Sure, I know it, but they'll criticize you just the same if you appoint me. My office is in Columbus, Ohio, not New York, Boston, Philadelphia, or Chicago. I'm from the 'sticks,' you know."

"So am I!" Harding countered. He paused and suddenly asked:

"Is Senator Knox of Pennsylvania a great lawyer?"

"One of the biggest in the country. A great man — why?"

"Because he is the one man in the Senate who has urged on me your appointment as Attorney-General from the first — "

"Well, I appreciate the compliment, coming from so high a source. But honestly now, man to man, you shouldn't ask of me this sacrifice. I can make money practicing law in Columbus, relieved from heavy responsibilities, enjoy the balance of my life with my wife and family — and go fishing. That's what I want to do."

I left him still firm in my resolution to decline all public office.

As the time drew near for the announcement of the selection for Attorney-General, the *New York World* and its St. Louis associate paper, and the Wolfe papers in Columbus, made a concerted attack on me that was unparalleled in the history of Cabinet making.

Mark Sullivan and Louis Seibold, two brilliant newspaper men, representing this faction, were constant in their efforts to obtain from the President-elect an expression of opinion on the subject. Mr. Sullivan informed his constituents as follows:

> Even if Harding should feel that Daugherty's position in Ohio politics would be still further improved by a tender to him of the office of Attorney-General, he would immediately rely on Daugherty to decline the office . . . .

This generous morsel of wisdom was freely handed out to an eager public at the moment I was resisting every effort of the President-elect to induce me to accept the office.

The persistence of Sullivan and Seibold in circulating all sorts of wild rumors about the Attorney-Generalship finally got on Harding's nerves.

There had been worked up a story about the offer of the post of Secretary of Agriculture to an Ohio man, which would have kept any other man from the state out of the Cabinet.

Sullivan and Seibold arrived in St. Augustine just before the hour for the interview of the newspaper men with Harding. Their appearance roused the ire of the badgered President-elect.

And when one of them asked:

"What about the Attorney-Generalship?"

Harding flushed with anger, pointed his finger at his questioner and said:

"I am ready to-day to invite Mr. Daugherty into the Cabinet as my Attorney-General. When he is ready, there will be an announcement, if he can persuade himself to make the sacrifice. Daugherty is a splendid man, an able lawyer, and he will make a great Attorney-General if I can persuade him to accept the post — "

He paused and continued with emphasis:

"You can say that I love him for the enemies he has made. The opposition to his appointment has strengthened the conviction that I need him."

He shot a straight look at Seibold and added:

"And you can set that up *in block* on the front page of your papers!"

I arrived from a walk unexpectedly on the scene and saw that there was considerable excitement.

I gripped a reporter by the arm:

"What's the matter? What's happened?"

"Harding has just announced to the press that he is going to make you Attorney-General if you will accept the post."

My heart sank. I knew that he had, on one of his rare occasions, lost his temper. He had committed me in such a way that it would be next to impossible to embarrass him by a public refusal.

Surprised, I went to his room:

"My God, why have you done such a thing?"

"I couldn't stand it any longer, Harry," he said, with deep feeling. "I'm sick and tired of filthy tirades against you from the men who did their best to discredit and defeat me. They make me furious with their cheap posing as the guardians of the nation! I made up my mind to put an end to it."

"But see what you've done to me! You've forced me into a corner."

"Well, it's up to you," he answered firmly. "Are you going to continue to stand by me, or desert me after all these years? I've never needed you in my life as I do to-day."

"I advise you again to appoint Sutherland."

"And I tell you again that Sutherland is my choice for the Supreme Court. I know you. I know your ability as a lawyer. I know you better than any other man. You will help make my administration a success. Others will contribute their skill and loyalty, I know, but while I hold the wheel of the ship I want you in the lookout in storm and stress. In you I'll have an adviser always reliable, honest, fearless, frank."

He stopped and leaned close:

"Surely I should expect to have the man by my side on whom I have learned to rely implicitly through years of trial and association. I demand the opportunity to show these people my faith in you. Aside from my wish to have your services in the office you will fill, I wish to do you high honor, to show you that I don't forget. But above all things I'm asking you to become my Attorney-General because I need you – "

There was nothing I could say. He knew that he had me.

I think the conflicting elements in this personal drama were best summed up at the time by an editorial in the *Philadelphia Public Ledger:*

The fierce, white heat of those who wish to discredit Mr. Harding's administration before it has begun beats upon Harry M. Daugherty, who will serve as Attorney-General in Mr. Harding's Cabinet. Since Mr. Daugherty's entrance into the Cabinet had been foreshadowed almost from the day of the election, he has been for nearly three months a shining mark for hostile criticism.

But our purpose here is not to make a case for Mr. Daugherty. It runs deeper than that. It is an attempt, feeble and probably futile, to induce in the American public the habit of straight thinking and fair play. It is an appeal to those who habitually mistake insidiously inspired prejudice for righteous emotion.

If there is a preconceived case against Mr. Daugherty, it yields readily to analysis. He has been a potent figure in Ohio politics for thirty years. He has fought a thousand battles, and in every battle he has made bitter, formidable enemies who not only believe the worst about him, but who lend a certain authenticity to it by spreading it.

No man may actively participate in politics through a period of years without becoming the object and the victim of animosities. Politically Mr. Daugherty has wielded power. Every man who wields power automatically becomes a discredited and disreputable citizen in the minds of those against whom he wields it. There will be stories 'on' Mr. Daugherty, but they establish nothing and prove nothing to any fair-minded man who knows politics.

And there is this to Mr. Daugherty's credit. No weak or crooked man survives for a long period of years the concentrated fire of political enemies. He curls up and dies and another takes his place. Mr. Daugherty has long been subjected to concentrated fire. He did not curl up and die. Instead, he remains a conspicuous figure on the horizon of politics, and never was so deeply intrenched within his party's lines. There must be something to him.

So in a moment of mental aberration I accepted the post of Attorney-General in the Harding Cabinet, and made the tragic blunder of my life.

CHAPTER IX

The Fight Over the Selection of Mr. Hoover

IN WHAT I shall say about Mr. Hoover I sincerely wish to disclaim any purpose of captious criticism.

It is an accident that this book appears on the approach of the Presidential Convention of 1932.

I am not trying to interfere in any way with the President's renomination by the Republican Party. As I have said before, I repeat, that under the rules of a responsible party government he is entitled to a renomination. The party would stultify itself to refuse it.

I said this in 1912 for Mr. Taft. I say it again for Mr. Hoover.

There can be no successful opposition to the renomination of a President by his party. Roosevelt, the most powerful leader the Republican Party had developed since Lincoln, tried to break this rule in refusing Taft a renomination. He failed signally, and he ought to have failed. He didn't play the game. He refused to abide by the rules under which he had lived and grown to greatness. He thought that he could smash those rules by the strength of his individual good right arm and his magnetic personality.

But Roosevelt hadn't the power to break the rules even when pitted against an opponent of Taft's kindly and nonaggressive temperament.

To-day we have a very much stronger case for the incumbent. There is no man of Roosevelt's daring and powerful personality to lead the opposition to Mr. Hoover. Mr. Coolidge is the only one in sight. And he would not enter a contest against a man he had retained in his Cabinet. He is a man of friendly, peaceful instincts. He has served two terms exactly as Roosevelt did. He would have to be dragged out of his retirement by main force. And there is no one in the Republican Party to-day with any influence who will undertake to do the dragging.

Mr. Hoover's renomination is in order according to rule and right in a government by great responsible parties. This is exactly as it should be under our system.

Nothing therefore that I may say about him at this time can be construed as disloyalty to my party.

When Harding first broached the subject to me of Mr. Hoover's appointment as his Secretary of Commerce about the first of December following the election, I was surprised.

But I did not say a word in opposition. In fact I did not lift a finger in opposition to any man the President-elect had under consideration for a cabinet portfolio, except to my own appointment as Attorney-General.

Herbert Hoover was probably the best advertised man in the United States. He had been a conspicuous figure in the Wilson administration. The country had the impression that he had rendered great services abroad in feeding the suffering and starving children of Belgium. This appealed to every mother. The press of the country boosted him constantly.

He had never been identified with the Republican Party and he was not acquainted with our policies. It was not a popular appointment among the men who took an active part in the nomination and election of President Harding.

There are always objections to any appointment to a cabinet position. No man in the world who amounts to anything or who has accomplished anything is without enemies.

Mr. Hoover was strenuously opposed by a great body of men in the Republican Party. He had his supporters too, and many of them, but not among those active in the councils of the organization.

From the beginning I took the position that I would not intrude my views as to the Cabinet unless the President-elect asked for my advice. But when he asked for the facts in regard to the opposition to Hoover I was compelled to tell him where the protests came from.

I intimated no purpose on my part to oppose Mr. Hoover. Had I been President I probably would not have appointed him, and he likely would not have chosen me.

Harding first discussed the selection with me early in December 1920, when he was in Marion.

"I have a hunch," he said, "that it's the best thing to do and the big thing to do to pick Herbert Hoover for Secretary of Commerce. He can be a big factor in a constructive way in our reconstructive period."

He asked me to send for Mr. Hoover. I conveyed the message that the President-elect would like to see him any day after December tenth. He wired a reply fixing the eleventh.

His visit to Marion immediately started protests in the party against his selection.

The opposition grew, especially among the Republican members of the Senate.

Harding requested me to make an investigation and find how serious the opposition was.

We were in St. Augustine at the time and I made a trip to Washington, remained several days, spent a day in New York, and continued to Columbus.

I made a written report to the President-elect as to the exact situation as I found it, and advised him that there was determined rebellion. I reported the facts, which he was entitled to, but gave no hint as to how I felt about it.

In reply he wrote me as follows:

St. Augustine, Fla.
February 9, 1921.

Hon. H. M. Daugherty,
Huntington Bank Building,
Columbus, Ohio.

My dear Daugherty:

I have yours of February 6. I had not read it at the time I telephoned you because we called you up immediately after our arrival. I am sorry that so many people impress you as hostile to Mr. Hoover for a place in the Cabinet. Of course, I do not want the administration to start out with a quarrel with Senate or any considerable faction in the Republican Party. I do hold him in very high esteem and think his appointment would appeal to the cordial approval of the country. The more I consider him the more do I come to think well of him. Of course, I have no quarrel with those who do not think as I do, but inasmuch as I have the responsibility to assume I think my judgment must be trusted in the matter. The main thing to consider at the present is whether Mr. Hoover will accept the post which I am prepared to offer him. Of course, I shall do nothing in the matter until I have an opportunity to see you again and get such information as you have to offer. It is always fine to have somebody scouting around to get expressions which very naturally do not reach me. I think it is fair to say, however, that the opposition of a number of the men mentioned in your letter does not deeply impress me.

[signed] Warren G. Harding.

The President-elect was amazed at the growing opposition to his wishes in the matter and delayed the announcement of Mr. Hoover's appointment to almost the last.

He asked me to make another trip to Washington and see the men who were opposing Hoover's confirmation, and I arranged to leave that night.

"Have you notified Mr. Mellon as yet of his selection as Secretary of the Treasury?" I asked.

"Not yet."

"Good. Don't do it until you get a long distance call from me in Washington. I'll have some information for you."

"All right, old man," he affectionately said, "take care of yourself and try and get this situation ironed out."

On arrival I found a number of Senators organizing to oppose the confirmation of Mr. Hoover. I did not think they could accomplish his defeat, but it would be embarrassing to him and to the President if there was a fight over his confirmation.

I wasted no time in general conferences. I knew whom to go to, and went. I had wired Senator Knox that I would take breakfast with him on my arrival in Washington.

Knox and Penrose were the two most powerful men in the Senate. Johnson also was opposed to the appointment of Mr. Hoover, and Senator Lodge. Both were standing shoulder to shoulder with Penrose and Knox.

After breakfast I asked Senator Knox to call Penrose and tell him we were coming over.

Meantime I had given no intimation of my business. Knox and I had been friends for a long time, and he had helped force me into the Cabinet. I felt I had a right to talk frankly to him.

We called on Senator Penrose and our visit created great excitement among the vigilant newspaper men who thought something of importance was about to be done, or undone. They waited for two hours to get the news.

Penrose was cordial. He had not been advised of my coming until we telephoned him. He asked me if the entire Cabinet was decided on. I told him it was not.

"Well," he observed, "you are going into the Cabinet as Attorney-General, aren't you?"

"Not if I can help it!"

He was surprised, having talked with Senator Knox, who thought I should accept the Attorney-Generalship.

"The President-elect proposes to put his friends into the Cabinet, doesn't he?" Penrose went on.

"Yes, I have no doubt about that."

"Well, what about Uncle Andy?"

"I do not know yet what he will do about Mr. Mellon," I fenced.

"What's that?" growled Knox.

"Well," Penrose put in, "he's not going to appoint Hoover, is he?"

"I think he is," I promptly answered.

And I stood my ground:

"The President-elect should be allowed to assemble his own Cabinet without interference and you're the last man in the United States to lead a revolt against his prerogative."

"I agree with Senator Penrose," Knox broke in.

"Well, I came here," I replied, "to tell you that Harding proposes to appoint Mr. Hoover, and he expects both of you to support his confirmation, as you should."

Penrose was getting madder every minute.

He still spoke with restraint, however:

"And you are not sure about Mellon, you say? You are friendly to Uncle Andy, aren't you? You were the first to propose his name. What's the use of this backing and filling?"

"I don't back and fill any more than you do," I countered. "I did suggest the name of Mellon. The only name I've backed for a Cabinet position, except Sutherland for Attorney-General."

"A good man," he said, "but you must take the place yourself."

"I must not," I firmly replied. "And gentlemen, to be plain about it — with two United States Senators from Pennsylvania leading a rebellion against the choice of the President for an appointment in his Cabinet — if I were in Harding's place after I took possession of the White House I would not allow either of you on the grounds. I'd sick the dogs on you. You are getting more Cabinet officers than any other state. Here is Secretary Davis to be appointed to the Department of Labor, and possibly Mr. Mellon as Secretary of the Treasury, and you are leading the opposition to Mr. Hoover's appointment."

Penrose got my ultimatum — no Hoover, no Mellon — and rose to heights of profanity I have never heard equaled. He swore in every mood and tense. I had "cussed" a little at times when unduly provoked. But I listened in awe to my master's voice.

"Well, gentlemen," I interrupted, "here is the situation. You expect to make a fight on the President's choice for a cabinet position and then urge him to select two members from your state."

"You actually mean to tell us," Penrose growled, "that the appointment of Mellon is not yet decided?"

"I've tried politely to convey just that."

"If Uncle Andy gets wind of this hesitation over his name, nothing will induce him to accept the place," he said. "I want you to see him to-morrow morning. I'll have him over here."

"That is a waste of time," I objected. "I have nothing to say to him. I am not selecting a Cabinet for the President. I'm helping him get the one he wants."

"But you will stay over a day and see him if he comes?"

"It will be no use," I answered emphatically. "Don't ask him to make the trip."

"You mean you won't see him!" Penrose shouted.

"I am trying to give you that idea," I said. "Of course, I do not wish to be disrespectful to Mr. Mellon but I will not advise the President, if he asks me, to appoint any man from the state of Pennsylvania while its Senators are ringleaders in a rebellion to discredit his administration on its opening day."

Penrose smiled:

"All right. You win. You want the opposition to Hoover

to subside and then you will announce Mellon's appointment?"

"I will make no announcement," I replied. "What the President wants to do, he will do in his own way and in his own time. I'll see Mr. Mellon if you wish in the morning, but I will not stay over to see him unless I have the assurance from you that the opposition to Mr. Hoover will be withdrawn."

"Well, I'll send for Mellon," he said.

Mr. Mellon came over and I saw him in Senator Knox's office the next morning. I talked with Harding over long distance telephone after the conference and told him that the opposition to Hoover would be discontinued. The following morning the President-elect called Mr. Mellon at Senator Knox's office and the appointment was made.

To my surprise, the morning after the conference between Knox, Penrose, and myself, Louis Seibold wired a story from St. Augustine about the meeting in Washington. I don't know how he got the information, but the uncanny news man wrote the article with accuracy, and wound up by stating that I had read the riot act to Penrose and Knox and laid down the flat proposition − "No Hoover − no Mellon!" Result, both Hoover and Mellon.

If I had joined Knox, Penrose, Lodge, and Johnson in their protest, the President-elect would have yielded to our opposition and Hoover's name would never have appeared on list. But I stood by my chief against all critics and Herbert C. Hoover was started on his way to the White House.

Herbert Hoover

Boies Penrose

Philander Knox

Andrew W. Mellon

"Penrose and Knox got my ultimatum.
No Hoover. No Mellon!"

Trinity (Baptist) Church of Marion, Ohio of which President Harding was a Trustee.

The Riverside (Baptist) Church of New York of which Charles Evans Hughes is a Trustee.

CHAPTER X

My Work as Attorney-General

THE inauguration passed, a splendid pageant in glorious weather that augured well for the future. For the first time in history the entire Cabinet of an incoming President was confirmed without a dissenting vote before the President could reach the White House from the Capitol.

Mrs. Harding was in good health on entering her duties as the First Lady and met every responsibility with courage.

I took a house on H Street near the old Shoreham Hotel as a temporary residence, a comparatively small building conveniently located between the Department of Justice and the White House. Here I received callers, and held conferences with men having business with the government, with Senators and Congressmen in matters of political patronage or other business of their constituents, and with many applicants for office.

I held conferences while eating my breakfast, during the lunch hour, at dinner, and late in the evening, until finally the whole house became a public office, and a change became necessary.

For many years Mrs. Daugherty had been a sufferer from arthritis and unable to walk. I had sought every means to restore her to health, and as a final resort she was taking treatment at the Johns Hopkins Hospital in Baltimore. Every Sunday, and often after business hours during the week, I drove over to see her. Hoping that she might be able to come to Washington, I took an apartment at the Wardman Park Hotel, where we made our home during the remainder of the time I was in office. Here she spent many pleasant weeks between hospital treatments and winters in Florida. When I retired as Attorney-General we returned to our home in Columbus. And just at a time when the doctors held out hope of relief, her strength failed and she passed away on November 24, 1924.

Jess Smith again proved his services invaluable. He ran the house on H Street for me with great skill.

I equipped an office on the first floor in which to meet the men that it became necessary for me to see. There were from fifty to five hundred in Washington daily trying to talk to me. Those that I couldn't see, Smith jollied along, taking them to luncheons, dinners, baseball games, and shows until they left town.

No man could have dreamed at this time of the sinister interpretation enemies would put on this association with a helpful friend in my home and official life.

I entered into the work of the office of Attorney-General with energy, determined, grimly determined, to make good the faith President Harding had placed in me.

The disorganization of the Department of Justice discovered in the change from Wilson to Harding was appalling.

But there were extenuating circumstances. For the entire year from the summer of 1919 to the Democratic Convention in San Francisco, June 27, 1920, A. M. Palmer, my predecessor, had been a leading candidate for the Presidency against Wm. G. McAdoo, Al Smith and James M. Cox. His hands were full of politics during the same period that I was managing the campaign for Harding. How he found time to do anything in the office of Attorney-General and run for the Presidency is beyond me. He had a few able assistants, or the Department of Justice would have broken down entirely.

The work of his office was still further confused and crippled because for the last year and a half President Wilson had been an invalid and could not possibly give the Attorney-General his personal backing in any great undertaking. I think this is the reason why no war frauds had been prosecuted.

The dockets of the Federal Courts were piled with cases untried. Many of these were out of date and impossible for trial. The number of judges was utterly inadequate, with the rapidly mounting thousands of cases under the Volstead Act.

The war had ended in 1918, yet in two years not a single action had been filed by the government against war profiteers, although the loudest clamor had arisen against hundreds of contractors.

Two thousand claims against the government, amounting to more than a billion and three-quarters, were to be pressed, many of them pure frauds, many of them silly, many of them vicious, and many of them − fair.

Under cover of war the grossest violations of the Sherman Anti-Trust laws had gone unchallenged.

The Federal prisons were crowded. They are under the jurisdiction and control of the Attorney-General, and his duties in this connection alone would be enough for three men to handle.

There was no Federal prison for women. Scattered over the country were hundreds in state penitentiaries and jails, housed under contract with the government. They had no protection, no work to do, and it was a horrible situation. I presented the matter to the President. He was in accord with my ideas on the subject, and agreed that there should be erected a prison exclusively for women.

Under my direction a bill was presented. The government was short of money. But I laid the matter before Congress with urgent facts and data and the bill was passed. Now there is at Alderson, West Virginia, a well-constructed institution for women violators of the Federal laws. They are safely confined, humanely treated, and given employment, with facilities for recreation, good food, and proper teaching.

The Department of Justice was reorganized earlier than any other under the Harding administration.

I saw the immediate need of a strong personnel in my staff and determined to bring to my assistance the ablest men in America who could be induced to accept the positions.

The first man I sought was the Assistant to the Attorney-General. I selected Guy D. Goff of West Virginia, who had been in the public service, a man of substantial wealth, not dependent on a salary for a living, and a lawyer of splendid reputation. He remained with the Department two years and later was elected to the United States Senate.

The selection of a Solicitor-General, a man who devotes his entire time to the preparation and argument of cases in the Supreme Court, was very important. This is the outstanding appointment in the Department of Justice, next to the Attorney-General.

It is not easy to find a capable man who is patriotic enough to accept this place, requiring ability, integrity, and unlimited energy that could command at least a hundred thousand dollars a year. I selected James M. Beck of Pennsylvania, a man familiar with government work, who was universally recognized as one of the greatest lawyers in America. His record as Solicitor-General of the United States has never been surpassed, though many great men have held that position.

In making this selection I offended Senator Pepper, also of Pennsylvania, who was a candidate for the office. The President had asked me to consider him. He afterwards turned up as my troublesome antagonist.

The Bureau of Investigation, another important branch of my office, is to the Department of Justice what the Secret Service is to the Treasury.

Under the law, the Chief of the Bureau of Investigation is appointed by the Attorney-General. The President is not responsible for him, and his appointment does not require confirmation by the Senate.

I had known William J. Burns for thirty years. I was familiar with his work while he was formerly in the service of the government, and afterwards, as head of his own detective agency. I had confidence in his integrity and loyalty. He had many enemies, as any man would have who had accomplished as much. He had built up a large business. The Pinkertons were his enemies. He was also a Catholic, and there are people who foolishly believe that Catholics should not be appointed to public office.

Burns had been engaged some years before on a case for the government. He was charged with having unduly interfered with the selection of the jury. He only did his duty. He investigated each juror in the case. This had always been done by the government.

There was sharp criticism of Burns on account of this case, and I laid the matter before President Harding, showing him the records. He read the entire case and said:

"If I had any doubt as to the appointment of Burns, I would, if I were in your place, appoint him on this record."

"That's what I purpose to do," I replied.

I was criticized for it, of course, but no charge reflecting on . Burns's integrity or efficiency was ever made. His selection was a deterrent to criminals. They were afraid of him, for he generally got his man. He was without question the greatest detective in America, and for this reason alone I appointed him.

Mr. Samuel Gompers, however, as President of the American Federation of Labor, was Burns's implacable foe. He had savagely denounced the arrest of the McNamara brothers, had rushed to the jail in Los Angeles, and had a picture taken standing loyally beside the two men.

While Gompers was admiring the pose and shouting his faith in their innocence, Burns produced the indisputable evidence of their guilt, and they confessed to wholesale murder, leaving poor Gompers' right hand still uplifted proclaiming their innocence.

I had never been unfriendly to Labor, but I could not allow their Lobby in Washington to dictate to me the personnel of the Department of Justice. Baiting the Attorney-General had been a favorite program of theirs for years. I refused to listen to the clamor against Burns, and from the hour I put him at the head of my Information Bureau organized Labor became my relentless enemy.

To this fact I owe the long series of personal attacks and persecutions which followed me to the end of my term under Mr. Coolidge.

The tasks before the department were colossal. We began suits for the recovery of $300,000,000 paid to profiteers under war contracts. Congress was demanding that suits be brought. We determined not to until we felt certain, after full investigation, that they were justified. We believed that the citizen was entitled to as much consideration as the government.

The ordinary force of the Department of Justice worked industriously on these claims and cases. Congress continued to complain that nothing was being done, though we were at work with every force at our command.

Finally I went before Congress and asked the Appropriations Committee for half a million dollars with which to install a separate branch of the Department of Justice to handle this work. Members of Congress who had been loudest in criticism admitted they were surprised and misinformed, and offered to make the appropriation a million dollars immediately. I asked them not to do this; I would ask for more as it was needed.

The War Transaction Section was organized. In the appropriation bill I was authorized to hire a man to take charge of the work at a salary of $25,000 a year. I wanted the biggest man available, and offered the post first to Henry L. Stimson, now Secretary of State, and then to Senator Deneen of Illinois. Neither would accept. The salary for this position was more than twice what I was getting.

Unable to find the man I wanted for this important position, I decided to take charge of the work myself, and save the government the $25,000 a year. I appointed three judges of the highest character, two Republicans and a Democrat, as an advisory council. And finally, when fully organized, this branch, next to the Department of Justice, was probably the largest legal department in the world.

Millions of dollars were collected by suits and otherwise, and many criminal prosecutions were instituted and successfully concluded.

These proceedings in the performance of duty made neither the President of the United States nor his Attorney-General popular with many people.

Another group of offenders prosecuted with vigor were millionaire violators of the Sherman Anti-Trust Law.

This law has been on the statute books a long time, sometimes vigorously enforced, at other times indifferently.

But up to this time no American millionaire had ever gone to jail for its violation. As a young lawyer I had trained under John Sherman, the law's author. I had an abiding affection and admiration for his genius as a lawyer and for his patriotism as an American citizen. I happened to be in his house as his guest and spent the evening with him in his library on the night he concluded the final draft of that law.

When the millionaires were sentenced the administration was criticized and attacked. No opportunity was overlooked to attack the Attorney-General. But it was from behind the scenes, and outwardly for trivial reasons, concealing the fact that a high-powered organization was fighting the administration and putting up the money to discredit everybody connected with it, from the President down.

In the bitter fight to enforce the Sherman Act the President stood squarely by me as he did in every battle for the enforcement of law during his administration.

The following letter from President Harding when the convicted men were finally sentenced is characteristic. I was suffering from the approach of a nervous breakdown caused by overwork and had gone to Asheville, North Carolina, to recuperate.

THE WHITE HOUSE
WASHINGTON

April 23, 1923

My dear General Daugherty:

I have noted the contents of yours of April 19th. I had not seen the sentences which were imposed in the pottery cases, but I had known of the conviction. I suppose there will be an outcry that we are persecuting our friends, but I know of no way to conduct the government except in accordance with the law. If men will deliberately offend they must expect to take the consequences.

I quite agree with you about the wisdom of the procedure in the sugar matter. Of course, Mr. Seymour told you that the matter was thoroughly thrashed over before the Cabinet and all of the members of the Cabinet were of one accord in recommending the proceedings. I have been observing the reaction as expressed in the newspaper comments. There is a division of opinion quite naturally. I note with amused interest that many of the newspapers which flayed the injunction proceedings against the railroad unions are strongly commending the action taken in this case.

I am immensely pleased to learn of your improvement. I hope it will not be long until you can return to Washington.

Very truly yours,

Gen. H. M. Daugherty,
Grove Park Inn,
Asheville, N. C.

Another hornet's nest was stirred up over the enforcement of the Volstead Act. Because of the part I had taken in the Ohio Convention which committed the Republican Party to Prohibition, I had few friends among those who had loved the saloon.

It was not a question of whether the President took a drink, or whether I took a drink. We were not saints and did not pretend to be. The law was there and it was my duty to enforce it, and the records of the Department of Justice will show that it was enforced as adequately as was humanly possible under the conditions.

Under my personal direction the Remus case in Cincinnati was prosecuted, the first of its kind of national proportions. Remus was convicted and sent to prison. I got my reward from him later when he testified against me before the Senatorial committee organized for the purpose of reflecting on the Administration and the Attorney-General.

My Department had nothing to do with the issuance of liquor permits. It was only my duty to prosecute cases when the testimony was presented by the Prohibition Enforcement Division of the Treasury.

And when I issued an opinion against liquor being brought into port under protection of foreign flags, the wets reached for my scalp. The Supreme Court sustained me, the ruling became a law, but my name became a byword where glasses clinked and men shouted:

"Here's to crime!"

After the war many young fellows were sent to Federal prisons for violations of the Volstead Act, automobile thefts, and minor offenses of various kinds. The prisons were crowded. The inmates had nothing to do. I consulted with the President. He was in favor of a plan being worked out to see these young offenders separated from the hardened criminals, given something to do, and saved if possible. We established a duck mill at Atlanta where the material was made and mail bags manufactured for the use of the Post-Office Department. Congress appropriated a half million dollars for the undertaking. When the mill was started, two or three hundred young men were put to work for which they were paid wages; these were small it is true, but it was an incentive to industry, and their earnings were either sent to their families or retained and given to the boys at the expiration of their sentences.

The government saved money and the boys were saved.

From time to time I selected young men from the prison and secured employment for them, some in the Department of Justice, where they were not known as ex-convicts. We secured positions for over a hundred in different industries, and they all made good.

At Leavenworth we enlarged the shoe factory so as to give work to additional men, extended the farming facilities, and the government was supplied with milk and meat.

The prisoners took interest in their work and were encouraged and helped, and on their release were fitted to take honorable employment.

To my surprise Samuel Gompers and the Labor leaders affiliated with him pounced down on me. The Labor organizations maintain one of the most powerful of the modern lobbies built up in Washington, and they used this engine of propaganda for all it was worth. I stood my ground and challenged Mr. Gompers to a public debate on the issue. He refused to meet me, and Labor papers renewed their systematic pounding at my department.

I knew that I was right and went ahead. At how great a price I was to learn later.

I am particularly proud of the work done in my administration of the office of Attorney-General in the expansion of the judiciary and the filling of its vacancies.

More judges were appointed under Harding and Coolidge up to the time I resigned as Attorney-General than during any other like period in the history of our government. Not one man that I recommended to the President for a Federal judgeship was refused confirmation by the Senate, and not one man failed to acquit himself with credit and honor to the Bench.

I made those selections with the greatest care.

They had to be confirmed by the Senate. And while a Federal judgeship is not and should not be a political appointment, it is often made so by Senators and Congressmen who are interested in the advancement of a particular man.

I recommended some Democrats, many Republicans. The most careful investigation was made as to the applicant's character, his family, ability, health, class of business handled in his profession, and everything about his life and habits. It was done quietly but thoroughly.

In the appendix to this volume will be found the list of eighty-eight judges appointed on my recommendation. Their record speaks for itself.

Even my old friend, the enemy, the *New York World*, expressed its approval.

Men who make loose assertions about bribery and corruption in the office of the Attorney-General of the United States are usually hopeless fools or vicious liars who know better.

No judge of any court, and no person for him, would think of bringing improper pressure to bear upon the Attorney-General, and no such thing was ever attempted, within my knowledge, during either my administration or that of any predecessor.

The Attorney-General lives in a glass house. He makes ten enemies where a President makes one. The fiercest light of publicity beats on his office and follows every step that he takes, day and night. The touching of a single bribe by such an officer of the government would immediately make the tenure of his position an impossibility. A thousand hostile eyes are watching him.

No other cabinet officer is subjected to such scenting. In all the clamor, the hue and cry, trials and investigations covering months that were instigated against me in the Senate, the House, and the courts, not one illegal or questionable act was discovered. If I had made a slip they would have found it. Concealment under such conditions is an utter impossibility.

One of the most troublesome questions on which an Attorney-General must pass is the pardon and parole of Federal prisoners. At least a thousand are submitted every year. This averages three a day. The amount of work involved for a conscientious officer is enormous. The bare reading of the record in each case would take half his life if not passed on to assistants.

The pardon branch of the Department of Justice is composed of twenty-five men and women under a competent head. This branch investigates and prepares all cases to be submitted to the Attorney-General. I read personally at least half of the cases, I should say, and all of the important ones.

Pardons and commutations of sentence are finally passed on by the President, upon the recommendation of the Attorney-General.

There is a widespread belief that money is used in such cases. This is of course silly. But families of unfortunates in prison are constantly preyed upon by vultures who claim to have pull or influence.

A widely circulated fable of my misuse of pardoning power originated in the part I played as an attorney for Charles W. Morse when President Taft released him from Atlanta. I never was employed in a pardon case in my life. The President believed, I believed, and every doctor who examined him at the time believed, that he was in a dying condition. I was not an officer of the government when his case was presented to the Department of Justice. I was a practicing attorney and had the right to appear for Morse or any other man, if I desired to do so. But because Taft was from Ohio and I had managed his campaign I refused to appear before the President or present Morse's case to him.

Geo. W. Wickersham, Attorney-General at the time, took the matter under consideration, and upon his recommendation President Taft was advised by the Department of Justice to release Morse.

I was anxious that Morse be released so that he might testify in a civil case in which I was counsel for a number of persons who owned holdings in the Metropolitan Steamship Company. The New Haven Railroad had secured possession of two steamships, the *Harvard* and the *Yale*, taken them out of service and thus destroyed competition. The stockholders, including Morse and his sister and others, were asserting a claim against the New Haven Railroad.

Morse was released and lived for some time.

The government was also interested in the testimony of Morse and it was useful in a case which the government itself had against the New Haven Railroad.

I never discussed the case with President Taft or attempted to influence him in any way.

My calling the attention of Attorney-General Wickersham to Morse's condition in order that he might be released if the facts, upon investigation by the government, justified it, and that his testimony might be used, was incidental. My action in the matter was confined to conferences with the Attorney-General himself.

Later much talk was indulged in and I was charged with having influenced President Taft. The President wrote a letter which was extensively published, in which he said over his own signature, as did also General Wickersham, that I never undertook in any way to influence them in the matter, and General Wickersham stated that I did nothing more than any man might do with strict propriety. These letters killed the story for a time.

The matter was revived in the Senate by Senator Caraway, inspired, no doubt, by Morse and others, when suit was brought against Morse's company by the Department of Justice while I was Attorney-General, to recover fifteen million dollars in war frauds. Morse was indicted by the Federal grand jury for criminal war frauds. Caraway's action was inspired to keep the pot boiling and to create prejudice against the Department of Justice and the Harding administration. Judgment was obtained by the government in the case, and the object of the attack failed by a court decision.

While Attorney-General I prosecuted Morse with vigor on another charge.

By far the most interesting case presented to me for release of a prisoner during the Harding administration was that of Eugene V. Debs. And for my decision in the case I was as usual held up to the scorn of the Nation by my old friendly enemy, the *New York World*.

Before his inauguration, after I had accepted the post of Attorney-General in his Cabinet, the President-elect, while we were in Florida, asked me to give my early attention to the case of Debs, who was then in Atlanta serving a ten-year sentence for seeking to obstruct the conduct of the war.

"I know a lot about the case," I informed him. "But have never given it any careful study."

"I wish you would. I've long been interested in Debs and I'd like to know all about his case."

"I'll make it one of my first duties," I promised.

Within two weeks after the inauguration I began to study it.

I found that his record as a prisoner in Atlanta was remarkable. His personality had been like a breath of fresh air to the men with whom he came in contact. He was a great help in the maintenance of discipline. The Warden couldn't say enough good things about him.

And this, too, in the face of the fact that he didn't believe in prisons or criminal law. If he could he would have opened the doors and released every convict. He did not believe crime a subject for punishment or that men could be reformed that way.

His views on social order were woefully wrong, but his personality was a benediction to all the criminals with whom he came in contact. He soothed their troubled spirits and healed more than one disordered mind.

He never cursed the government for his imprisonment. He showed no desire for revenge. He harbored no bitterness. He was at all times sincere, gentle, and tender.

His record in prison stirred in me a desire to see and talk to him at once.

The sooner his case was disposed of, the better. His followers and sympathizers were making a martyr of him and daily adding to national unrest. Hundreds of strikes were on or under way.

In sending for Debs, my first desire was to do him justice, to know the man personally and find out at first hand what he really stood for, and to contribute something, if possible, toward the restoration of industrial peace.

I called the Warden of the Atlanta penitentiary, and asked him to put Eugene Debs on the train and send him to see me.

"Right away, sir," was the prompt answer.

"And listen. Don't send a guard with him. Let him put on a suit of citizen's clothes and come on his parole alone — no detectives, no espionage, I'll trust him absolutely. Give him money for his food and transportation and say nothing to any one. Send him straight to the Department of Justice to see me."

On the morning of his arrival I cleared my desk of urgent matters to give him all the time necessary.

Colonel Goff, my assistant, was with me in conference at

the time he arrived and met him in the little anteroom, and he waited there half an hour.

I met Debs at the door of my office, extended my hand and he pressed it warmly.

I spoke the first words:

"You were a prisoner of the United States when you stepped across the threshold. Now and until you leave you're as free a man as I am."

"Thank you, Mr. Attorney-General," he slowly answered.

"I want you to remember that anything you may say to me, and you can say anything you please, will not be held against you."

His rugged face lighted and he looked at me as if he couldn't quite believe his ears.

"Any admissions you make," I went on, "will not be used against you in any way. And if you do not wish to answer any questions I ask, your refusal will not be held against you."

"You are very kind," he breathed.

"I will answer every question you ask me, frankly and without reserve, except one," I said.

"And that is?"

"What I am going to do in your case — you understand?"

"Perfectly."

We talked freely for several hours. He unfolded frankly his ideas on government, his ideas on religion, his own case, the cause of Socialism with which he was identified, his beliefs and disbeliefs. A more eloquent and fascinating recital I never heard fall from the lips of any man. Because he was sincere. So simple in his faith.

I found him a charming personality, with a deep love for his fellow man — to my mind, of course, absolutely wrong in his ideas on government and society, yet always sincere, truthful and honest.

I could understand why he was a man of influence and had polled a million votes for a poor cause. He did not flinch at anything. He looked every fact squarely in the face. He made no apologies. And I asked for none. He was a little excited and nervous, but quick to observe that he was talking to a man who would try to be fair to him.

I had an appointment for lunch and left him in the anteroom for an hour.

On leaving I said:

"Rest here a while where you will not be exposed or disturbed. I'll send in your lunch. It's a cold, wet day. Your clothes are thin for this climate coming up from Atlanta. I don't want you to take cold."

A gracious smile again overspread his strange face.

"You are very kind to me. I appreciate it more than I can tell you."

"What do you want for lunch?" I called from the door.

"A little fruit, if you please."

I sent him the fruit, and upon my return we resumed our talk and continued it until time for his train to leave for the South.

Toward the end I said:

"Is there anything else now you would like to say to me?"

He rose quietly.

"I think, my dear Mr. Attorney-General, that I have said about all I have on my mind at this time. And you've said a lot for me to think about. Which I'll do."

"All right," I said, "you can go now. My car's at the door to take you to the station. You've money for a dinner on the train. If you prefer a lunch prepared I'll send it to you."

"Thank you, I'd like a warm dinner."

"My only request is that you talk to no one of this interview."

"Rest assured of that."

"Of course," I added, "I've reached no conclusion on your case and can't for some little time. I'll study all its phases. I want to be as fair and generous with you as the law will allow. If I hadn't been deeply interested, I wouldn't have sent for you. That you know, of course. Take care of yourself. The President, too, will be fair and just as he always is. Your political beliefs and activities will have nothing to do with the decision."

He got up and hesitated a moment as if trying to decide whether it was proper to offer me his hand. I extended mine. As my hand clasped his the tears were streaming down his cheeks as he said:

"Mr. Attorney-General, may I say a personal word as we part?"

"Anything you like."

"I just want to say that I thank you from the bottom of my heart for your generous and manly treatment of me in this meeting. No matter what you feel it your duty to do in my case, I'm grateful that we have met and I shall always respect you."

He paused and spoke with deep feeling.

"And I shall always remember this as one of the happiest and most inspiring days I've ever spent."

He left me with the conviction that I had never met a man of more appealing personality than Eugene V. Debs.

I studied the whole record with care. A conscientious judge had tried his case and pronounced his sentence. The Supreme Court had unanimously affirmed it. Hundreds of other men who had resisted the military draft and sought to interrupt the prosecution of the war were in prison and it was a problem what to do with them.

I regarded Debs's case as in many respects unique. He was a fanatic in his faith. He was in no sense a criminal except that he had broken a law which he believed an invasion of his most sacred rights, although in my opinion he was wrong.

I finally decided that as he was sixty-four years old and had suffered three years' imprisonment, the ends of justice had been met.

I recommended that his sentence be commuted to expire December 31, 1921. Before approving, Harding changed the date, and wrote:

"Commuted to expire December 24, 1921."

"I want him to eat his Christmas dinner with his wife," the President smiled.

The *New York World* promptly proclaimed my act that of a poseur and fool who was playing to the galleries.

No man with any brains or character can hope to please his enemies.

THE WHITE HOUSE
WASHINGTON

September 25, 1922.

My dear General Daugherty:

Please accept a belated acknowledgment of yours of September 14th with which you enclosed to me the Order in the Debs case and that recently made in response to the petition which you filed in behalf of the government. It is all very interesting reading.

I note by the papers this morning that the Court has taken a firm attitude in sustaining you at Chicago. Meanwhile, the country has greatly profited by the justifiable activities of your Department.

Very truly yours,

Warren G. Harding

Hon. H. M. Daugherty,
Attorney General,
 Washington, D.C.

CHAPTER XI

The Great Strikes

THE STORY of the great strikes of 1922 that called out more than a million men and threatened the foundations of the Republic has never been told.

The Harding administration was put to a supreme test.

Of the tremendous issues at stake but little is known today by the general public. Yet this country, in my judgment, never passed through a graver crisis. The principles involved were fundamental to our existence as a free people, and how near we came to the destruction of those principles may never be fully known. As a leading actor in the scenes it is my duty to give their inside history.

The Red agents of the Soviet Government who had bored into the organizations of our coal miners called a strike of six hundred thousand men. These miners, acting under the orders of radicals, worked day and night, by inflammatory circulars and fanatical speakers, to precipitate a clash of arms.

I found out that a few weeks before the miners' strike began on April 1, 1922, Zinoviev had sent from Moscow to his Communist agents in the United States the following explicit orders:

"The Central Executive Committee of the Communist Party of America must direct its particular attention to the progress of the strike of the miners of America . . . . "

The sinister thing in this first paragraph of the proclamation from Moscow was that it was written *weeks before* the strike on April 1. Zinoviev knew it was coming because he and his associates in Russia had sent the order to America calling the strike through the Reds who had bored into the labor unions!

The instructions from Moscow continued:

"Agitators and propagandists must be sent to the strike regions.

"It is necessary to arouse striking coal miners to the point of armed insurrection. Let them blow up and flood the shafts. Shower the strike region with proclamations and appeals. Thus arouse the revolutionary spirit of the workers and prepare them for the coming revolution in America."

I called the President's attention to the facts, and kept him fully informed.

Uneasiness was growing in the nation. Behind the coal strike of 600,000 miners began to loom the threat of a strike of 400,000 railroad shopmen, which would tie up every artery of commerce in America.

The *Boston Herald*, which had helped elect Harding President, came out in a fiery editorial, typical of the crisis, under the title:

"WARREN G. HARDING ON TRIAL!"

It was headed by a poem of J. G. Holland which will bear repeating to-day:

> God give us men! A time like this demands
> Great hearts, strong minds, true faith, and willing hands!
> Men whom the lust of office does not kill:
> Men whom the spoils of office cannot buy:
> Men who possess opinions and a will:
> Men who have honor, men who will not lie.
> For while the rabble with their thumb-worn creeds,
> Their large professions and their little deeds,
> Wrangle in selfish strife, lo! Freedom weeps,
> Wrong rules the land, and waiting justice sleeps.

Among other things, the editor said:

In this situation of affairs the President, after receiving Mr. Lewis at luncheon on Monday, summoned the Union operators and the United Mine Workers' officials to a conference at the White House.

Our organic law provides that all people are entitled to life, liberty and the pursuit of happiness. The laws of the United

States provide that men may work without interference from outside, and the law provides for their protection.

At the time of the Pullman railroad strike, Grover Cleveland, as President of the United States, acted in no uncertain manner.

We have believed that prior to conferring with Mr. Lewis, President Harding should have announced that murder must cease; that those who desired to operate their properties should be protected; that those who desired to work would be protected; that those who were guilty of the Illinois murders must be punished, and that no conference could take place with the leaders of the United Mine Workers until they at least showed a willingness to obey the law; but Mr. Harding has evidently thought otherwise.

The President is on trial. Will he prove himself a Grover Cleveland? Will he prove to the people of the United States that this is a free country; that any man has a right to work without getting the consent of a labor organization? Will he show that the owner of property has a right to operate his property without the consent of a labor organization? Will he declare that a man wishing to work in this country will be protected; that a man not wishing to work may strike, but must not murder the man who wishes to work? Will he in clear and forceful language notify the people of the United States that murder and violence must cease in labor disputes; that this is not a Soviet government? Or will he supinely yield to Mr. Lewis and his associates and attempt to coerce the operators into yielding their constitutional right to operate their properties in safety under the laws of the land? The conference Saturday should answer this question.

The coal operators are not on trial; the United Mine Workers are not on trial; Warren G. Harding, President of the United States, is on trial in this conference to be held on Saturday.

Order as well as law must be maintained.

The conference held in the White House ended in smoke. I watched the situation with keen interest and growing alarm, yet hoped against hope that a settlement might be reached without the intervention of the legal arm of the government. If the Department of Justice entered this controversy it would mean more than polite conversation.

I finally told the President that the coal strike would have to be broken, or we must surrender to the gentlemen in Moscow who were directing it.

"We'll not surrender," he answered firmly. "Make sure of that."

It lasted five months. At least a hundred million dollars had been lost by wage earners, transportation lines, general industry, and the American people. Widespread suffering covered the entire country. Every scheme to prevent the distribution of coal was used without scruple. Production was paralyzed. The coal-carrying railroads were crippled. Thousands of cars loaded with coal were sidetracked and piled up at switching points. Thousands of cars were damaged and their movement became impossible.

At one point of concentration in Kentucky many thousands of cars were piled up at a junction. Four thousand of them had been disabled by vicious vandals.

The movement of these cars was absolutely necessary to the continued life of interstate commerce.

The Northwest was anxiously awaiting fuel for the winter. But the barges could not be loaded because coal could not reach their docks.

For months unsuccessful efforts had been made by the Secretary of Commerce, the Secretary of Labor, and the President to settle the differences between the operators and the miners. Every effort had failed.

There were hidden forces at work that defied reason.

I called Senator Richard Ernst of Kentucky into conference with the President, and asked that he send him at once to see Governor Morrow at Frankfort.

If the Governor of Kentucky would call out the State Guard and move those seventeen thousand cars that were blocking transportation in his coal fields, I believed the backbone of the strike would be broken.

Senator Ernst undertook the mission. Morrow called out the militia and smashed the blockade at a single stroke.

The moment cars began to move in thousands, a panic struck the rank and file of the strikers, and their leaders immediately began a series of illegal conspiracies with the members of the Railroad Shop Crafts Union who were considering a strike.

They held a secret meeting in Cincinnati at which plans were formulated for the railroad strike. We caught them red-handed in the conspiracy. The penalty for the act was imprisonment in a Federal penitentiary.

When they were notified of their danger, the coal strike was called off, production resumed, and coal cars moved on every line in the Nation.

The Reds inside the Shopmens' Union called the strike on the railroads.

Here was a situation of far graver significance and more sinister import. For the striking railroad workers had boldly demanded that the roads be surrendered to the labor unions under the Plumb plan.

Here indeed was a conspiracy worthy of Lenin and Zinoviev. The Red borers controlled the Shop Crafts Union. If the roads were confiscated by the government, they would ultimately be turned over to the labor leaders to run. From that hour our time-tables and freight rates would be made out in Moscow, and the first step would have been taken in a revolution to overthrow our government and substitute a Soviet régime.

No more subtle and dangerous move had ever been made by a group of American citizens since the foundation of the Republic.

I saw at once the scope of the movement and the vast issues involved, and early determined to set every wheel in motion within the Department of Justice to meet the crisis.

The real issue of the strike was the radical determination to force the government to take over the railroads.

Men connected with the Administration, inside and outside the Cabinet, including Senator Cummins, co-author of the Esch-Cummins Act, believed this to be the only solution.

When the situation reached a point where every one seemed paralyzed, the President called a conference on the *Mayflower.* Senator Cummins, who had already prepared two tentative bills to take over the roads, was invited. The entire problem was discussed. The President at no time committed himself to any proposition.

The following week Harding called Cummins, the Chairman of the Interstate Commerce Committee of the Senate, into a conference with me at the White House, and the situation was discussed for an hour and a half.

At our week-end conference on the *Mayflower* the matter was again discussed at an informal meeting of some Cabinet members and others with Senator Cummins, who now boldly advocated government control of the roads. Harding was not present. After the discussion had continued for two hours, I made my first personal declaration on the issue. I said with deliberate emphasis:

"I'll consent, gentlemen, to the take-over of the railroads by the government only when all authority is shattered. When there is no government. When the strikers and their radical leaders in the labor unions have the railroads and the government tied up in bundles. When everything — government, industry, law, and order — has gone to pieces. And when we are willing to admit that there is no law in existence. With my last breath, before I become unconscious, I shall say: 'Let them all go to hell together and we'll go down with them.' "

The President, who was taking a walk on deck, paused at a window and heard my closing words.

Later in the day he told me that Senator Cummins had reported to him that I would never consent to the government's taking over the railroads, and that he had answered:

"The Attorney-General will play the game of the administration, or he will voluntarily resign — rest assured of that."

At a later conference with the President and Mr. Cummins, the Senator expressly declared that under the Clayton Act an injunction against the strikers could not be obtained. Harding was of that opinion. I held the contrary but made no reply. I was not ready to show my hand. The Department of Justice was preparing a bill in equity to test the question. The railroads were of the opinion that the government should join with them in filing a bill.

My advice was emphatic: "File your own bills."

I persisted in the position that the Government of the United States should go into partnership with neither the railroads nor the strikers. If we brought a suit it would be solely in behalf of the government.

I gave no indication of the course I had mapped out, but under authority of law appointed more than three thousand deputy United States Marshals to assist in preserving life and property. I also called on all state and municipal authorities for aid.

Secretaries Hoover and Davis were trying to bring about a settlement, but on terms which the Attorney-General considered unsound, terms that meant a surrender of principles of government which could not be yielded, and that in the next general railroad strike would have meant a surrender that would have brought national disaster.

The President, in distress over the growing tragedy of the situation, consented that Secretary Hoover present to the railroad executives a plan of settlement.

They unanimously and angrily rejected it

After the Cabinet meeting that day, in a conference at the White House, I told the President that I did not agree with the plans which had been proposed and that no possible good could come out of it. And none came.

In the order to strike, issued by the radical leaders of the Shop Crafts, the decision of the Railway Labor Board had been boldly flouted. This Board was the creation of the labor interests and they had secured an increase of wages by its orders. But when wages were reduced in the depression and readjustment following the war, the radical leaders repudiated their own Board and struck a blow at government, public authority, and the foundations of law and order.

The damage now done had resulted in the loss of half a billion dollars. A thousand trains, carrying passengers and United States mail, were forced out of service. Trains were being derailed, bridges blown up, tunnels destroyed, switches and tracks wrecked.

In this sabotage the strikers were assisted by radical and lawless elements outside their unions. It was a common evening sport for these men to attack workmen, drag them into the woods, strip them naked, and tar and feather them.

Many murders were committed.

While the crews of abandoned trains on Western deserts were idle by orders from their radical leaders, women and children were crying for food and water. Babies were born in the aisles of day coaches.

The strikers finally dared to picket the White House, the office of the Attorney-General, and his automobile. Nothing was left undone to intimidate the administration and cripple its action.

I hastened the completion of the outline of drastic action on which I had been at work for two months, called the President, and asked for a conference. I decided to spring the plan immediately. There was not a minute to lose.

THE WHITE HOUSE
WASHINGTON

July 31, 1922.

My dear General Daugherty:

          I am writing to acknowledge yours
of July 29th, with which you send to me the very
complete digest of the strike situation, and an
outline of your policy and your reasons therefor in
dealing with it officially for the Department of
Justice. I do not think that your treatment of
calling for deputy marshals, in order to maintain
law and order and conserve property, will ever be
questioned by any official authority.

                    Very truly yours,

                    Warren G Harding

Hon. H. M. Daugherty,
Attorney General,
Washington, D. C.

CHAPTER XII

The Conspiracy of 1922

IN MY conference with the President I took pains to make clear the increasing threat against civilization which the strike now made.

"I've a war map on the wall of my office," I began, "in which pins are stuck daily marking the spot where a train has been wrecked, a bridge dynamited, a riot has broken out, a worker been kidnaped, another assaulted, a murder committed. Hundreds of cases are covered up. Men are maimed and killed and the crimes concealed.

"I have the records piled high in black and white, from eye-witnesses whose words are beyond question. Of known murders by the strikers. A thousand and five hundred cases of felonious assault with intent to kill. Sixty-five accounts of kidnaping accompanied by brutal assault, eight cases of tar and feathers, fifty-one cases of dynamiting and burning railroad bridges for the purpose of wrecking freight and passenger trains, two hundred and fifty records of bombing of railroad property or the homes of nonstriking employees, fifty cases of train wrecking by derailment, hundreds of flagrant practices of sabotage in the crippling of engines and cars — with the story of the pulling off of more than a thousand mail trains on account of these mobs.

"This is not the work of American union laborers. The rank and file of the unions involved don't know what it's all about. They are honest, patriotic men when we come to know them.

"The real import of this movement is not on the surface. You must look deeper to find it. We are face to face with a determined conspiracy to overturn the government itself.

"There are at this time a little over two hundred organizations in the United States controlled by the revolutionary leaders. Some of them are local, others nationwide. Forty-five of these organizations are engaged in the Soviet effort to seize control of the labor unions of the country and convert them into fighting units. Fifty-two leaders hold three hundred and twenty-five organizations, thus fusing them into a single whole. There is no gap or breaking point. Ten of these directors constituting the core of the conspiracy appear both in the radical and in the 'Liberal' groups and at the same time among the 'Civil Liberties,' 'Parlor Bolshevik,' and 'Intelligentsia' groups.

"They have established a news agency known as the 'Federated Press,' financed by the Central Communist organization under direct orders of the Third International at Moscow. It serves two hundred newspapers, publications, and agencies in America and a hundred and twenty in Europe. It has established branches in thirty cities including the national capital.

"In one of the Communist orders to their borers into the labor unions we read:

" 'The workers' revolution cannot succeed without the great bulk of labor organizations. We cannot be satisfied with the formation of a few new unions of revolutionary purpose. We must control the existing units of labor.

" 'The class struggle, which so long appeared in forms unrecognizable to millions of workers, develops now into open combat, civil war.' "

"It looks like it, doesn't it?" the President muttered.

"Looks like it!" I scoffed. "It *is* civil war. And it's so widespread and serious we don't dare allow the facts to be known! The Labor Lobby in Washington that attempts a strangle-hold on legislation is no longer conservative.

It is controlled by the Red borers in its ranks." I paused and fixed the Commander-in-Chief of the Army and Navy with a serious look.

"And don't think these instigators have overlooked the soldiers. In a manifesto to the Communists of America, Bukharin and Berzin of the Executive Committee of the Moscow International say:

" 'We consider that one of the most important tasks before you is the organization of Communist groups in the army and navy, where you should carry on energetic propaganda in favor of soldiers' and sailors' Soviets, and denunciatory addresses against officers and generals. Act centrally. Do not fall asunder. Organize new revolutionary headquarters.'

"We can't afford," I went on, "to proclaim a condition of civil war at this time, though we are actually in it. The reckless young of the rising generation, who have caught the spirit of anarchy from the war conditions, have begun to question all things you and I hold sacred and worth while. They have written an interrogation point before Law, Order, Government. This insanity will pass. But it is a real force to be reckoned with in the ugly crisis in which we find ourselves."

The President settled in a chair and looked at me anxiously.

"Well, what is your answer to this?"

"Direct, drastic, firm action by the United States Government. Can it live and move and assert its power? Have we a government?"

"I believe we have," Harding snapped.

"So do I. And believing this I've worked out a plan for obtaining the most important injunction ever issued."

"Injunction?"

"Exactly."

"But Cummins declares it can't be obtained. The law specifically says that during a strike neither an employer nor the employees can ask for or obtain an injunction."

"I know that," I answered. "But there's a fact that Senator Cummins has overlooked. The Government of the United States is neither an employer nor an employee. We will demand an injunction in the name of the government representing a hundred and twenty million people."

Harding sprang to his feet, his face flushed.

"You think that will hold in law?"

"We can try it. We can at least find out whether the government of the Nation has perished or still lives."

He paced the floor for a moment, came back to my chair, looked at me a moment, and said with deep emotion:

"Your plan's an inspiration. I'll back it with all the power at my command."

"Remember," I warned, "the question is a far bigger one than appears on the surface. It means, have we the government of our fathers or not?"

"All right," he eagerly agreed. "What's your first move?"

"The first thing necessary," I answered, "is to prepare the country for the drastic action I propose to take through the courts. There will be a tremendous outcry from the Reds, Pinks, Yellows, and deluded labor leaders. We must have the backing of the masses of the people."

"What's your suggestion?" he broke in with a little impatience.

"I suggest," I said, "that you immediately send a message to Congress on the question. Special legislation is not needed. We have all the laws necessary. Will you send the message?"

"Yes."

"Your argument will be addressed to Congress. In reality you will speak over their heads to the whole people of America."

"I see."

The President surprised Congress and the nation by the startling and vigorous message which he delivered on August

18. Sympathetic strikes had been called by radical labor leaders, and more strikes were in the offing.

Harding went straight to the point and struck from the shoulder, saying:

"We must assert the doctrine that in this Republic the first obligation and the first allegiance of every citizen, high and low, is to his government — "

A ripple of applause swept the House, struck the packed galleries, and swelled into an uproar of approval.

"And to hold that government to be the just and unchallenged sponsor for public welfare and the liberty, security, and rights of all its citizens.

"No matter what clouds may gather, no matter what storms may ensue, no matter what hardships may attend, or what sacrifices may be necessary, government by law must and will be sustained."

Again a burst of applause swept the House.

"Wherefore I'm resolved to use all the power of the government to maintain transportation and sustain the right of men to work."

No clearer statement of patriotic purpose ever came from the lips of a Chief Magistrate but there was no burst of applause. His words cut to the bone. The powerful labor lobby had their scouts in the gallery. Members of Congress sank a little lower in their seats. Cowards dreaded the million enrolled voters in the ranks of organized labor. They dreaded the curse of the labor leaders.

The President went on with relentless purpose:

"Deserted continental trains in the desert regions of the Southwest have revealed a cruelty and contempt for law on the part of railway employees, who have conspired to paralyze transportation. And lawlessness and violence in a hundred places have revealed the failure of the striking unions to hold their forces to law obeyance.

"We have a state of lawlessness shocking to every

conception of American ideals, violating the cherished guarantees of our freedom.

"It is fundamental to freedom that all men have unquestioned right to work and live and choose their own lawful ways to happiness.

"In these strikes, those rights to live and choose their own lawful ways of happiness have been denied by assaults and violence, by armed lawlessness.

"In many cases the municipal authorities have winked at these violations, until liberty is a mockery and the law a matter of community contempt.

"These conditions cannot remain in free America!

"It is not my thought to ask Congress to deal with these fundamental problems by legislation at this time.

"No hasty action would contribute to the solution of the present critical situation.

"There are existing laws by which to settle the prevailing disputes. There are statutes forbidding conspiracy to hinder interstate commerce.

"There are laws to assure the highest possible safety in railway service. It is my purpose to invoke these laws, civil and criminal, against all offenders alike."

No more rigorous blow was ever struck in Congress by a President of the United States to preserve the liberties of our people. No braver words were ever spoken by any President for any purpose. His enemies scoffed. His friends applauded.

And all eyes were turned on the Department of Justice. Such words could not be the signal for more conferences. They meant business.

It was realized at once by the thoughtful public that the crisis was one to be met without truckling to the interests of either party in the conflict. The rights and liberties of millions were involved against the claims of a small class of organized labor now dominated by the leaders of a revolutionary conspiracy.

Solely on this principle I marshaled my facts and prepared the papers in one of the most important cases any Attorney-General had handled in half a century.

It was a case that held my own life and career in its strangling grip.

I knew the forces which I had challenged. I couldn't foresee the heights to which they would go in their thirst for revenge.

CHAPTER XIII

The Cry for Revenge

IN ANSWER to the President's bold message to Congress, crimes increased and the situation became daily more threatening.

Everywhere thoughtful men were asking, "Have we a government?"

Mrs. Harding was driven to her bed by persistent criticisms of the President. Harding was greatly depressed and sent for me.

It had taken two months to prepare the case. It was an enormous task. The crimes recited covered half the states of the Union, and the bare recital of the offenses against law filled volumes.

I had given opportunity to both sides to settle their differences before we appealed to the courts.

I read to the President a draft of the bill prepared by the Department of Justice and outlined to him what the restraining order would contain.

Harding was enthusiastic.

"How soon can you get action?" he asked.

"I have arranged," I replied, "if I can secure a Federal judge to hear the case, to be in Chicago on Friday morning, September first, at eleven o'clock — five days from now — "

"Can't you act sooner?" he interrupted.

"It will take until that date to complete the full draft of the bill. I'll be there with it ready Friday morning, and if my assistants have secured a Federal judge the case will be heard immediately — "

I paused and leaned closer.

133

"But Mr. President, you must promise me not to say a word to any one, inside the Cabinet or outside, as to my plans and what I propose to do."

"Certainly, I'll say nothing," he agreed.

"What I'm going to do is the last resort before calling out the troops and shooting down citizens — "

"You don't propose to argue the case yourself?" the President interrupted.

"Yes," was my prompt answer. "Solicitor-General Beck and two assistants are away. I've lived this situation for two months. I can save the government a hundred thousand dollars in counsel fees. Besides, the engaging of special counsel would cause a long delay. The ablest lawyer would require many days to master the details of such a case."

Harding frowned.

"I don't want you to go to Chicago. You're taking too many chances. I don't see how you will get there alive."

"I'll get there all right," I assured him. "It's my duty to go. And I'm going. I'll take all the responsibility on my own shoulders — "

"I don't like it," he persisted.

"And I want you to understand, Mr. President," I went on, "that you can change your Attorney-General by the stroke of a pen, but once I start on this case you cannot change my course."

"Couldn't you intrust the case to the United States District Attorney in Chicago acting with your associates, and avoid the dangers of this trip?"

"No," I answered. "I'm going myself. And I'll keep a telephone line open between the White House and Chicago until eleven o'clock Friday morning. If up to that minute a settlement has not been made I'll take the first step to ask the Court for the injunction. After that hour, it will be too late for further conferences."

The next morning while the bill was being completely

typewritten I went to see the President. He asked me again to reconsider my decision to go in person to Chicago.

And again I stuck to my plans.

"All right," he nodded, "drop in to see Mrs. Harding a minute. She's still in bed from worry over this crisis."

She shot at me a leading question the moment I approached her bedside.

"What's coming of all this?"

"Now look here," I said genially, "I've just dropped in to say good-by, as I'm going away on a trip. To do something I can't tell you about. Just take another bet on me, and if I fail there'll be another Attorney-General here soon."

"Can't you tell me what you're going to do?" she asked.

"No. Only the President knows and he has promised to tell no one. Don't ask him. Just wait and see what happens in the next few days."

I left her curious but reassured. Harding was still uneasy over my going and said:

"I don't mind repeating to you that I'm uneasy for your safety. I've had many evidences of an ugly spirit abroad since I delivered my message to Congress. It was well received by the leading papers. And they're speculating as to what drastic step we're going to take. Your action will be a thunderbolt. But I'm going to back you to the limit."

"I've counted the cost carefully," I replied. "We are going to drive the radical leaders into a frenzy. They'll not strike at you. But they'll leave no stone unturned to get me. By a derailed train, a broken cross-tie, or a stray shot. But I'll take my chances."

"I understand," he nodded. "I'll not stop you. You've undertaken a great service for the country. I wish you Godspeed on your mission."

I took with me to Chicago C. J. McGuire, Colonel Goff's secretary, who was a lawyer as well as a capable stenographer. Colonel Goff was in Europe. On the train we went to work immediately, and at four o'clock in the morning, just as we entered Chicago, the draft of the temporary restraining order which I had prepared to present to the Court was finished.

We reached Chicago the day before the case was presented in court. Mr. Blackburn Esterline, of the Department of Justice, and Mr. McLaughlin were there some days in advance, getting things ready.

It being summer vacation there were no Federal judges in Chicago to whom the application could be made. My assistants were still trying to find one.

Judge Wilkerson was finally located. He was out of the city but came back to Chicago. I was willing to submit it to any judge, but was most fortunate in getting Wilkerson. He had long been in the service of the government as District Attorney before being appointed to a judgeship by Harding on my recommendation. But I had little or no personal acquaintance with him. He is the distinguished judge who recently sentenced Al Capone to prison.

I went to the Blackstone Hotel and sent for the District Attorney, Charles F. Cline. Under the law the bill had to be signed by the District Attorney where the bill was filed, as well as by the Attorney-General.

I instructed Mr. Cline to say nothing about the matter, and I am confident that the judge, when he arrived at the Federal Building the first of September, knew nothing of the business that was to be brought before him.

At ten o'clock I asked Mr. Cline to notify the newspapers that there would be something of importance before the Court and entered the room cheered by the thought that real Americans with red blood in their veins would back the move I was about to make.

Judge Wilkerson took his seat on the bench.

I had sent one of my assistants to the telephone at eleven o'clock to inquire if there had been a call for me from

Washington. In a few minutes he returned and told me there was no message.

Judge Wilkerson remarked:

"The Court observes that the Attorney-General of the United States is present. Has he any business to bring to the attention of the Court?"

I arose and said, "I have an important application on behalf of the Government and will ask Mr. Esterline to read the bill."

The judge was furnished a copy which he followed as it was read by Esterline. It was very long and I had asked that it be read in order to save my own strength, which had been drawn on considerably, for the argument.

The moment my purpose to move against the strikers was known the room was alive with the activity of a prodded wasps' nest. Newspaper men ran empty-handed for telephones, court officials moved frantically to restore order, and waiting attorneys leaned forward with alert interest.

As the reading of the bill of complaint continued, the court throngs grew, and the eager interest of the crowd advanced to dramatic excitement and expectancy.

I addressed the Court without delay.

"The Railroad Labor Board is an agency of the government. The President issued a proclamation calling upon the strikers to return to work, obey the Board's decisions, and not interfere with the transportation service or with men willing to enter or continue in service.

"The defendants, in refusing to accept the Labor Board's decision cutting wages, have repudiated the Board and its authority and hold the Government of the United States in contempt. The government can have no chart for its course except the law.

"Legal safeguarding against such menace in the future must be worked out when a chance has been given to appraise the entire situation.

"I repeat the words of President Harding in his recent message to Congress: 'We must reassert the doctrine that in this Republic the first obligation and the first allegiance of every citizen, high or low, is to his government, and to hold that government to be the just and unchallenged sponsor for public welfare and the liberty, security, and rights of all its citizens. No matter what clouds may gather, no matter what storms may ensue, no matter what hardships may attend or what sacrifices may be necessary, government by law must and will be sustained.

" 'And I will use all the power of the government to maintain transportation and sustain the right of men to work.' I do not appear as a representative of the roads but represent the people of the United States.

"The government is friendly to all labor. It is not opposed to labor unions if they perform such functions as can be performed in lawful America. Never while the labor unions limit their activities to legitimate acts and lawful pursuits not injurious to society, at least while I speak, and to the extent that I can speak, for the government of the United States, shall a blow be struck at them. But it may be understood that so long and to the extent that I can speak for the government I will use this power to prevent the labor unions of the country from destroying the open shop. When a man in this country is not permitted to engage in lawful toil whether he belongs to a union or not, with full protection and without interruption, the death knell to liberty will be sounded and anarchy will supersede organized government.

"Unions should not be destroyed, but they should be corrected and restrained. If the acts of violence and murder are inspired by the unions, then it is time for the government to call a halt. No organization or association, no matter how powerful it may be, can hold its constitution or its laws supreme over the government, the Constitution, and the laws of the United States of America. No union or combination of unions can under our laws dictate to the American Union.

"No organization or association of organizations will be permitted to laugh in the frozen faces of a famishing people without prompt prosecution and proper punishment."

After citing authority under which the Court could enter the restraining order I continued:

"The right to work in this country is as sacred as the right not to be compelled to work, if a man is not disposed to do so. And every man must be equally secure in his choice.

"The time has not yet come for taking over the roads by the government.

"The defendants could do no wiser thing for organized labor than to consent to making the restraining order permanent.

"The dispute between the employers and employees is not involved in this proceeding. We have passed that point. A governmental body entitled to recognition and obedience has decided that dispute. I am not taking sides at this time as an advocate of either.

"It so happens in this instance that the railroads are willing to render the service the government requires they shall render. They are trying to serve the American people. They are trying to observe the law. They are endeavoring to furnish transportation. On the other hand the defendants are preventing transportation and are offending against the law, as alleged in this bill, and by acts of violence are antagonizing and opposing the Government of the United States.

"Shall the American people suffer? Shall property be destroyed? Shall commerce be destroyed? Shall the laws be broken? Shall society be disorganized? Shall prosperity and all labor cease? And the poor be in want because employers and employees engaged in interstate commerce, obligated to the government and to the people of the United States by a greater obligation than that which rests upon any other set of men in the country, because of a dispute between them, refuse to obey the law?

"No! The answer by the government is that if they cannot agree, others will be given the privilege and protection of performing this service who will obey the law."

Judge Wilkerson listened to my argument with profound attention. I knew him to be one of the most fearless judges on the bench and one of our greatest lawyers.

He agreed with me on every point raised and granted the temporary injunction without a minute's delay.

An ugly murmur swept the crowd of labor agitators. They had heard my demands – the most stringent and far-reaching order ever asked of any court in the history of the Republic. I not only asked the Court to enjoin the conspirators, I asked it to forbid in the injunction any attempt to aid and abet a refusal to obey its provisions.

The wildest excitement swept the courtroom when Wilkerson gave his decision, and the news spread with lightning rapidity into the corridors and streets now jammed.

As I left the Court I was surrounded by United States Marshals and deputies. The President himself had requested that the Secret Service send their men for my additional protection. I knew nothing of this, of course.

A hollow square was formed at the elevator and I left the building. I was not in sympathy with this display of caution, but whether I liked it or not, I was escorted to the street and we started for the Drake Hotel. They had transferred me from the Blackstone, where I originally registered, to the Drake. And when we reached the hotel the same precautions were in evidence. From the entrance to the elevator and on the floor to which I was assigned Secret Service men were everywhere.

They decided that I should not leave Chicago from the regular station. Instead I was escorted to Englewood where I took the Pennsylvania train to Columbus, stopped for a day, and returned to Washington in a manner to attract as little attention as possible.

On my arrival President Harding congratulated me most cordially and rejoiced in my safety.

At the next Cabinet meeting, I was surprised to find that Secretary Fall in a vicious and pronounced way opposed the policy of securing the injunction.

He was joined by Mr. Theodore Roosevelt Jr., who had secured permission of the President to take a seat at the Cabinet meeting in the absence of Secretary Denby, his chief. The young gentleman sat beside me. And when the subject of the injunction was brought up he had in his hand a copy of the bill. He opened the discussion as to the legality of the procedure and made a long speech to the Cabinet. It was the only occasion I can recall where an assistant to a Cabinet officer was ever allowed to sit in his absence, even on his own invitation. The bill young Roosevelt held was marked quite liberally. His discussion was scattered, excited, and very emphatic.

Several times he repeated that his father never would have approved such an injunction.

I was greatly amused at his argument and when he had exhausted himself I quietly remarked:

"You seem vastly interested in the subject. Perhaps you should appear and lay your views before the Court."

Fall proceeded to criticize the policy of the injunction with much bitterness.

In a recent newspaper serial, Fall has said that this attack occurred during the coal strike. The old man's memory fails him in this. It was after the injunction had been asked for and granted in the Railroad Shopmen's strike. He got the whole subject hopelessly confused in his statement, declaring that I had attempted to force the railroads into a receivership and then bring an injunction against the labor unions.

The one thing I opposed at all times with every energy I possessed was the suggestion that the government take over the railroads. They had been taken over during the War with appalling results. The government had lost a half billion dollars in their management, and the railroads had been brought to the brink of ruin. One of the first acts of Harding's administration was to return the roads to their rightful owners — the people who had invested eighty billion dollars in their construction and equipment.

Fall says that he shouted at me:

"You don't know any law, and you can't learn any. You say you will take your army of United States Marshals and settle this strike. They're not your marshals. They're officers of the court. You have nothing to do with them except to nominate them for appointment by the President."

The first part of this paragraph Mr. Fall did not speak.

He did say: "The Attorney-General has laid this Cabinet, Mr. President, open to criticism. The public is going to think you and the Cabinet have sanctioned his acts!"

He says that he paused and added:

"If the Attorney-General is going to be permitted to do such high-handed, damn-fool things, my resignation is in."

Again his memory fails. He said nothing of the sort. No man ever uttered an oath in a Cabinet meeting presided over by Harding. If he had done so, he would have been rebuked on the spot. The President was a lovable, human man, but was a stickler for the proprieties of life and official position.

The President suddenly rose, faced the Cabinet and said firmly:

"Gentlemen, the discussion is closed. I do not care to hear any more and I hope there will be no further discussion of the matter here or on the outside. The law makes it the duty of the Attorney-General to take the action which he has taken, and that is his responsibility. I was fully informed before he went to Chicago and I heartily approve every act of his in this matter."

A painful silence fell on the other end of the table as he abruptly ended the Cabinet meeting and left the room.

Within forty-eight hours the strike was broken and the railroads again became the King's Highway which no man might obstruct.

At a mass meeting in Chicago, Charles G. Dawes made one of his daring, characteristic speeches in which he said:

"He who reasons that a halt to weakness in law enforcement has not been called and that conditions will not become better, little understands the American people.

"Progress has been made from the Adamson law of surrender to the Daugherty injunction. In my judgment future generations will regard this court decree as the beginning of a new era of law and order. Through it our government declares that the right of a man to work is as sound and sacred as the right of a man to stop work."

As I had anticipated, a manager of a newspaper deliberately tried to incite riots by urging defiance of the Court. I immediately secured his arrest, put him in jail, and we had no more proclamations of violence.

The Red leaders, of course, played this injunction for all it was worth in spreading the spirit of recklessness among the strikers.

The national campaign for the election of a new Congress was on. The labor leaders held a meeting in Canton, Ohio, denounced me in bitter terms, and demanded that the President ask for my resignation.

I was urged by the National Committee to speak in the campaign and I decided to reply to this attack. I selected Canton as the place to make the speech, as it was the scene of the attack

The big hall was packed with five thousand men and women. I expected to be hissed as I rose to address the meeting. Instead, I was received with respect and moderate cheering. The expression on the faces of the crowd plainly said: "Come on now, Mr. Attorney-General, and show us what the injunction is all about."

I told the workmen in as plain words as I could use how their organizations had been betrayed by rats who had gnawed their way into them. I told them how honest Americans had been deceived by those fanatics and had followed them blindly into a state of crime and anarchy.

I explained what an injunction meant. It was merely laying the hand of the government on the shoulders of a man about to commit a crime and warning him not to become a criminal. If he stops, no crime is committed. If there is a question as to his rights involved, he is given a speedy hearing before the court which decides the issues of right and justice and injustice.

I explained that the injunction is already as old as our common law, as old as the laws of Rome, as old as civilization itself. It embodies the fundamental principles, "Where there is right, there is a remedy," and "An ounce of prevention is worth a pound of cure."

In the middle of my speech a terrific crash behind me caused me to turn. I thought a bomb had exploded under the platform. A man who weighed three hundred pounds had moved in his chair and crashed it into kindling wood.

I smiled and went back to my speech. And a curious thing happened. Whether it was a fancy of my imagination or a reality I've never known. But every time I drew near an enormous bouquet of flowers that stood beside the speaker's stand I caught a strange pungent odor that made me dizzy. The second time I smelled it I caught my breath and thought I was going to faint. It immediately flashed over me that someone had slipped onto the rostrum before I reached it and concealed a deadly gas trap in the flowers.

I moved to the other side of the speaker's stand out of line of the breeze that crossed the flowers, felt no further inconvenience and closed my speech with a round of applause.

From the rear I saw a workingman rise quickly and make

his way to the platform. He was followed by seven or eight companions.

I said to myself: "Here's where trouble begins." I walked to the other end of the platform to meet them.

"Well, gentlemen, what is it?"

The leader said:

"Mr. Daugherty, I was on the committee that demanded of the President that you resign. Labor men were opposed to the action of the government and we were all prejudiced against the Attorney-General, for we held you responsible for the injunction. We never knew what the strike was all about, and for myself and my associates I want to thank you for coming to Canton and telling us the truth."

I thanked him, shook hands with him and his friends and felt myself more than repaid for my pains in preparing and delivering that speech. It was printed and thousands of copies mailed to workmen all over the United States. That its effects were wholesome, there was no doubt.

But within ten days from the granting of the injunction and collapse of the strike, Ralston, the attorney for the American Federation of Labor, and its powerful Lobby, moved, through their representative on the floor of the House, Mr. Keller of Minnesota, my impeachment as Attorney-General for "High Crimes and Misdemeanors."

Keller's resolution was the opening act of a drama of revenge in which I was to be hounded by the men whom I had struck in the performance of my duties. "Get Daugherty" was the slogan. And through their organizations it became at last a national anvil chorus.

CHAPTER XIV

Impeached for High Crimes and Misdemeanors

THERE is perhaps no parallel in the history of our Republic for the brazen attempt of the labor lobby to impeach and destroy a Cabinet officer for performing the duties of his position.

For insolent effrontery this answer to a suit in equity brought in our courts in behalf of the American people caps the climax.

In the bitter struggles between President Johnson and his enemies following the assassination of Abraham Lincoln, the attempt was made to force on him a member of the old Cabinet to which he objected. But in the wildest flight of blind anger no Congressman had dared to offer a resolution of impeachment against one of President Johnson's Cabinet for performing the duties of his office.

Amid the insane passions of the period of 1866-67, there might have been excuse for such an act. In 1922 there could be none for the attempt to impeach and remove from office the Attorney-General of the United States.

He was working in perfect harmony with the President, who had plainly outlined his course of action in a message to Congress. If he was guilty of High Crimes and Misdemeanors his chief was equally guilty.

President Harding was incensed at this move to discredit his administration by such a dastardly subterfuge. He backed me to the limit and asked me to fight the insult with every ounce of manhood I possessed.

A delegation called on the President and announced that impeachment proceedings were pending against the Attorney-General.

Harding said:

"That's all right. Go ahead. He has been in wars before and can take care of himself. He is only doing his duty. But I would advise you before you start to prepare yourselves. For you have a long road to travel in a fight against the Attorney-General and the government."

The conspiracy to destroy me made no effort to conceal the origin of its movement. It appeared at times as a direct and brazen attempt to intimidate me in the performance of my duties.

On September 11, I was absent from my post in Washington. On that date I appeared before Judge Wilkerson in Chicago in the hearing for the temporary injunction, the temporary restraining order having been in existence for ten days, as the law provides.

The business of the labor unions was to appear against me with their lawyers and fight the case. They failed to do this because they had no defense to seventeen thousand crimes of which I had accused them in my bill in equity. They made none on September 11 and they never made one at any later date.

Instead of defending themselves against the charge of conspiracy in committing those crimes against the peace and dignity of the nation, they rushed their agents into Congress and stabbed me in the back by an asinine resolution charging me with High Crimes and Misdemeanors in office and asking for my removal.

It was in many ways a very shrewd move. I had many bitter political enemies in my own party and in the opposition who would believe any and all evil spoken against me. The language of an "impeachment for High Crimes and Misdemeanors" sounded formidable. Many simple people would believe the charges merely because they were spoken and recorded in the House proceedings. The bare accusations would put the Attorney-General on the defensive and cripple his standing in the courts and before the people. In this they were correct.

Hostile partisan newspapers, of course, pronounced me guilty without discussing the absurd "hodge-podge" which Keller read into his resolution.

This remarkable document was drawn by Jackson Ralston, the attorney for Samuel Gompers, the American Federation of Labor, and their legislative lobby in Washington.

Keller had been elected in a strong labor district. He called himself a Republican, but he was never considered one. He followed every radical movement and was their useful tool as a Congressman.

He rose in his seat in the House while I was arguing the injunction in Chicago, and made the first move in the drama of revenge entitled "Get Daugherty." The stage was set for a tragedy, which came very near developing into a farce on the first day.

The only elected member of the House representing the Reds proclaimed:

"Mr. Speaker: I impeach Harry M. Daugherty, Attorney-General of the United States, for High Crimes and Misdemeanors in office."

The little man puffed out his chest and sat down.

Speaker Gillette leaned over his desk:

"When the gentleman rises to a question of high privilege he must present definite charges at the outset."

"Very well," said Keller. "I will do so."

He read from Ralston's outline:

"Harry M. Daugherty, Attorney-General of the United States, has used his high office to violate the Constitution in the following particulars:

"By abridging freedom of speech.

"By abridging freedom of the press.

"By abridging the right of the people peaceably to assemble.

"He has conducted himself in a manner arbitrary, oppressive, unjust, and illegal.

"He has used the funds of his office to prosecute individuals and organizations for certain lawful acts." (He meant, of course, the lawful acts of the conspirators who directed the campaign of violence which resulted in seventeen thousand crimes.)

"He has failed to prosecute the malefactors of great wealth." (This in the face of the fact that I was the only Attorney-General in history to put a millionaire in jail for violating the Anti-Trust Act.)

In a soap-box speech he asked that his resolution be referred to the Judiciary Committee for action.

Immediately, a Democrat, Mr. Blanton of Texas, a distinguished lawyer on this Committee, rose and said:

"Mr. Speaker, I rise to a point of order."

"The Gentleman from Texas will state it," Gillette, the Speaker, answered.

"I make the point of order," Mr. Blanton said, "that the recitation of generalities does not under the rules of this House constitute impeachment of a public official; that this recitation is nothing but generalities, no specific charge of malfeasance in office, no specific charge of improper conduct in office, but a mere recitation of generalities which could be lodged against any official of the United States. I make the point of order that it does not come within the rule."

The Speaker scanned the formidable-looking document prepared by the labor lobby's attorney and decided to admit it to record.

On my return from Chicago I addressed to the Chairman of the Judiciary Committee the following letter:

DEPARTMENT OF JUSTICE
Washington, D. C.

Hon. A. J. Volstead,
Chairman, Judiciary Committee
U.S. House of Representatives

My dear Mr. Chairman:

My attention has been called to a proceeding, or an attempted proceeding, pending before your Committee to impeach me as Attorney-General.

When this proceeding was instituted I was engaged personally in the trial and argument of an important government case in the Federal court in Chicago, and had no opportunity to give the matter any attention, if it was, in fact, a matter deserving attention.

I am advised that December 4 has been set as the date your Committee will hear the testimony of those who preferred the charges and instituted the impeachment proceedings. I do not think a matter of this sort should be allowed to rest in the Committee, and I am exceedingly anxious that prompt action be taken. I shall be glad to furnish the Committee any information desired and all data necessary, excepting only such information as might be inimical and prejudicial to the interests of the government to make public. Any such information will be given to the Committee in confidence.

I have not received from your Committee a copy of the charges preferred. Will you kindly have the same sent to me at once?

Very truly yours,
[signed] H. M. Daugherty
November 18, 1922.   Attorney-General.

I had known from the beginning that the plan was not to press the proceedings but to let it lie there and be talked about, and to keep up the gossip and prejudice as much and as long as possible.

I forced the Committee to take up the resolution and push it. Keller and his associates wanted delay. Even when they gave up the fight, I insisted that the matter be vigorously handled by the Judiciary Committee. The Committee investigated thoroughly and made its findings.

At the first meeting which they held to hear Mr. Keller's charges and review the evidence to sustain them, he had nothing to offer beyond the vague statements which he had presented.

And then a remarkable scene was enacted.

The Chairman, Mr. Volstead, frowned and Keller drew himself to his full height:

"The Committee should take the charges which I make, and they are true until they are proven not true — "

Every lawyer in the room laughed aloud.

"Is it your intention," inquired Yates of Illinois, with an amused surprise, "that this Committee ought now to report this resolution favorably without any showing of facts whatever by you?"

"I have made my charges," Keller cried, "and they are true until they are proven not true!"

Again the Committee laughed without restraint.

The Chairman restored order and mildly remarked:

"In the United States, Mr. Keller, the burden of proof is always on the accuser. Every man under our flag is held innocent until he is proven guilty. In Russia I hear the process is the opposite. We must work under the rules of evidence as practiced in our courts on this side of the water."

For the third time Keller repeated:

"I have made my charges and they are true until they are proven not true."

His idiotic reiteration of an absurdity at last angered the Committee and they demanded that he produce his evidence without further oratory.

Confronted by the stern demand for facts Keller could do nothing but ask for delay.

The hearing was postponed again and again, and always because he was not ready.

The agitator continued in the meantime to make vicious attacks in the House on me, protected by the law granting him immunity from the prosecution for libel. The radical Red "Federated Press" repeated those speeches far and wide.

The *Locomotive Engineers' Journal* said: "Daugherty should be impeached because he has illegally prosecuted and persecuted the working class and shown himself the friend of the malefactors of great wealth."

Samuel Gompers, the conservative who was then forced into the leadership of the radical class, issued a proclamation in the official organ of the American Federation of Labor:

"It is our purpose to do everything possible to bring the impeachment proceedings to a successful conclusion. Labor will participate in the work through its representatives, through its council, and through the presentation of the testimony of witnesses."

The labor men were now completely under the spell of their radical advisers. They made no effort to conceal their program of revenge and warning. They were not merely after my scalp. They were serving notice in this vicious political procedure that they would crush any Attorney-General of the future who dared to interfere with their plans.

Samuel Untermeyer, as chairman of the finance committee of the "People's Legislative Service," a Pink Soviet organization, for some mysterious reason made a feint at producing evidence before the Committee, but contented himself with a couple of abusive letters and dropped out of the case.

When pressed to the wall by the Committee in its demand for facts, Gompers's attorney, Jackson Ralston, weakened and began to crawfish on the charges.

The Committee finally issued a peremptory demand on Keller to appear, produce his evidence, and call his witnesses. He was just outside the room, hiding behind his vacillating attorney.

The Committee then caused a subpoena to be issued. The Speaker of the House called the Sergeant-at-Arms and ordered that Keller be brought before it under arrest. On hearing the call of the Sergeant-at-Arms, Mr. Keller dashed down the corridor and ran at breakneck speed. The ancients believed that the bowels were the seat of the human soul. In this mad flight, the radical leader gave positive proofs of the truth of this faith. Scrubwomen were called at an unusual hour.

This hearing before the Judiciary Committee thus ended in a filthy fiasco. It would have been a joke but for the important fact that it was a preliminary move in a more powerful attack already in preparation.

The Committee, after a full hearing which I insisted upon, reported with but a single dissenting voice that all charges were unfounded. The House adopted its report by a vote of 204 to 77, a group of radical Democrats joining the Soviets at the last moment merely to discredit a Republican Administration.

The Democratic members of the Judiciary Committee led in ridiculing the attack.

Keller had fled South for his health. He needed a rest. But the paper *Labor*, organ of the Railroad Brotherhood, and Mr. Untermeyer's Conference for Political Action, boldly announced:

"Congressman Keller has already served notice on the Attorney-General that unless he gets out of public life, the impeachment fight will be renewed as soon as the new Congress convenes."

Mr. Keller sank into oblivion, but the work he had so clumsily begun was taken up now by more skillful and unscrupulous hands backed by unlimited resources.

At this juncture the American press gave striking evidences of its ability to see through humbug. I began to believe that an official of our government could do his duty without being hung for it.

For the moment I had the laugh on my enemies.

From every state of the Union came a chorus of

condemnation of the proceedings and a vigorous defense of my position. The injunction was still before the courts, and the attack had been rushed to intimidate both the judge and the Attorney-General. I read the papers with growing interest.

The *Boston Transcript* observed: "A greater fiasco could not be imagined than this attempt to destroy a Cabinet officer, who notwithstanding that he has been made the center of the most bitter attacks on the Harding administration, as a matter of fact has proved one of the most energetic and capable prosecuting officers that has ever conducted the Department of Justice."

The *Hartford Courant* said: "Daugherty's determination to bring civil and criminal prosecutions for war frauds has resulted in a great deal of anxiety among people who thought that they had gotten away with it. His prosecution of Anti-Trust law violators has resulted in the first jail sentence ever imposed in such cases. To heap abuse upon the Attorney-General is to their interest and they have done it and are continuing to do it as badly and clumsily as they can."

The *Niagara Falls Gazette* hit the mark in a brief editorial: "During the rail strike last August about twenty trains were marooned in the deserts leaving passengers to suffer hunger and intolerable heat. Daugherty secured the indictment and conviction of eight union trainmen responsible for this crime. For this he is being hounded by Gompers and his vindictive associates. The attempt to impeach the Attorney-General has failed, but the future will see other trumped-up charges coming from the same source."

The *Atlanta Constitution* said: "It is doubtful if in the history of this country there has ever been a more generally unwarranted, unprovoked, and in the end disgraceful persecution of a high official of the Government than represented in the attempt to impeach the Attorney-General.

"The charges against Mr. Daugherty were aided and

abetted by an element of Radicals who sought his downfall as a penalty for his firm and courageous position in recent industrial troubles. A position demanded in the interest of public welfare."

Mr. Arthur Brisbane in the *New York American* did not mince matters:

"What Big Interests Have Set Out to Get Daugherty?

"What is all this attack on Attorney-General Daugherty about?

"Anybody who has had experience with persecutions of this kind knows they are not due to failure to be aggressive in performance of duty, but are always due to powerful enemies that have been offended by a just and impartial performance of duty.

"The plain question in Attorney-General Daugherty's case is, therefore, not what has he failed to do, but in what vigorous way has he enforced the law, which has caused some big interests to hate him and to go out to 'get him,' and to stir up its big hired lawyers and its little owned politicians to attack the man who has offended this interest and to say things that will be printed in newspapers even though they are never proved nor even attempted to be proved?

"The investigation of Attorney-General Daugherty has fallen utterly flat.

"No proof of any allegation has been presented. The chief accuser, and on the flimsiest of pretexts, has even refused to testify.

"What is needed now is another investigation, to find out who the big interests are who are attacking the Attorney-General of the United States, and who are trying to discredit and weaken him and weaken the force of his official procedure.

"Is it the whisky ring, against which the Attorney-General's office has been especially active?

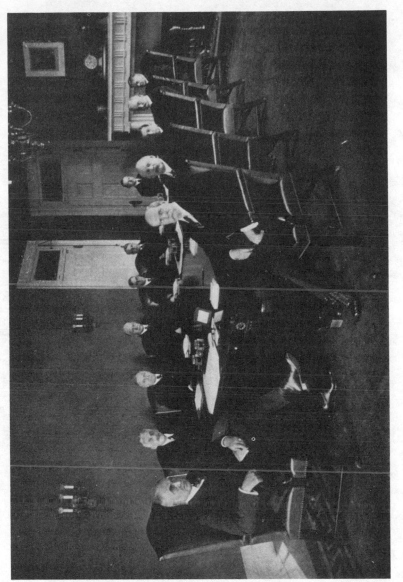

The Harding Cabinet

Senator W. E. Borah   *Samuel Gompers*

Among those who tried to get Daugherty's scalp.

"Is it the war profiteers, who were so powerful with the late Democratic administration?

"Is it the Palmer-Garvan outfit, who fraudulently confiscated alien property and delivered it to their friends, and whom the Attorney-General has exposed?

"Most surely there is some interest, and some corrupt interest, responsible for the attacks which up to this time have been so utterly baseless and futile as to make them an insult to the American people whom the Attorney-General represents."

I will say that the morons who led this attack on me hadn't the brains to realize the gravity of their acts. I have never believed that Gompers knew how completely the Red Wing had made a fool of him. As the head of the American Federation of Labor he had more than once before been made to walk a tight rope by the dynamite squads in his unions. Once started on their march, these dynamiters had always dominated the leaders of labor.

Mr. Louis Adamic has just written a brilliant and powerful story of class violence in America entitled *Dynamite*, in which he traces the history and achievements of this group in the labor unions. He shows that they have not only done as they pleased when it pleased them, but have forced their superior officers to obey their orders.

I am inclined to think that Gompers was acting under orders from this radical group of habitual criminals when he directed Ralston, his attorney, to draw the impeachment indictment against me.

Mr. Adamic, in his book, proves beyond the shadow of a doubt that these dynamite groups in the labor unions were the pioneers of racketeering in America. They taught the modern criminal the rudiments of his profession. And the racketeers have now become such experts, under present conditions, that they have begun to lay tribute on their teachers!

I was the first Cabinet officer whom these racketeers attempted to dynamite in the performance of duty. I will not be the last. For their ultimate success in my case was intended to intimidate every man who succeeded me, and make the American Republic thereafter cower under a new Reign of Terror.

My victory was short-lived. The forces at work behind the scenes engaged more skillful generals to lead in the next attack.

Senator William E. Borah has always played a lone hand in the United States Senate. No man in his party, or outside, ever knows exactly where he will turn up. For some unaccountable reason the great Western orator played into the hands of the radicals of the labor unions by announcing himself in favor of the recognition of Soviet Russia.

Our distinguished Secretary of State, Charles E. Hughes, saw the danger of this unexpected attack on the fixed policy of the American government. He asked for the Harding Administration records in the Department of Justice of Soviet activities in the United States. We gave them to him when he locked horns with Borah.

The Senator learned of my assistance to the Department of State, became my enemy and began to back the conspirators who had organized in the Senate to drive me from the Cabinet.

I noted Senator Borah's position with uneasiness. He and I had been friends for many years, and while we had not always agreed, I appreciated his friendship. There is no question as to his ability and integrity. I thought he was too big a man to be the agent of those determined to get their revenge on me. But his activities were helpful to the movement.

And they were not long in showing their hands. They found a leader after their own heart and rallied to his standard.

In the little borough of Montana, masquerading as a state, boasting two United States Senators who represent a population about the size of a county in Ohio, there suddenly appeared, as a candidate for the Senate, a District Attorney appointed under Wilson. On his banners he had inscribed the slogan: "I'll get Daugherty!"

On this issue he rallied the cohorts of the I. W. W. "Big Bill" Dunne, the Communist associate of William Z. Foster, had taken refuge from warrants out for his arrest in Burton K. Wheeler's Federal District at Butte. He had discovered that the Department of Justice was not functioning against the radicals in Mr. Wheeler's territory.

"Big Bill" became a leader in the movement to send Wheeler to the Senate to get my scalp.

The scandal of the open alliance between an officer of the United States Government and the men who were preaching its overthrow at length developed a row in the State Legislature. Thirty members demanded the resignation or removal of Wheeler from public office. The I. W. W. defeated their resolution by three votes.

Alarmed by the dangerous alliance of an officer of the government with its implacable foes, the State Council of Defense summoned Wheeler and "Big Bill" to appear before them and explain their alliance. The hearing was a heated one and lasted five days. At its conclusion the Council of Defense voted unanimously that Wheeler had been guilty of close affiliation with the I. W. W. and other seditious elements, and that as an officer of the law he had refused to prosecute them for crimes committed against the state and nation.

The Council promptly asked President Wilson to remove Wheeler from office. A meeting of the County Councils of Defense of the entire state joined in this request.

In spite of this "Big Bill" Dunne reached such power in the councils of the Democratic Party in Montana that he named Wheeler as its candidate for the Senate. They had been "comrades" in the campaign of 1920, and Dunne knew that Wheeler's election would be a victory for the cause of Communism in the United States.

The question has been asked, how such a man with such a backing ever won a seat in the Senate of the Nation.

The answer is simple. The voting population of the whole state is less than many counties of the East. Only thirty-four per cent of those entitled to vote went to the polls. The Reds, Pinks, Yellows, and their associates turned out in force as they always do. Wheeler was elected a United States Senator by 30 per cent of the voting population of his little borough.

So Burton K. Wheeler, comrade of "Big Bill" Dunne, Communist and champion of Red Russia, took his seat in the United States Senate and began preparations immediately to "Get Daugherty."

CHAPTER XV

The Real Mrs. Harding and Her Home Life

I WAS too busy with the work of the government to give time to Senator Wheeler's first attacks. And I let the winds blow. I can see now that I made a mistake in permitting lies to go unchallenged. A lie repeated long enough will be hailed at last as a revelation.

A lull in the open activities of my foes gave me time for the injunction suit, which I now pressed with every force at my command.

When the case came for the final trial on the issue of a permanent injunction which would have the effect of established precedent and a working law, we were ready to the last detail. The evidence in the 17,000 crimes recited in our bill was complete and overwhelming. Not a single witness appeared for the conspirators. Not one of them dared to show his face in Court. Not one of them would risk an appearance on the witness stand and subject himself to the merciless cross-examination in store for him.

The Court issued a permanent injunction against the men conspiring to destroy our government by criminal acts, the most far-reaching ruling of its character recorded in the history of the Nation.

It has ever since been the avowed purpose of the labor lobby in Washington to destroy this power of the government. If they succeed in destroying the right of injunction and deprive us of this principle of law, as old as civilization itself, we start on the toboggan that ends in Moscow.

I cannot believe our lawmakers will ever stoop to this surrender of the liberties of the American people. But we live in a new, strange world. And things may happen that now seem impossible.

Eternal vigilance is the price of liberty.

And I warn the nation that this attempt to destroy our institutions in the great strikes of 1922 is still to-day a secret, tireless, militant force at work undermining our ideals and corrupting the mind of our youth.

I found in Mrs. Harding always a strong champion and an inspiring friend.

She had carried into the Executive Mansion the sweet spirit of her Marion home life, and never attempted to play the "Great Lady." She was natural — always herself. In an age of jazz she was simple and old-fashioned and made no attempt to change either the world or her own outlook on it.

She took life as it came, always finding her happiness in the success of her husband.

In the old days in Marion, when she was the circulation manager of the *Star*, she used to ride a bicycle and pedal home half an hour ahead of the editor to broil the steak. There were no butlers then. Not even a servant.

She had been a great help to him in running his newspaper, a close observer of public events, a student of men, and one of the best-informed women in the country.

They were of more help to each other than any man and woman I have ever known. She was intensely interested in his work and watched carefully to see that he made no mistakes. If he did she was keen to "pick him up," though she did it in a way that never nagged. Their discussions were heated at times, but never quarrelsome or bitter.

A charming and brilliant hostess at gatherings of state, she was tactful and helpful to all.

In the dangerous illness which developed from her

anxieties over the great strikes her life hung in the balance. I had never seen a man more utterly crushed than Harding over this tragedy. I went to the White House three or four times a day.

When the crisis developed the President phoned me to come at once. I found him in his study pacing the floor:

"I think the end is near!" he said tensely.

Dr. John Finney of Baltimore and Dr. Charles Mayo of Rochester were in consultation with Sawyer and Boone and President Harding's brother, Dr. George T. Harding.

At the President's request I remained all night, and at 12:30 persuaded him to get some rest. Mrs. Harding passed the crisis at two a.m. The doctors gave her husband a cheering message. And his face lighted with a great joy.

Her love for Harding was of the deep, eternal things of life, and he knew it. She had never stooped to petty jealousies, and I never heard them quarrel, though they spoke their inner secrets in my presence with freedom.

She was a woman of the keenest intuitions and sharpest insight into any vexed question of state. Her intuition almost amounted to second sight.

The most spirited discussion that I ever knew to take place between them was over a clause in one of his messages relating to the League of Nations. The President was opposed to the League, and Mrs. Harding was even more tenacious in her opposition. Yet a clause had slipped into his message that would be considered favorable to America's ultimate affiliation with the League.

He had conferred with Secretary Hughes on the message the night before, and I have always wondered how this clause found its way into the text of the message.

The President was a great admirer of his Secretary of State, whom he considered the biggest man in the Cabinet. I agreed with his estimate.

Early in the administration I had a personal test of

Hughes's character which I can never forget. I had rendered opinion as Attorney-General on a question of law involving an important issue — so important that I said to the President that I would like to hear the opinion of Secretary Hughes.

"You're a great lawyer, Mr. Secretary," the President remarked, "as well as a diplomat. This is a matter of grave importance. The Attorney-General and all the Cabinet will be glad to hear your opinion."

Hughes gave it without any false modesty or apologies. It differed from mine. In fact it was the contradiction of my views.

I immediately replied and called his attention to an important point of law which he had forgotten or overlooked in his hurriedly given opinion. I went into the details of this point and showed its relation to the issues.

When I finished my argument he looked at me and smiled genially:

"I'll have to withdraw my first opinion. I had overlooked the point the Attorney-General has presented. I've made a mistake in an offhand decision. He is right and I am wrong."

Only a big man — one of the biggest — could do a thing like that. Harding was quick to get this, as he was quick to recognize every element of greatness in the Secretary of State.

Usually the President tried his messages out on me much as a showman tries out a new play on the dog.

The night before this message was to be delivered, I was scheduled to make an address before the Ohio Society in Washington.

Early in the evening I received a call to come to the White House.

I spoke to the chairman of the meeting and whispered:

"Don't like to disappoint you but I must go to the White House — "

"Wait just a few minutes, I'll call you at once. Make us a little speech first."

He introduced me, I spoke for five minutes and hurried to answer the call.

The President and Mrs. Harding were waiting for me in the library.

There was an air of restraint between them. I caught it instantly. I thought at first it might have been a little domestic spat over something trivial, but changed my mind the moment Harding spoke:

"I want to read to you the message I'm going to deliver to-morrow."

I knew in a flash what had happened. He had read it to her and she had disagreed with something in it. They had engaged in an argument that had ended in a heated discussion.

I threw her a glance, caught a twinkle in the corner of her eye, and said to the President:

"By all means let's hear it — go ahead."

"It's an international affair," he said, "and maybe you'll have a suggestion to offer."

Mrs. Harding's face was still flushed and the President's was set in unusually stern lines. She took a seat on a long stool before us, and I sat in my usual chair beside his desk.

The message was now in final form ready to be printed in the morning before the time of delivery.

The President read in even tones, and when he reached the paragraph relating to the League of Nations, I stiffened in my chair and saw Mrs. Harding smile as I said:

"Wait — a — minute — Mr. President — are you saying there exactly what you intended?"

"Certainly," he said.

"Why," I interrupted, "my interpretation of that would head us straight into the League of Nations, destroy the policy of your party, and ignore the pledge of the last election."

Mrs. Harding sat bolt upright, her eyes flashing:

"Exactly what I've been telling him."

The President fumbled the sheets in his hand as I suggested:

"We're in no hurry. Let me read that on paper. Maybe I didn't catch its real meaning."

He handed me the page, I read it over carefully and firmly said: "Mr. President, you certainly don't mean what this says. If you do, the Republican Party collapses. I don't know what it will mean to the country, but it will mean the death of your administration."

"I don't agree with you at all," he answered.

I looked at the President and said:

"Let me write out my idea of that paragraph."

"Go ahead," he agreed.

I took a pencil and pad and wrote my views in about as many words as the original paragraph. The three of us argued it for an hour or more.

At a quarter of twelve Secretary of War Weeks unexpectedly came in. Driving by from some engagement he had dropped in for a late call.

I was glad to see Weeks. He was fond of Harding, but he was a man who always had opinions of his own on any public question.

I immediately suggested:

"If you think I'm wrong about this, here's a fairminded man; read that paragraph to him and let's see what he has to say."

The President read the sentences, and Weeks flushed as he spoke almost the same words I had used:

"Why, Mr. President — I don't think you mean this at all."

Harding began to laugh now and reiterated his stand with the greatest firmness.

We argued until nearly two o' clock and I rose:

"Well, there's nothing more to be said about the matter. We'll go home and get some sleep, and you can think it over."

"I've thought it over," he smiled.

"Well, as far as I'm concerned," I said, "I think you're dead wrong. But if you decide to let it stand I'm with you. Though it means the destruction of your administration, the ruin of your party, the repudiation of the pledges on which you were elected. It means you're going into the League of Nations and I'm going home right now."

We three walked down the stairs from the library.

The President held my overcoat, and quietly said:

"I'll hold your overcoat for you even though I didn't get much help from you to-night."

"Well," I laughed, "if you want to kill me I'll wrestle with you all night over this thing. But I must tell you what I think."

"You are all right," he muttered, "but no good to me on this question."

He opened the door and in the gentlest way said:

"Good night."

I rode home in Secretary Weeks's car, and mine trailed. Weeks was worked up to a high pitch of excitement over what he had heard and so was I.

We planned to go to the Capitol together the next day to hear the fatal message delivered.

We sat beside each other in our seats assigned to the Cabinet in the House where the President delivered his messages. The Secretary of War asked me:

"Have you an idea of what he's going to do?"

"Not the slightest."

"Haven't you heard from him since last night?"

"Not a word."

"Then we'll say farewell to glory." He glanced at the packed galleries and sighed: "Good-by, Washington. I'll go back to Boston beans and good old cod-fish cakes."

We listened with bated breath as he came to the fatal paragraph.

I gripped Weeks's hand:

"Well, good-by, old friend. It won't be long now — "

He began to read the paragraph before I released my friend's hand. I felt the muscles tighten as he whispered:

"Glory to God. We're saved. He's reading the substitute word for word."

"A wise little woman!" I murmured.

"What's that?" growled Weeks.

CHAPTER XVI

Miller and Forbes

IN THE three years preceding the Harding Administration 100,913 criminal cases were prosecuted.

In the three years beginning with the Harding Administration, 168,606 criminal cases were prosecuted.

The former Attorney-General collected from convictions a total of 14 million dollars in three years. During my three years, collections from the same sources, for which the Harding administration is entitled to credit, amounted to over 32 1/2 million dollars.

These figures are shown by the records of the Department of Justice, and might well account for the attacks made on me by those anxious to lift the pressure.

No administration in the history of the country can show a more vigorous prosecution of criminals, great and small, than President Harding's.

In the appointment of a personnel of 50,000 men and women, the President of the United States can know but few he chooses for office. And no matter how close the scrutiny applied by him and his assistants, untrustworthy men will gain positions.

They do in all administrations.

No man ever applied for a subordinate public office with higher credentials or stronger backing than Colonel Thomas W. Miller.

His business record was varied, but clean of all suspicion. He had managed a ranch in Nevada and had worked for the Bethlehem Steel Company. He was Secretary of State in

Delaware for two years and a member of Congress from 1915 to 1917.

He was a graduate of Yale University, a member of the Episcopal Church in good standing, a member of the Union League Club of Philadelphia, the Yale Club, the Bankers of America, the National Press, the Racquet of Washington, the St. Elmo of New Haven, and the Wilmington Country Club.

He had hundreds of warm friends who gave him the highest recommendations.

His public career had been inspiring. He was one of our young Congressmen who volunteered for war from the floor of the House of Representatives, rushed to Plattsburg for training, enlisted as a private in the U.S. Infantry in 1917, fought eleven months in France, received citations for gallantry in action and especially meritorious conduct. He rose to the rank of Lieutenant-Colonel and was honorably discharged from the service in September of 1919.

He was one of the original incorporators of the American Legion and a member of its National Executive Committee. He was an Eastern Director of the Republican National Campaign Committee, and was appointed by Harding as Alien Property Custodian March 12, 1921.

No man ever entered the service of any administration under more auspicious conditions or greater faith in his ability and honesty.

President Harding died before the charges were brought against Colonel Miller which resulted in his imprisonment.

Such was not the case with Charles R. Forbes. Of all the experiences Harding had in the White House, the one with Forbes was the only one that cut him deeply.

He was also a veteran of the World War, a Colonel in rank, a member of the Executive Committee of the American Legion for the State of Washington, and a leading figure in the Military Committee of the Chamber of Commerce of Spokane.

On a visit to Honolulu, Senator and Mrs. Harding met him at a social function. The Colonel was the star featured guest of the evening. He was handsome, genial, plausible, and very popular. Mrs. Harding liked him from their first meeting, and she was a keen judge of character, both in men and women. Colonel Forbes was the type of man around whom women have always buzzed. I have often wondered how he got past Mrs. Harding's piercing eyes and held her good opinion almost to the end.

Harding and Forbes became personal friends. Whether the Colonel saw in him a coming man in American politics I don't know. But the fact is that, although a Wilson official, he took pains to cultivate the Hardings. He showered them with attention and added much to the happiness of their tropical outing.

The future President returned to America with a vivid impression of his new friend — an impression which he carried through the next few years.

Colonel Forbes, when he heard of Harding's candidacy for the Presidency, left the Hawaiian Islands, returned to Spokane, and began fighting to swing the delegation from the State of Washington for the Senator.

Senator Poindexter of that state was a candidate for the Presidency. Our plan of campaign was never to enter a contest against another candidate in his own state. Forbes was not friendly to Poindexter, and set out immediately to secure the delegation for Harding. I soon put an end to it.

The encounter was unpleasant and laid the foundation for a personal antagonism between us.

When Harding was nominated Forbes plunged into the campaign and fought valiantly to elect him. He was a man of tireless energy, popular and a good campaigner.

A conspicuous leader of the American Legion, he desired a place on the Shipping Board. But this was a regional office and the position Forbes sought had already been offered to another man.

He then selected the position as head of the Veterans' Bureau as his next choice, and got the enthusiastic backing of the American Legion.

The President made the appointment with considerable pleasure and did not consult me about it. He merely informed me:

"I've put Colonel Forbes into the Veterans' Bureau. With his fine record as a soldier and his genius for making friends he'll do great work there."

From time to time the President remarked: "Forbes is making a fine record," and would recite what was being done in the Veterans' Bureau.

During the time he was in Washington I probably saw Forbes about two or three times. I never met him at the White House, nor did we ever discuss politics or the work of his department.

He engaged a shrewd lawyer by the name of Charles F. Cramer as his chief counsel. I never met Mr. Cramer and no questions were ever submitted to the Department of Justice, or to me as Attorney-General, by the legal staff of the Veterans' Bureau.

This Bureau is an independent department of the government directly under the President, and Harding was intensely interested in its work because of its services to the veterans. Its establishment was one of the achievements of his administration.

Dr. C. E. Sawyer, the President's physician, was also deeply interested. Sawyer and Forbes, however, soon began to have difficulties.

When Congress, in response to a widespread public demand, appropriated seventeen millions to the Veterans' Bureau for the purpose of buying sites and building a chain of hospitals for wounded soldiers, many of us feared that

Senator Brookhart

Senator Ashurst

Senator Wheeler

Senator Moses

Senator Jones

The Wheeler Committee
investigating Attorney-General H. M. Daugherty.

Gaston B. Means
America's Baron Munchausen.

*Means' farcical appearance in the Wheeler melodrama,
as its general manager.*

Forbes was not the man to assume responsibility for such a tremendous expenditure of money. And not long after the work started our fears were realized.

Ugly rumors began to fly. I did not think Forbes dishonest, but felt he was not big enough for the job. Dr. Sawyer was sure he was not. The doctor was a man of splendid capabilities and experience, and was one of the most helpful advisers to the President during his entire administration.

Sawyer called my attention to the situation. I joked with him at first, and told him he was prejudiced against Forbes. He frankly admitted it.

"For that reason you can't be fair," I said to him. "Give him a chance. The President thinks he is capable of great things."

Later Dr. Sawyer came to me and said:

"Forbes has had his chance. There's no use locking the stable door after the horse is gone. He is not a man to be trusted and he is going to play hell with the President."

He repeated this to me more than once and after hearing complaints from varied sources I set in motion the machinery of my department to see if I could find out what, if anything, was wrong. I learned enough in a short time to justify me in taking it up with the President.

I found him sitting for his portrait with Howard Chandler Christy. When I entered the White House he asked me to his study.

There behind closed doors I said:

"Mr. President, I have a very unpleasant duty to perform."

"You and I have had many unpleasant duties," he replied, and added, "what's wrong now?"

"Dr. Sawyer has informed me that strange things are going on in the Veterans' Bureau."

"The doctor hates Forbes," he broke in.

"For your protection," I continued, "I have made an investigation."

"And you are sure of facts and not stupid gossip?"

"Sure. I've learned that Forbes is leading a life of dissipation. A thing no man can do and handle the people's money. A thing that no officer of the government can do in any position. To say nothing of a job where he has the spending of seventeen millions from the public treasury."

"What has he done?" the President asked.

"He is running with a wild crowd. Some of the men of millions who step too high for Forbes to follow and keep his head. He is your appointee. I have no feeling about the matter except that I want to do my duty toward you and your administration. It is hard for you to believe evil of a friend but there are limits to the application of this principle and you have reached the limit in this case. You are walking on the crest of a volcano."

I started to go. The President was very much impressed and, of course, depressed.

I suggested to him:

"You have your own facilities for getting the facts. I would be glad if you find everything all right. I don't want you to act entirely on my advice. I may be prejudiced against Forbes, but I don't think so. I suggest that you send your own men to check my report, get the facts, and get them as quickly as possible."

It was late, about dinner time. And for the first time since the inauguration, he did not ask me to stay when I happened to be at the White House at this hour.

He was worried and upset and took no pains to conceal it. I was disturbed myself and hurried back to my house.

I did not see the President on the following day, which was unusual. I generally had a few minutes' talk with him every day.

At eleven o'clock the second morning he called my telephone and asked me to lunch with him.

He was as cordial as ever, Mrs. Harding as gracious as usual, and we had a pleasant luncheon without reference to business.

As we rose he said:

"Come into my study a few minutes."

He looked at me in silence and then asked:

"Did I hurt your feelings the last time you were here?"

"Why, I don't know what you are talking about," I fenced.

"Yes, you do."

"The Attorney-General can have no feelings. He is only a machine. What do you mean?"

"The Forbes matter, of course — "

I lifted my hand:

"You didn't hurt my feelings. You couldn't. I know you too well. You were surprised and shocked. And doubtful of what you had heard. And you did what I would have done myself. You've made a little investigation of your own — "

He nodded dolefully.

"Yes, I have. And found you were right. I'm awfully sorry about it all. I'm heartsick over it."

"What are you going to do?" I asked.

"But one thing is possible. Get rid of Forbes."

"Then quickly — we have no information as yet in our hands of an actual crime he has committed. It will come out only too soon. He should be removed at once."

The President asked Forbes for his resignation. He refused at first to give it. Then Harding removed him and sent him on a minor foreign mission to save him from immediate disgrace.

I begged him not to do this. But he was adamant. He couldn't find it in his heart to crush, at a single blow, a man whom he had trusted. He couldn't be cruel.

He asked me to use the Department of Justice to make a

thorough investigation of the Bureau. And, at once, I set a staff of men on the job.

While I was conducting the case for the President, and he was giving me information obtained elsewhere, a Senate investigation of the Bureau was started.

Cramer, chief counsel for Forbes, who doubtless saw the handwriting on the wall, committed suicide.

Senator Reed of Pennsylvania, Chairman of the Investigating Committee, had a conference with me and I told him that we would take no part in the proceedings of his committee, but would continue to investigate on our own account.

The double investigation left no doubt of the guilt of Forbes and his associates.

I sent for Mr. John Crim, Assistant Attorney-General in charge of the criminal division of the Department. He was one of the ablest men we had. In Senator Reed's presence I put him in charge of the case, told him to investigate it thoroughly and find an indictment if the facts justified one. I promised him all the help needed. He took charge immediately and left for Chicago, the scene of one of the first charges.

To expedite the case I went, myself, to Chicago and appeared before the grand jury. Forbes was indicted, convicted, and sentenced to a term in prison.

I think nothing in Harding's life ever cut him so deeply as this man's betrayal of the trust he had placed in him.

Forbes was not indicted until long after the President's death, but my activities in the case were well known to Mr. Coolidge, under whose Administration the case was concluded.

As in the Remus case, the Means case, and many others, the *New York World*, my old enemy, could find no fault with anybody except the Attorney-General. And immediately on Forbes' release from prison, the *World* secured from him and published in its Sunday edition a vicious tirade against me.

CHAPTER XVII

The Amazing Collapse of A. B. Fall

THE President was planning his trip to Alaska. The enormous work which he had done in two years had begun to tell on his strength and he was compelled to take a rest that had been too long delayed.

He died on August 2, 1923. No matter what the cause, it is a subterfuge to say that his death was in any way hastened by the betrayal of his friends.

Early in the spring of 1923 the President knew that Forbes was false to his trust. He was quickly dismissed. While President Harding was keenly disappointed in Forbes, it was all in the day's work and created no worry that affected his health.

Colonel Miller was then in the government service, and no suspicion existed in the mind of anyone as to his integrity. It was long after the President died that any charges were brought against the Alien Property Custodian.

A. B. Fall, Secretary of the Interior, resigned on March 4, 1923.

There was, therefore, up to the time of the President's death, no suspicion that Fall had betrayed his trust.

Scandalmongers, mud-throwers, and lying publications have attempted to make the country believe that there was something connected with President Harding's administration that caused or contributed to his death. This is not true. At that time the country was freer from disturbing elements than it had been for years. Prosperity had returned. The President was as happy when he left Washington on his Alaskan trip as he had been at any time during his term of office.

He died a natural death, as shown by the certificates of his physicians. No doubt the end was hastened by a weakened condition from the strain of three years of the hardest work and the countless demands on his time and strength, and the excessive heat at the time.

If there were disturbing guilt on the part of anybody in the Harding administration, Mr. Hoover himself was as innocent of such knowledge as the President. For exactly eight days after the resignation of the Secretary of the Interior, Secretary Hoover wrote Mr. Fall the following letter, quoted in a recent serial of the North American Newspaper Alliance:

DEPARTMENT OF COMMERCE
Office of the Secretary

Washington, March 12, 1923.

Hon. Albert B. Fall,
Three Rivers, N. M.

My dear Fall:

This note is just by way of expressing appreciation for the many kindnesses I had at your hands during the last two years in the Cabinet. I know that the vast majority of our people feel a deep regret at your leaving the Department of the Interior. In my recollection, that department has never had so constructive and legal a headship as you gave it.

I trust the time will come when your private affairs will enable you to return to public life, as there are few men who are able to stand its stings and ire, and they have got to stay with it.

Yours faithfully,
[signed] Herbert Hoover.

The last service I rendered the President was of the most personal and confidential character. After I assisted him to clear his desk, he requested me to draw his will, which I did. We discussed many matters. And he again insisted I must not fail to meet him on the coast and assist him in work which he proposed to do aboard ship as we went through the Canal to

Puerto Rico, and Cuba, and thence to New York. In New York he expected to make the final speech of the trip. Five members of the Cabinet were absent from their posts. I did not go West with him because he wanted me to keep shop in his absence and see that certain policies and orders were carried out while he was away.

No act of mine, therefore, could have weighed on his health or caused him a minute's uneasiness. I had never taken an important step in his administration without his full knowledge and approval. The sources of the attacks on me he knew as well as I, and that the purpose of critics was to discredit his administration and lay the groundwork for the campaign to defeat him for reelection.

The Associated Press reporter at Marion, on June 16, when President Hoover dedicated the monument, was quick to catch the weakness of his remarks on this subject. He hurried to my room in the Hotel Harding after the ceremonies to ask me for a statement.

I covered it in the fewest possible words appropriate for such an occasion and simply said:

"I thoroughly approve of the orations made here today by the distinguished speakers. Their fine tributes to President Harding form a fitting climax to the work of the Memorial Association and reflect honor on themselves, their country, and its future."

It was all I felt that a gentleman could say under the circumstances. I reserved my full comments for this book, at that time in preparation.

Ex-President Coolidge's address at the Memorial exercises was a model of vigorous, Yankee thinking and perfect English.

We can get no intelligent or just conception of the Fall tragedy until we realize the high standing of the man in the Cabinet, in the Senate, and before the country. I repeat that his selection was among the most popular that Harding made. The Senate not only approved the choice, but its members

January 26, 1923

My Dear General Daugherty:

Birthday greetings and good wishes. Knowing you to be temporarily laid up, I have the wish to call and offer greetings and good wishes in person, but since that is impossible you will please accept written assurance deeply, friendly interest in your health, your good fortune and your happiness. Health is so essential, so I wish you speedy and permanent recovery. Pray do not be impatient. Sometimes we draw so heedlessly on our energies and reserves in order to carry on,

Letter from President Harding to

that nature wants a settlement
on her own account.

I can make no reference
to the birthday anniversary
which is pleasing to my fancy.
After one passes fifty they
come with such seeming swiftness
that I sometimes incline to
let them pass unnoticed. I
note you are the eldest but
one among those sitting
around the cabinet table,
yet I declare you the
youngest of all in spirit,
and if I added "in appearance"
I do not know who would
dispute. As was memorably
said at Vero — "There's a
man."

I hope you soon register
Normal. Sincerely Warren G Harding

Attorney-General Daugherty on his birthday.

went out of their way to show it in a demonstration never before accorded another man in the history of the Nation.

If Fall's collapse was a reflection on Harding it was an even greater reflection on the United States Senate, which had so signally celebrated his entrance into the Cabinet.

Brushing aside passion, prejudice, charges and counter charges, what are the simple facts about Fall's case?

I'll try to give them in plain words.

The oil leases made by the Secretary of the Interior were not an invention of Fall. The laws under which they were made were enacted under the outgoing Democratic administration.

Senator Thomas J. Walsh of Montana, the prosecutor of Fall and Doheny before the Senate Investigating Committee, was the original sponsor of these laws. The *Montana Record-Herald* of February 8, 1924, gives with verbatim quotations from the *Congressional Record* the full story of Senator Walsh's connection with this phase of legislation. On September 3, 1919, he boasted on the floor of the Senate that he was the father of the original oil-leasing bills.

He urged the passage of the leasing act on the ground that the naval reserves were being drained by private wells on adjoining territory, and quoted in support of his statement his old personal friend and Democratic associate E. H. Doheny.

He argued in favor of leasing the naval oil reserves to private parties for development, on the ground that it was unwise for the government to undertake it.

His speech is in the *Record*.

This Federal Leasing Act, under which all public oil reserves were leased, whether naval or otherwise, was enacted into law in February 1920, under President Wilson. It was amended on June 1, the same year, so as to give the Secretary of the Navy complete control of all naval reserves. Secretary Josephus Daniels is credited with writing this amendment and Senator Walsh supported it.

The Senator therefore is within his rights when he claims that he is the father of the original oil-leasing measure.

In securing the passage of this bill Senator Walsh, the Inquisitor, fought LaFollette and his radical group to the last roll call.

LaFollette offered an amendment to the bill which would have exempted from its provisions the naval reserve lands, particularly the Teapot Dome and Elks Hills. He branded the bill as a Standard Oil measure and attacked Doheny and Phelan and other oil men. He did not oppose the principle of the government leasing its public lands for oil development, but bitterly fought the extension of leases to the naval reserves.

But for the active and skilled leadership of Senator Walsh, LaFollette's amendment might have been adopted. Walsh defended Doheny, and defeated the LaFollette amendment. And that opened the way for the leases that were afterwards made to Sinclair's company and to Doheny by A. B. Fall.

When the Harding administration came into power March 4, 1921, these laws were all on the statute books, and their scope was clearly defined.

The general work of leasing of public lands was in the hands of the Secretary of the Interior. Hundreds of such leases had already been made and more were being made daily. The Navy Department, however, controlled the leasing of the naval reserve lands only.

About three months after he had taken charge of the Navy Department, Secretary Denby was informed that private companies whose leases surrounded the naval reserves were drilling wells within a few feet of the line and rapidly draining the government's oil from the pools below. And unless something was done these valuable reserves would be exhausted and the nation would lose its treasures.

It was Denby's duty to conserve these national resources. Under the law enacted by the former administration, he had the right to lease them if he deemed it wise.

He immediately consulted the Secretary of the Interior, Mr. Fall, as to how he could go about this and protect the government. Fall was an oil expert. And while Denby was a lawyer, a graduate of the Naval Academy, and an expert on naval affairs, he knew little about oil.

This information was given to the President.

The legality of the leases was never discussed in the Cabinet by anyone, and at no time was the opinion of the Attorney-General asked concerning them.

Secretary Denby asked Fall to take over in his Department the handling of the leases. The Secretary of the Interior agreed, and the two asked the President for an order authorizing the transfer.

The Navy Department had no leasing force, while a staff of about one hundred and fifty lawyers and experts were in the Department of the Interior to look after the leasing of public lands. It would have been impossible for Secretary Denby to undertake to handle the leases without duplicating in part Secretary Fall's big staff. He had neither the time nor the inclination to study the complicated laws involved.

Harding issued the order without hesitation and without consulting me, either personally or as Attorney-General. He had implicit faith in Fall's ability as a lawyer and expert on oil lands. No man had ever questioned his honesty.

Harding provided, however, that the leasing under the transfer should be made subject to the supervision of the President. And that no general policy as to drilling or reserving lands located in a naval reserve could be changed or adopted, except by agreement of the Secretary of the Navy.

LaFollette watched the events of the oil leasing program with keen, suspicious, hostile eyes. And without any concrete facts on which to base his suspicions, he offered a resolution in the Senate asking Fall for all the documents in his Department that covered the leasing of the lands in the naval reserves.

Fall himself must have had some doubt as to the legality of the President's authority to issue the executive order transferring to the Interior Department the naval reserve lands, for when the leases were executed Denby as well as Fall signed them. If Fall was certain that the President's executive order was supported by law, there would have been no necessity for the Secretary of the Navy to join in the execution of the leases.

In all the testimony subsequently taken in the courts and before Senatorial committees investigating oil leases, Secretary Denby was never charged with or found guilty of a single dishonest or corrupt act. There was no more honest man in the Cabinet. And yet his name, like those of others as innocent as he, was bandied about in the public prints with foul insinuations.

The President received from Fall a report on the leases made under him. This report contained nothing of an illegal or suspicious nature. And the Secretary of the Interior, concealing from the President the fact that he had secured no competitive bids and had received a "loan" of $100,000 from Doheny before these leases were made, allowed his chief to send to the Committee a letter of endorsement. This was a gross betrayal of confidence.

In this letter he permitted the man who had honored him with a Cabinet position to announce:

"I think it is only fair to say in this connection, that the policy which has been adopted by the Secretary of the Interior, in dealing with these matters, was submitted to me prior to the adoption thereof and the policy decided upon and the subsequent acts have at all times had my entire approval."

Harding died without a suspicion of the ugly fact that Fall had excluded competition and had obtained a loan of $100,000 from Doheny.

And Mr. Hoover knew as well as I that Fall's resignation

was in the President's hands to take effect March 4, 1923, long before the Teapot Dome scandal broke.

Fall did not resign because he was under fire. He was not under fire when he gave Harding his resignation. He resigned to go abroad on a mission of oil development and a prospective merger.

Again I recall Mr. Hoover's remarks at Marion with increasing amazement: "Warren Harding had a dim realization that he had been betrayed by a few of the men whom he had trusted. That was the tragedy of his life."

Did Mr. Hoover have this realization when he wrote Fall his letter of sympathy and confidence on May 12, 1923? If not, surely Harding did not, for he died within less than ninety days of that date.

Was President Hoover hinting ever so vaguely that Harding had found himself involved in the muck of the oil scandal?

I cannot believe that he would make such an insinuation. Though, of course, one of the scurrilous books which he may have read, and which perhaps kept him from Marion so long, says as much.

A muckraker by the name of Samuel Hopkins Adams, in a coarse, filthy screed in which he used fictitious names and shifted scenes to escape the laws of criminal libel, insinuates that the Harding family, without Harding's knowledge, was given by force of arms a slice of oil land, and that the President received from this an income until he died.

Unfortunately for this cheerful fiction writer, he specified the particular strip of land handed over to the President without his knowledge by a mysterious gang of political pirates.

In order to get possession of it for the President's family, he says, the Navy Department sent a squad of Marines to the field, shot off the owners, and gave the grounds to the President's family.

A more stupid and malignant lie was never circulated about a public official within my knowledge of American history.

It is a well-established fact that Colonel James G. Darden of Maryland and his associates held this particular strip of land under a lease which Colonel Darden believed valid. It adjoined the Teapot Dome.

In an interview with Harry S. Sherwood, correspondent of the *Baltimore Evening Sun*, at Ellerslie Farms, Colonel Darden's home, and published in the *Sun* March 18, 1924, the Colonel said:

"Fall and I had been enemies for thirty-five years. When I heard of the Teapot Dome lease and his purpose to send Marines from Denby's Department to shoot me off the ground, I went to see him and we had a three-hour session.

"His last words were: 'Sinclair's lease covers that land. He'll take care of you as he will of the others. I don't care a damn. I'm going to quit anyhow.' "

In his statement Darden continued:

"When the President heard of what Fall was doing in the matter, he sent for me. I would never have embarrassed him with a discussion of it if he hadn't called me in. Harding was the fairest, finest man I've ever known.

"When I entered his office in the White House he was cordial to me. But he was worried over the situation.

"He said finally:

" 'What can I do? You're my friend and I'd like to help you. Fall says he's going to send the Marines out there. He is T.N.T. on the subject.'

" 'Please don't mix in the row, Mr. President,' I urged. 'There's only one thing we can do about it, take it into court.'

"And that's what was done. Fall sent out a squad of Marines. They 'ousted' our company, gave the land to Sinclair, and the evicted concern brought suit for the recovery of $500,000 worth of oil taken off it, and tied the money up in court until operations were stopped."

If every dollar of the money received from the development of this property was paid into court, as Darden says, it could not have reached the Harding family.

I repeat. A more stupid and infamous slander was never uttered than Mr. Adams gave about this strip of oil land. The name of Adams is an honored one in American history. I marvel at the cheek and irresponsibility of a writer who could sign his name to such a book. It is a disgrace to American literature and a reflection on the sense of honor and decency in modern publishers.

Fall's action in using his official power to strike an old enemy was not surprising to those who knew the man. I knew Darden and sympathized with him in his fight. The attack was in harmony with Fall's tyrannical temperament.

The furor raised over the Teapot Dome scandal brought to my I. W. W. enemy in the United States Senate the opportunity for which he was waiting.

In a tirade of abuse Wheeler sought to connect my name with Fall's in the oil leases.

Nothing was more clearly established in the records of the government than that I was in no way associated with Fall and had nothing to do with the management of his office.

Attorneys for Fall asked me to testify in his case that the oil leases were legal and that I had so stated in the Cabinet meetings. Such a thing never took place and I refused to so testify. My opinion as to the legality of the leases was never given, verbally or otherwise. The Attorney-General gives no verbal opinions. And if a member of the Cabinet wishes his opinion on any matter a request for it is presented in writing, supported by the files, and the opinion is rendered formally in writing. As I have stated repeatedly, I knew nothing about the execution of the oil leases until the matter came up for investigation, and Senator Pomerene and Mr. Roberts, now Justice of the Supreme Court, were appointed to prosecute the oil cases.

I asked President Coolidge to appoint special counsel in

Office of the Attorney General
Washington, D. C.

Jan.23,1924.

MEMORANDUM.

In addition to the investigation now being made of
the Teapot Dome lease, I wish the records of the Department investigated
with reference to the lease on California Reserves 1 and 2 to Mr. Doheny
or any of his companies. Let me have a memo, as quickly as it can be
prepared showing what, if anything, has been before the Department in
connection with any of these leases.

Attorney General

those cases as I had been an associate of the defendant in the Cabinet.

One of the charges the distinguished counsel brought against Fall is printed in their complaint as follows:

"Section 24: The said Albert B. Fall, acting as aforesaid, although a question was raised as to the legality of such a lease, steadfastly refused to take the opinion of the Solicitor of the Department of the Interior (his own Solicitor-General) or of the Attorney-General of the United States concerning the legality of the same."

I had known H. F. Sinclair for many years, but I had never done any business for him and had never discussed with him any government matters.

I had never met Mr. Doheny, but knew him as a leading Democrat and was curious to see him when I heard that he had given a million dollars to the campaign fund of his party.

The attempt to associate me with Fall's transactions in oil is a thing I have always resented. But the lie has been repeated so many thousands of times, millions of people probably believe it.

For irresponsible Senators, under immunity, continued to charge that the Attorney-General of the United States was guilty of irregularity and corruption in connection with the oil leases.

The minute Fall's fate was finally settled by his imprisonment, I had Hon. Paul Howland of Cleveland address a letter to the United States Special Counsel, Atlee Pomerene, who had handled the case for the government.

In his reply Senator Pomerene in his concluding page quoted the decision of the Supreme Court on this point:

"But he (Fall) refused to submit the question to the Attorney-General; and as a reason for not taking such legal advice said that the chances were at least even, or at least there was some chance, that an adverse opinion would be given. And if the Attorney-General signed such an opinion he (Fall) would be stopped from doing anything."

In conclusion Senator Pomerene says: "There is no evidence in the record of any of the oil cases, and none ever came to the knowledge of special counsel, so far as I know, indicating that Mr. Daugherty had any personal interest in any of the oil leases or contracts."

The full and exact text of this letter will be found in the Appendix to this volume.

Nothing could be more convincing than Senator Pomerene's final paragraph exonerating me as an individual as well as an officer of the government.

I have denied this ancient slander a hundred times, only to find my name linked with Fall's again and again. I suppose the lie is too good a story to be dropped by my critics, and it will probably roll on until the trumpet of the Archangel calls the end of time.

I am not the judge of any man's conscience. And I cannot say what was in the heart of Albert B. Fall when he took from young Doheny that little black bag containing $100,000 in cash. He has given a rational explanation of why he asked for cash instead of a check. Thirty-seven banks in New Mexico had closed. There was no bank open in his town. The men from whom he was buying the addition to his ranch demanded cash and refused to take a check of any kind.

There is the further fact in corroboration of this that he gave Doheny his note for the amount, which was, of course, a legal record of the transaction.

He swears that the money was a loan from one friend to another. This may be true or not. It does not justify in any way his telling a falsehood about the loan, his declaration that Ned McLean loaned it to him. It does not justify his deception of Harding, who died believing in his innocence.

Upon Fall's collapse, our radical Senator, Burton K. Wheeler, introduced his resolution for an investigation of the Attorney-General.

CHAPTER XVIII

The Degeneracy of the U.S. Senate

IN THE reign of Burton K. Wheeler and his particularly close associates as spokesmen of the United States Senate, that body touched the lowest mark of its entire history.

Senator Walsh of Montana, a resourceful and able lawyer, had gained wide notoriety as the prosecutor of the oil transactions. Wheeler became his rival for public acclaim. Without the ability of Walsh, he had not the faintest conception of the dignity or fairness which a United States Senator should possess.

Because much of its work is secret and confidential, the Department of Justice is more likely to be suspected of intrigue than any other branch of the government. For its own protection it must "go straight."

Wheeler listened to the whisperers. He had no regard for the truth, but sought sensational stories and made speeches in the Senate which spread his false statements. The public reads and jumps at conclusions. Nine times out of ten the things circulated as examples of the perfidy of public men turn out to be false.

On Fall's confession that he had received a "loan" of $100,000 from Doheny a wave of indignation swept the country. And the amazing falsehood which he told when he declared that he got the money from McLean further incensed the nation, to the injury of President Harding's memory and the standing of his Cabinet.

Hundreds of letters poured into the White House, to members of the Cabinet, to members of the House and Senate.

The Senate became a caldron of filthy gossip and slanderous accusations. The destruction of the character of public officials became a national sport. Red Senatorial gasbags poured poison fumes into the air until an honest man could scarcely breathe within the walls of the Capital.

Republicans were deceived and swept off their feet.

Democrats were deceived and swept off their feet.

When we contrast the personnel of this body with the Senate of earlier days, we realize the depths to which it has fallen. The bare mention of the names of Clay, Calhoun, and Webster condemns this modern assembly.

There were conscientious members, of course, entitled to respect. It was agreed among conservative Republicans to allow the clamor to go unnoticed and let it run itself out. The rough riders who were making the disgraceful speeches were now rarely seen in public offices. They never went to the Department of Justice to find the facts. They never went to the White House to get the truth. They listened only to the scandalmongers, and felt that they had accomplished something which entitled them to be called statesmen when the newspapers published their names!

Leaders?

There were no leaders.

The process of degeneration in the Senate had, of course, been going on for some time. It had proceeded rapidly from the invention of the direct primary election in the choice of its members. Under the old régime, as intended by the founders of the Republic, the Senators represented states, not the mass of voters. The House of Representatives was organized to voice the masses.

The Senate had been formerly organized as a body of conservative, big-brained men, removed from the threat of popular clamor. The powers intrusted to them by the makers of our Constitution rested squarely on the fact of their removal from the influences of the mob.

The moment we began to elect Senators by direct vote of the masses, instead of by the vote of state legislatures, we destroyed the foundations on which this branch of our government rested.

We established the rule of the demagogue and destroyed the possibility of great leadership. The primaries are utterly unfitted for the selection of conservative leaders. As a rule the number of men who give any attention to a primary election for a Senator is very small. The number of good citizens who give time and thought to it is too small to count.

Under such conditions the Senate of the United States has ceased to represent anything for which it was founded. In no sense is it a representative body of our national government.

I'll go further and say that under present conditions the Senate is fast becoming a menace to national progress, if not a threat against the principles on which our Republic was founded.

The Senate is constantly interfering with the Executive. No President has for years been able to perform the duties of his office without an open fight with the Senate, which has enlarged its claims of power until it threatens to take over both the Executive and Judicial branches of our government.

To remove the threat we must either strip this body of the enormous power supposed to be entrusted to it under our Constitution, or reorganize it from top to bottom.

If the Senators of the United States are going to represent voters, not states, a radical reform is the urgent need of the hour.

This representation must be honest, fearless, and fair. It must be based on the number of voters for which each Senator speaks.

On the present anomalous basis, two men from the state of

Nevada, for example, representing a total population of ninety-one thousand inhabitants, can nullify in the Senate roll call the votes of the two men from New York who represent twelve million people, whose chief city has become the financial center of the world.

This is not merely an anomaly; it is a political crime thus to disfranchise twelve million people in New York merely because they happen to live within the lines of a state, and give to a couple of men from a little Western borough two Senatorial votes based on a handful of people.

To put it more strikingly, seven of these little boroughs which we call "states" have a total population of only three millions. But because they are divided by state lines they send *fourteen* men into the Senate. The state of New York has four times their number, namely twelve and a half million, and only sends *two!*

It requires the combined votes of the great states of California, Ohio, Texas, Illinois, Pennsylvania, New York, and Massachusetts, with more than fifty-one millions of people, to equal in strength in the Senate roll call the fourteen Senators from the little Western boroughs with only three millions!

Such conditions cannot remain without threatening the foundations of the Republic.

The Senate, as it stands, is a dangerous solecism.

It represents nothing ever contemplated by the founders of the nation. Based on population, the seven states named, with fifty-one million people, should have more than two hundred Senators against the fourteen little Westerners.

I am not saying that these small boroughs in the West do not occasionally give us a man of big brain in the Senate. Borah is such a man. But his personal hold on the tiny constituency that votes for him in a primary makes him an irresponsible leader. He becomes a bull in a china shop, and goes on a wild rampage when he feels like it. No man can tell when he is going to do it. Borah himself doesn't know.

If this Senator had used his powerful personality to bring the mob of howling dervishes from his section to their senses, many of the disgraceful acts and scenes which followed the Fall debacle might have been avoided.

But Borah was again busy with his game of political solitaire. He permitted the little lawyer from Butte, Montana, to take the lead, if he did not aid and abet him.

Borah, of course, found himself in a position in which he could not antagonize the chief representative of Soviet Russia on the floor of the Senate. He had himself introduced the resolution for the recognition of the Soviets.

Up to this time I had counted Borah, one of the men of big brain and powerful personality in the Senate, my friend. I was to find now that I had hopelessly alienated him by the aid I had given to Secretary Hughes in his fight against the resolution on Soviet Russia.

The part I had taken in this drama had been given the widest publicity, not on my initiative, but at the request of the Secretary of State. I give here a personal and confidential letter written to me as Attorney-General by Mr. Hughes. I asked and got his permission to use it when I saw fit to do so, but it has never been published until now.

THE SECRETARY OF STATE
Washington

January 9, 1924.

Personal and
Confidential

My dear Mr. Attorney-General:

The morning newspapers carry correspondence with Assistant Attorney-General Crim to the effect that the Department of Justice had no evidence to warrant prosecutions under the Logan Act. This is evidently put out, and will be used, to indicate that the Department of Justice has no evidence to sustain the position that I have taken with respect to Communist propaganda in this country directed from Moscow. Of course, there is abundant evidence upon this, and I have an enormous file furnished me by the Department of Justice accordingly. It is, however, highly important that at this critical time, the idea should not get abroad, after all that has been said, that there is really no evidence to support it.

I hope, without embarrassment to your department, you will be able to give a line to the press at once indicating the real situation.

My suggestion would be a very brief statement along the following lines:

Apart from the question of prosecutions or of technical requirements to meet the provisions of particular status, it should be clearly understood that the Department of Justice has abundant evidence to support the position of the Department of State, with respect to Communist propaganda, directed from Moscow, in this country. With high regard, I am,

Faithfully yours,
(signed) Charles Evans Hughes.

I immediately gave to the press the desired information in an expanded form. It was carried by every newspaper in the United States and helped to defeat the Borah resolution for the recognition of the Soviets.

Mr. Hughes was grateful to me for the services I had rendered the Department of State, and at the next Cabinet meeting he pressed my hand and said:

"You're a brick."

"No," I answered, "I just play ball with the fellows on my team."

He laughed over it and was very agreeable. Hughes was a charming man to work with. Of course, a man of strong individuality, who liked to have his own way, and generally got it, when he was right. And he was as nearly right on most questions as any man I have ever known.

Borah was naturally furious at me for the part I had played in the defeat of his pet scheme. I did it from no antagonism to him. I did it from a sense of duty to the country and toward a fellow member of the Cabinet.

His resolution was against the settled policy of the American Government. And if we had followed England's lead in such recognition we would have been compelled, as England was, to retreat from an ill-advised act.

And I did it from the deepest personal convictions of the issues involved.

I believed then, as I firmly believe now, that Soviet Russia is the enemy of mankind. That unless the forces of civilization stamp out this nest of vipers who have enslaved a hundred and sixty million human beings, our social system as well as our form of government will perish from the poison that is being poured into our vitals.

Soviet agents are busy to-day as they were at that time, poisoning the hearts and minds of the youth and manhood of every nation of the earth. These madmen have launched a new religion with which they have set out to conquer not only America but the world, and every nation of Europe and Asia is to-day trembling at their approach.

In this new Paradise of Communism, the human race is reduced in theory and practice to the level of a herd of hogs. I call it the lowest, the most degrading, the most bestial nightmare the human mind has ever conceived.

It cannot succeed when put to the final test. Unless its progress is halted, humanity may be hurled back into the darkness of a thousand years of hopeless floundering and groping before it can emerge again into sanity. For these maniacs have destroyed the home, pulled down the churches, blotted the name of God from their skies, and reduced man to the status of chattel slavery.

What is slavery?

Involuntary service.

If a man can work and will not, he will be made to work!

On this axiom their whole system is built. They guarantee in return a meager supply of poor food, barely enough clothing to cover the body, and a rough bed on which to sleep and breed children they can never know or love. The lash of the overseer will ultimately be the only incentive for work.

How many years of such life will it take to crush out of the human soul the last spark of hope and aspiration and reduce man to a beast?

History is strewn with the bones of dead civilizations. Ours rests on the growth of the mind of man and the expansion of his soul. Reduced to the terms of Communism there is nothing on which the soul of man may feed, and little to sustain his body. If we surrender to this nightmare, our civilization is doomed and we, too, head for oblivion.

I know that Mr. George Bernard Shaw, the rich, literary clown of England, rushed over to Russia and for ten days hobnobbed with Stalin in the seats of the mighty. His mouthings filled our press with raptures over what he thought he had seen. As a matter of fact he saw nothing except his preconceived ideas of Communism. He saw only what he went there to see and came back to poison the human race with his insanity.

He ignores facts and preaches his crazy theories. The men who have studied the Russian Soviet experiment with open minds and clear eyes bring to us a different story.

Henry Wales, an American newspaper man, has just completed a journey of twelve thousand miles across the Soviet Union, going from west to east and from north to south, from the Arctic zone at Archangel to the sunbaked steep of the Caucasus, the Baku oil fields and the Riviera on the Black Sea coast.

Forty nights he passed in so-called railway trains, some of them of a type we use for cattle.

Always he traveled alone, a thing few foreigners have ever dared. He never allowed himself to be led about blindly or shown the things theorists wished him to see. He went where he pleased and studied conditions as he found them. When interpreters were used he secured good ones through American engineers whom he encountered in every district.

The agents of the government explained to him that the strange things he saw were due to the emergency of a state of siege through which the Soviet régime was passing. That is, a condition of war in which the entire population was reduced to slavery, or involuntary servitude.

At Archangel he succeeded in locating a horrible concentration camp of these slaves concealed in a church.

At Rostov, Kharkov, and Stalingrad he inspected huge factories and witnessed their utter failure through ignorance and indifference. They practically produced nothing, except when under American supervision.

Through the southern districts he saw hordes of tramps, bums, and child-waifs, homeless men, and boys, thousands of them only eleven or twelve years old — and girls! — on their annual migration from the warmth of the south to the larger communities of the north after the rigors of the winter had passed.

Men in hundreds of thousands, barefooted, ragged, black and filthy, with long matted hair and beards covered with vermin. Polluting the atmosphere with the stench of their unwashed bodies, drawn, haggard, and famished, these monsters walked the streets and towns, fighting with the dogs and crows for a morsel of stray food.

Or they sat day and night in the railway stations, furtively watching for a chance to rifle the pockets of a drunken peasant, or steal the luggage of a careless passenger.

In the Ukraine and North Caucasus he visited dozens of the new state collective farms, worked by peasants, forced to labor against their wills, and saw the terrible conditions there. So terrible that the local Communist slave-drivers begged

Moscow to ease the pressure to export grain, and give the poor devils who raised it enough wheat to eat to sustain life and save their stock from famine.

He visited their homes — mud huts without windows. He watched their apathy and listlessness, brought on partly by lack of food and partly by their spirit of fatalism, a full relapse to the herd life of undernourished swine.

He saw livestock dropping in their tracks to die of hunger beside swollen carcasses that already cumbered the earth. Vultures alone were rich.

These peasants, thousands and thousands of them, in their hunger, misery, and despair, were resorting to passive resistance. They refused to work their lands, and lay down in feigned or real illness when their overseers came to drive them into the fields.

With their wives, and gaunt, pale, yellow, listless children, they slept on piles of rags and straw in their huts waiting for the end, whatever it might be.

Here is a true story of conditions in Soviet Russia written by a fearless young American observer. It was printed and copyrighted by the *Chicago Tribune*, May 21, 1931, and copied the next day in the *New York Times*.

As yet no agent of Communism has dared reply to it.

In the face of these facts, a literary clown skips to Moscow, takes dinner with Stalin, comes back, and tells us we are fools unless we adopt Communism and scrap our homes, our churches, our ideals, our civilization.

And a growing number of morons are gathering around the Red Rag lifted in our country as the symbol of the Brotherhood of Man!

If these people are so enamored of Russia and her new scheme of life, why do they not migrate to her vast, undeveloped reaches of territory, and leave to honest Americans the inheritance of their fathers?

It happens that I was the first representative of the present order whom Burton K. Wheeler, the Communist leader in the Senate, picked for attack.

It should be borne in mind that Wheeler's determination to drive me from the office of Attorney-General was in no sense a movement of a responsible political party against its opponents. Wheeler is no more a Democrat than Stalin, his comrade in Moscow.

Brookhart and Wheeler had just returned from a state call on the Communist leaders in their Russian Capitol. They were received in the inner Soviet circles as "comrades," and came back to the United States to praise their teachers.

In his resolution in the Senate asking for a Special Committee to investigate the Attorney-General, Harry M. Daugherty, every charge in the wording was a lie out of whole cloth, and Wheeler knew that they were lies when he wrote them.

Every one of them was proven to be false in the statement which I submitted to Wheeler's Committee on the opening day — proven false by records in the Department of Justice with dates and details.

Wheeler charged that I failed to prosecute violators of the Sherman Anti-Trust Act.

A lie.

For the records showed in black and white that I had prosecuted more of these cases than any other man who had held the office of Attorney-General, and secured jail sentences for the first time.

The second charge was that I had neglected and failed to prosecute A. B. Fall, H. F. Sinclair, E. L. Doheny, Charles R. Forbes, and their conspirators.

Another lie.

The records of my office showed the prosecution of Forbes under my direction, and the prosecution of Fall, Doheny, and Sinclair through special counsel, as suggested by me to the President.

The Senate voted to appoint a Special Committee to carry out the provisions of this resolution. And in doing so, custom and precedent, as well as responsiblity, were swept aside. The Judiciary Committee should have conducted the inquiry. But Wheeler and those with him and behind him would not trust it.

Only in this way could the plan to create excitement and prejudice be carried out.

If the amazing full report of the proceeding of the Wheeler-Brookhart Committee could be read by the general public, it would be denounced as the most highhanded piece of rough work ever done to accomplish an unlawful and dishonorable purpose. Only Senators Moses and Jones represented our present civilization in it, and they were insulted and brushed aside by the Red Triumvirate from the beginning of the inquiry.

Senator Borah consented to this infamy.

An ominous sign.

For the corruption of his mind by Communistic theories had already set in. The Senator revealed its further development in his last Labor Day address, when he declared that the rich must feed the unemployed during the coming winter, and warned:

"If they do not do it voluntarily, *they will nevertheless do it!*"

CHAPTER XIX

Roxie Stinson Takes the Stand

THE Resolution of Investigation against me was not drawn to prove any specific charges. And no real effort was made to prove a single one.

It was drawn solely to set a stage on which Burton K. Wheeler, through the use of gossip and slander, lies and insinuations, would discredit our form of government itself, break down respect for its institutions and laws in the minds of thoughtless people, and advance the purpose to establish a Soviet form of government in the United States.

He relied on the appetite for sensation fed by our daily press to accomplish his purpose.

In the shadows behind him, of course, were strong men who gloated over the chance to strike back at an Attorney-General who had dared to strike them.

The attack was timed to play into the hands of all these hostile forces.

It was known that my report on the War Frauds cases was nearing completion and would show great achievements.

It was known that the real facts in the history of the railroad strike were about to be presented to Congress in a full report describing the seventeen thousand crimes on which the injunction was based.

It was known that the Phillips case, an important instance of War Fraud, was about to be tried, after a long fight by shrewd lawyers to secure its dismissal or continue indefinite postponements.

It was known that Charles W. Morse, whom I had indicted, was about to be called for trial after every possible effort had been made to postpone his case again.

A civil suit had been instituted by the War Transactions Section of the Department of Justice against Morse and his associates to recover a judgment of something over fifteen million dollars.

It was known that the Attorney-General was preparing an appeal in the case of Francis P. Garvan and the Chemical Foundation, in which the lower court had decided against the government.

It was known that I was pressing for trial one hundred and seventy-five other cases of War Frauds.

It was known that great pressure was being brought to bear on me as Attorney-General to indict for alleged criminal acts former officials under the Wilson administration whose record the Grand Jury was investigating.

I hold no brief for any member of President Wilson's Cabinet, but in justice to the men who served with him in that trying period, I want to say that after a thorough investigation I found no reason to bring indictments against a single one whom I was being urged to prosecute.

It was known that I had sent millionaires to jail for violating the Sherman Anti-Trust laws for the first time in history, and that I was moving against others.

The first purpose of these forces back of Wheeler was, of course, to discredit me and cripple the work of the Department of Justice. These men were not working with the Communist leader of the Senate to destroy our form of government. They were merely using him as the instrument of my destruction — and as far as they were concerned, to hell with the government.

The stage was set and the farce began under the most approved rules of Soviet Russia. My lawyers were insulted and bulldozed from the opening hour to its close. I was not allowed to call witnesses in my defense, or to appear in my own behalf, or to cross-examine their witnesses, except under limitations. I was never subpoened before the committee and never attended a session.

Wheeler's witnesses were allowed to say any foolish thing that occurred to them, from kitchen gossip to a discourse on the Einstein theory, which Gaston B. Means essayed on more than one occasion.

Gaston B. Means was one of three hundred or more investigators in the employ of the Department of Justice. A man I never saw but twice. A man I appointed with misgivings, at Burns' suggestion. When he was unfaithful to his trust I discharged him. He hated me for this, and because I had him indicted. Later, in an affidavit, he admitted that Wheeler and his Committee had promised that his case would be dismissed in return for his services to the Committee.

This man, Means, became the general manager of Wheeler and his two radical associates on the Committee.

This so-called investigation was conducted by Wheeler and Means in a riot of perjury and a parade of criminals, convicts, ex-convicts, and men under indictment for felonies.

The first witness called was "Miss" Roxie Stinson, divorced wife of Jess Smith. The story of how she became the prima donna of Wheeler's play is interesting.

I did not know Roxie Stinson, never saw her but twice in my life, and never spoke to her but once, when she happened to be in the hospital when I called to see Jess Smith.

This unfortunate woman had become my bitter enemy because I had refused to allow Smith to bring her to Washington while he was in charge of my house.

The moment the Wheeler Committee began its attack on me, she saw an opportunity to get her revenge.

A. L. Fink, a witness the Wheeler Committee summoned but whom they refused to put on the stand, afterwards swore before a notary to the facts thus suppressed.

Among other things Fink swore in his affidavit were the following – quoted substantially, but not verbatim:

"On February 18, I was in Cleveland, Ohio, on business and saw in the papers that Roxie Stinson, an old sweetheart of mine, had fallen heir to a great deal of money. As a dealer in stocks and bonds I thought I could sell her an interesting proposition. I called her at Columbus over the telephone and she came to Cleveland.

"We went to the Hotel Hollenden where we registered.

"On going up to room 452 I started to tell her my business proposition when she stopped me and said:

" 'I have a far bigger deal on right now and you ought to come in on it.'

"I asked her what it was.

"She told me that Harry Daugherty was cheating her out of what belonged to her as Jess Smith's wife and she could tell a story on Daugherty that would drive him out of office. She asked $150,000 for it and wanted me to help her get it.

"Senator Wheeler heard of Roxie Stinson's proffered story through my [Fink's] lawyer, Henry Stern, of Buffalo, and Stern, through Wheeler's influence, or orders, forced me to go to Washington and see him.

"Wheeler got me to go with him to Columbus and bring Roxie to Washington.

"He started the hearing immediately. After the first day I went to Wheeler and said: 'I don't propose for a moment that she is going to bring out this hotel episode because it will ruin my family.'

"Wheeler pulled her off the stand and sent for my wife to fix it up.

"She came and he promised her if she would make no trouble that he would secure for me the big job of Collector of Internal Revenue for Buffalo and make Stern a Federal Judge when he had ousted Daugherty.

"Wheeler promised Roxie if she would play the game with

him he would form a pool using his Democratic friends in Wall Street, give me the money to sell the market short in advance of the news of Daugherty's resignation, and give her twenty-five per cent of the profits."

Under these remarkable conditions "Miss" Roxie Stinson continued her testimony under Wheeler's guidance for days and days, weaving a fantastic tale of what "Jess told me."

Poor Jess could not speak from the grave and she let her imagination soar.

Unfortunately for her, A. L. Fink refused to go through with his part of the plot, did not appear as a witness for Wheeler, but made an affidavit with his wife that completely destroyed the value of Roxie's recital. Mrs. Fink swore that Wheeler repeated to her his promise of a Collectorship for her husband, a Federal Judgeship for Stern, and a big profit in a stock pool for Miss Stinson.

And yet in all the vicious tissue of falsehoods to which Roxie swore, she never once made a statement of her own knowledge against me. It was always what "Jess told me." She had been carefully rehearsed. The dead could not contradict her. She had stacks of intimate letters from Smith, and not one line in them could be found on which to build an accusation.

Roxie Stinson's inventions of imaginary conversations with a dead husband (testimony that would not be admitted under the rules of law in any court of justice) were, of course, blazoned in huge headlines in morning newspapers as if they were proven facts.

This was Wheeler's purpose in calling the witness, and he accomplished it.

The next star witness called by Wheeler was the notorious Gaston B. Means, whom I had discharged from the Department of Justice and had under indictment for two felonies.

The Committee promised this man "protection" if he

would play into their hands. And the poor fool walked into the trap.

For days, weeks, and months he strutted and posed and regaled them with stories that would have done credit to Baron Munchausen.

I had refused to see or speak to him before he appeared, although he made many efforts to have a conference.

After his farcical appearance in Wheeler's play had closed, and the Committee had dropped him, alarmed at the incredulity with which his lies had been received, Means again sought an interview with me, offering now to tell the truth and repudiate his entire testimony before Wheeler's Committee.

I received from him the following letter:

136 N. Union St.
Concord, North Carolina.

February 19, 1925.

Hon. Harry M. Daugherty,
Columbus, Ohio.

Dear Sir:

The reason for this letter is my request for a personal interview with you, and my sincere desire to speak to you of many matters, of which, I feel sure, you have no knowledge and of which I cannot adequately write. * * * *

I feel that by my testimony before the Brookhart-Wheeler Committee, I did you a great injustice, and am willing and anxious to make amends for what I did, as far as possible.

My wife and others close and dear to me, immediately after I testified, and who knew the facts, urged me to correct publicly, at once, the injustice done you. * * * *

On account of the stigma cast upon my little boy by my ingratitude and repudiation of you, and because I want to clear my name as far as possible for the sake of his future, I desire to do what I can in atonement. In my possession are authentic and unquestionable documents to verify every statement I will make.

Hoping and trusting that you will advise me when and where I
can, most convenient to yourself, see you, I am

> Yours respectfully,
> (Signed) Gaston B. Means.

I arranged for the meeting in the presence of W. J. Burns
and others, and Means voluntarily made an affidavit of eight
thousand words and swore to it before Jesse L. Knapp, a
notary public, repudiating his testimony before the Wheeler
Committee.

Among other things he swore: "From the day of my first
visit to Senator Wheeler up to the day that I took the stand
before his Committee, I held conferences with the Senator,
either at his office or at his home, both in the daytime and
night, or communicated with him on the phone, every day or
every night."

In substance he then says that he tried repeatedly to get in
touch with me and failed and that when he got my message
that "he, Wheeler and his Committee could go to hell," he
threw all scruples to the wind and went on the stand.

He adds (verbatim):

But I knew what Daugherty did not know, namely: That
Senator Wheeler had entered into a conspiracy to wreck his life,
the life of an innocent man.

Wheeler told me that he knew that I was the collector for Mr.
W. J. Burns, Mr. Daugherty, and Mr. Jess Smith. I told him
repeatedly that this was absolutely untrue, and if he really
believed, or anybody believed, that I had ever collected a dollar
and given it either to Burns, Daugherty, or Jess Smith, they were
fools.

In addition I explained that I would gladly give him my
records, documents and files to prove this statement.

He wrote an official letter asking for all my files for use in the
investigation.

After receiving the letter, I thereupon delivered to him all of
the records, files, data, diaries that I had, which enumerated
truthfully and accurately all my dealings. Which he admitted

confirmed the verbal and written statement I had given him pertaining to any alleged receiving of money for W. J. Burns, H. M. Daugherty, or Jess Smith.

In fact, after he got through with the papers he said he was "in a hell of a situation," and that his every hope in carrying out the plan as devised by himself was to begin at once to build up a case.

From the date of the passage of the resolution until I actually took the stand Senator Wheeler was apprehensive as to whether I would carry out the plan for him to "get Daugherty."

Until Senator Wheeler heard of Roxie Stinson his idea was to use me as his first witness. And the reason for this was that otherwise the newspapers would not carry the story as he hoped to be able to get it over.

He told me that he had been advised that Roxie Stinson had a number of letters from Mr. Jess Smith and that these letters were compromising to Mr. Smith, Mr. Daugherty, and their close friends.

I told him she had letters from Jess Smith but they would not prove compromising or be of any value in establishing charges against the Attorney-General. He went on to say that he heard she was quite a striking and handsome woman.

Prior to her appearance on the witness stand, Senator Wheeler was convinced, from his statements to me, that except for the fact that the situation smacked of social scandal there was nothing in any evidence she had. But it would be of enormous interest to a curious element of the public because of the scandal. And that to bring out any material essential matter Miss Stinson would have to be coached.

Her testimony is a matter of record, and by going over it line by line, and word for word, I can see through Senator Wheeler's motive for his questions and the prepared answers.

I will refer to one striking feature of her testimony when she alleges that she saw Jess Smith with seventy-five $1,000 bills.

This statement was absolutely a creation of Wheeler's mind to corroborate the statement he was asking me to make about being collector for a Jap in the Belleview Hotel in Washington of one hundred $1,000 bills and giving them to Jess Smith.

Senator Wheeler had told me that if they could not find anything else against the Department of Justice, Mr. Daugherty, and the administration, this evidence would have to be produced. They had gone too far in their insinuations and innuendoes as to graft and corruption. Otherwise he and his associates would be ruined.

He told me that the whole purpose and object of the investigation was political and that if it were properly handled he [Wheeler] could become the Democratic nominee for President, and if not, for Vice-President. And that if matters did not shape themselves along these lines a new party would have to be created.

It was after this meeting when Wheeler first made his ideas so plain to me, that I began to know Senator Brookhart. Any man, so I sized it up, in his opinion, who had any real money, was a thief and a scoundrel.

Brookhart approved of all Wheeler's plans. He would end most of our conferences with the expression:

"The American people are willing to believe anything and everything against the government and the thicker we can put it on the better."

Between the time I met Mr. Vanderlip and the date I appeared on the stand, I was going over with Senator Wheeler almost — if not every day — the charges in the questions and the answers as he had prepared them for my documents, files, and records.

When I called his attention to the fact that the records did not confirm the answers to any number of the questions that he was going to ask me, his reply was:

"Look at your records now [he had them in his possession for a long while] and you will find that the material has been supplied in which you can make good if pushed to it by anybody. But you are not going to be pushed to it, because I am not going to let the examination of you get out of my hands at any time."

How faithfully Wheeler protected his witness is recorded in the three bulky volumes of the Committee hearings, filling 3,412 closely printed pages. And not a single charge was established on which this Committee could ask for action against me in Congress, before President Coolidge, or in any Court of Justice.

The investigation was not begun or conducted through its months of meddling for the purpose of proving any charges. It was conducted solely as a scandal show with which to destroy the faith of millions in the Government of the United States.

My fate as an official was only incidentally involved, and no recommendation or report was ever made to the Senate on the issues involved in Wheeler's resolution.

The whole affair was a disgrace to the United States Senate and will ever remain a blot on its history.

Wheeler constituted himself from the opening day sole prosecutor, judge, and jury. The current cartoonists were quick to catch this phase and ridicule it.

Humorists covered them with scorn. The very name, "Senatorial Committee," became a by-word.

I quote a specimen of their humor from the *Clarksburg* (W. Va.) *Telegram*:

Senator: "What is your name?"

Witness: "John Doe."

Senator: "Ah, ha! A member of the notorious Doe family of England, which committed countless murders, robberies and other crimes. You have not denied this?"

Witness: "No — because — "

Senator: "We desire no opinions."

Witness: "Well now — "

Senator: "Have you left off beating your grandmother?"

Witness: "No — yes — that is — I protest."

Senator: "It will do you no good. You cannot bulldoze us!"

Witness: "Look here now — "

Senator: "Silence, sir! Where were you at 7:15 o'clock the evening of February 23, 1922 — and if not, why?"

Witness: "I cannot recall."

Senator: "Don't quibble, sir! The Committee will note that the witness fails to answer and is in contempt!"

Witness: "But I never — "

Senator: "Have you any debts or other obligations?"

Witness: "Why, naturally — "

Senator: "Answer yes or no, sir."

Witness: "Yes, of course."

Senator: "Strike out the words, 'of course.' You do not deny then that you have never affirmed having denied any statement of denial regarding your robbery of a watch and other valuables from William Jinks, have you?"

Witness: "No — that is — er — "

Senator: "And you do not deny, do you, that during your business career you have bought one or more shares of stock in an industrial corporation that pays taxes to the United States?"

Witness: "Yes — no — "

Senator: "Ah, ha! Serve a subpoena on Thomas A. Edison. We want more light on the subject."

A committee using such methods, violating every principle of English law, led by a radical who directed a procession of perjurers, sat for months handing out to the newspapers for headlines a mass of insinuations, innuendoes, vicious gossip, and shameless lies.

As a result of these proceedings, in answer to mob opinion, not to facts, I was the first public official who was thrown to the wolves by orders of the Red borers of America.

The object was to intimidate not only me but all those who followed in the office of Attorney-General.

Again I repeat: "Eternal vigilance is the price of liberty."

CHAPTER XX

The Scandal Mongers of Washington

THE thing that gave to Wheeler the deadly power which he wielded as an assassin of character was not the facts which he developed, but the impetus that his insinuations gave to venomous gossip.

A gossip which echoed first in Washington and appeared in headlines of the press throughout the entire country.

I have always wondered why reputable newspaper correspondents in Washington did not expose the disgraceful situation. They knew its purpose. I was told in confidence that they realized the proceedings were a farce and a fraud, but had to "play it up" in accordance with the policy of their papers.

For years Washington has been a cesspool of filthy gossip. Nowhere in the known world has there been anything like it, certainly in no capital of Europe, Asia, or Africa. The Emperor of Abyssinia, who claims descent from Solomon, certainly never heard anything like it in the harems of his palaces. It couldn't have flourished there. His Majesty would have chopped off the heads of such offenders without the formality of a trial.

And the Washington brand of gossip is the lowest, dirtiest, and most vicious small-town stuff.

Washington is really a very small town as American towns go. It looks big because of its magnificent buildings, its beautiful parks, its boulevards and monuments.

These are impressive but they do not make a real city, any more than the marble of an Italian cemetery constitutes one. The city which is a center of commerce, intelligence, and social progress can only be made by the pressure of the life of its people.

Washington lacks this composite mass of active intelligence and social vitality. Its real population is not unified and in the last analysis is extremely small in its effective groups.

Half the inhabitants of Washington are Negroes. And they are disfranchised.

This large body of Negroes was deprived of the ballot under the reconstruction régime that followed the Civil War. Thaddeus Stevens, the Radical leader, took the ballot from the white South and gave it to the Negroes to get control of the Southern states. He overlooked the important fact that the blacks outnumbered the whites in the capital! And when they moved to elect a Negro mayor, Congress promptly disfranchised the District of Columbia.

The Negroes of Washington can't go back to their native states of the South to vote, for they are practically disfranchised there by the Democratic South.

This vast Negro population in Washington, comprising more than half its inhabitants, lives in another world, and may be left out of account in estimating the social forces that determine the life of the city, though many reputable colored people live there and are good citizens.

The other half of the population, the white half, is composed largely of clerks, small officials, their kin, and laborers.

"Society" in Washington is a very small group of the idle rich and high officials. This unit is subdivided into still smaller cliques whose petty squabbles and jealousies are beyond reckoning.

For impossible, deadly, venomous gossip these people are unique in the annals of the human race. I have never seen anything like them in any other city in America or read of anything like them in history.

The Washington high official is always the shining mark of

their poisoned arrows. The higher the position he holds the greater the temptation to shoot at him early and often.

Harding at once became a favorite theme for these select tongue lashers. He was handsome, popular with both men and women, a good fellow, and they rolled his name as a sweet morsel.

One of the first crimes of which he was accused was that he was a frequent visitor to a strange house on H Street. This house happened to be my home, which I had rented from the McLean estate, with an office on the first floor in which to meet people who desired to see me regarding political matters which I had no time to discuss at the Department of Justice.

It naturally became the rendezvous of all sorts and conditions of men, who sought favors of me as a Cabinet officer, or as the successful manager of a presidential nomination, and, as they concluded, the friend and confidant of the President.

Their missions were in no case criminal. The desire for public office in this country is a widespread ambition and it is not confined to any one party.

Seeing the number of people who called at my home, the loose-lipped began to wonder and whisper. Instinctively to their minds I early became the leader of a band of criminals bent on looting the government.

The men who called to see me were personal friends from Ohio, leaders of politics from every state, business men whom I had known for years who came to pay their respects and congratulate me on what they considered my success.

Lists of these callers Wheeler sought from my cook, my butler, my chauffeur. To every name of prominence a sinister motive was attached. He spoke the name of this old McLean house on H Street with bated breath. Its foundations were supposed to have been laid by criminals and cemented with the blood of many victims. Only a thief or a murderer could live in such a house!

And the Hardings were seen going there and coming away from there. On several occasions. It was awful. It was unbelievable. It should be investigated.

And they did. Wheeler raked its history from the day its foundations were laid until I moved to the Wardman Park Hotel.

Mr. and Mrs. Harding on a few occasions honored me with a call at the H Street house as they had at my home in Columbus. I recall that they took dinner with me twice there. President Harding never took a drink there in his life, and I never knew Mrs. Harding to take a drink anywhere. The President never played cards in this house. There was too much work to do and too many callers to permit card playing.

After I moved to the apartment at the Wardman Park Hotel, the President and Mrs. Harding called on me, of course. Quite often they had dinner with other friends accompanied by their wives. There was no drinking. After dinner there were social games. Current stories of these affairs are the grossest slander. Nothing took place in either house that the whole public might not have seen.

There was no cheap vulgarity at these gatherings, no calling each other by first names. No man ever addressed the President in my house or apartment except as "Mr. President." I never did. And I would have resented such lack of breeding in any guest.

The picture which Samuel Hopkins Adams draws of these games is a vicious libel. Every character in his book is a filthy caricature, false, slanderous, and untrue to life. He has shamelessly prostituted his talents as an author in a way I have never known a man of repute to do before. He dipped his pen in the poison of cheap, impossible gossip and wrote as fast as his hand could fly. I repeat again that his screed is a disgrace to American literature.

"The Little Green House on K Street" is another myth

created by the tongues of Washington's scandal mongers. I never entered this house in my life. I never saw it. Harding never entered it, nor saw it, to my knowledge. Two men of my acquaintance, one a former Columbus citizen, occupied a house on K Street. What took place there I had no means of knowing, had no interest in, and never had occasion to investigate.

I have been accused of the darkest crimes because Miss Roxie Stinson testified that I was a visitor at this house.

Her testimony on this point is very instructive when we recall that her part had been carefully rehearsed by her director, Senator Wheeler. She proved herself quite a clever actress.

Wheeler star-featured her scene in "the Little Green House on K Street." The name lent itself to romance, mystery, and crime. It suggested fascinating scenes of revelry, plots, intrigue, and devilment.

The inquisitor rolled the name under his tongue. When he mentioned it Roxie grew very quiet and demure.

"What, if anything, do you know," he asked, "of the Little Green House on K Street?"

"I'd rather not answer," she shivered, assuming an attitude of shame and tearful distress that she should be compelled to speak of things so terrible.

She hemmed and hawed, as directed, saying:

"I would rather not answer!"

Wheeler finally gave her the cue which they had rehearsed:

"You know that Mr. Smith and the Attorney-General met at the K Street house on a number of occasions?"

"I don't mind saying that," she replied and then enraged Wheeler by adding the damning clause: "I was told by Mr. Smith!"

The cat was out of the bag before Wheeler could stop her mouth. She had never been in the house and knew absolutely nothing about it!

Senator Moses inquired mildly:

"Do you know the number of the house?"

And to Wheeler's dismay she cried:

"No. I never saw it in my life!"

As a matter of fact she had never heard of it in her life until she came to Washington to testify, and was engaged to play the rôle of prima donna in Wheeler's show, and he had rehearsed her in the part. She wasn't a quick study and went up in her lines in the opening performance.

The same peddlers of dirt who had attacked Harding had pounced on his predecessor, Woodrow Wilson, the day after he entered the White House. They told the world without hesitation or an if or a but that the austere scholar was in reality a Lothario of the deepest dye — a devil with the women. That his "affairs" before his election were outrageous. That he was now prowling around the streets of Washington under the cover of darkness seeking blacker adventures. And that his wife, the mother of his children, was already arranging a suit for divorce.

There was just as little truth in these vicious lies as in the ones told about Harding.

I regard Mr. Charles Willis Thompson as one of our most brilliant political and historical writers. He is a real student of the times. He writes soundly. He never goes off half cocked. And he always says something worth reading when he tells his story.

He began as a lawyer and has a trained mind. His first newspaper job was as Washington correspondent in the early days of the *New York World*, from which he graduated within a year to the *Tribune*, and then began a twenty-three-year service with the *New York Times*, ending as one of its leading editors.

He is now a free-lance writer and has published a notable book, *Presidents I've Known*, which should be read by every student of American history.

He had a personal antipathy to Harding which he frankly confesses:

"It seems there must be something odd and queer about me for Harding never attracted me in the least. He rubbed me the wrong way every time I saw his standardized smile and heard his comfortable good-fellow voice, and finally, though I had not a thing against him personally, I grew to have a feeling of impatience in his presence."

He reserves his highest praise for Theodore Roosevelt.

The point I'm making is that Mr. Thompson would not knowingly bring any grist to my mill as Harding's champion and Roosevelt's critic.

But in one of his chapters on Roosevelt he has something of tremendous importance to say to the American people which I wish to repeat verbatim. It was written in a discussion of the vicious lie, so long circulated, that Roosevelt was a drunkard.

The ex-President finally brought a libel suit against an editor for printing this lie. People thought he was making a mountain out of a molehill, but Roosevelt said in reply:

"Any man familiar with public life realizes the foul gossip that ripples just under the surface about almost every public man, and especially about every President.

"It is only occasionally printed in reputable papers and set forth in explicit form. But it is hinted at in the press and set forth with circumstantial mendacity in private. And if left unrefuted until after the man's death it lasts as a stain which it is then too late to remove. From Lincoln and Garfield to Cleveland and McKinley this gossip has circulated and still circulates.

"In the case of Mr. Cleveland, for instance, it took the form of accusing him of actions so atrocious that even to think of them makes one indignant. And in this case I know personally there was not the smallest shadow of foundation for the charges.

"Yet it is such an unpleasant task to call the slanderers to account that any man tends to shrink from it."

"I do not know why," Mr. Thompson continues, "Roosevelt said, 'from Lincoln and Garfield.' He could have started earlier.

"When I went to live in Washington, Negroes were pointed out to me on the streets, with the information:

" 'That man belongs to the − family. You know − the illegitimate descendants of George Washington.'

"After I had lived there a while I became accustomed to hearing this sort of remark about every President. Sometimes with meticulous details, such as that President Arthur's mistress was the daughter of a certain Supreme Court Justice. That Harrison had suffered a heart attack and died in a house of prostitution, and so on.

"President Wilson's friendship for Mrs. Peck was made the handle for numberless utterly impossible stories, all scandalous and all related on the authority of somebody 'in a position to know.'

"I do not know how many times I was confidentially and mysteriously assured, always on 'unreproachable authority,' that Justice Brandeis got his appointment to the Supreme Court as a reward for his services in stealing, or buying, Wilson's letters to Mrs. Peck.

"One day, Cleveland H. Dodge, calling on Colonel Edward M. House, said:

" 'I've just learned that I paid Mrs. Peck one hundred and twenty-five thousand dollars for her letter.'

" 'When were you informed of that?' asked House.

" 'This morning,' replied Dodge.

" 'I beat you,' said House, 'I learned the day before yesterday that I paid her one hundred and fifty thousand dollars.'

"I made a Western tour with Woodrow Wilson," Mr. Thompson goes on. "In Denver the Press Club gave a dinner to Wilson and his party, and entertained us sumptuously. My neighbor at the dinner, a refined and pleasant Denver gentleman, thinking to say something that a member of the Wilson party would like to hear, said smilingly to me:

" 'This is rather different from last month. Roosevelt was here then and we intended to give him the same sort of entertainment. But he got so drunk he couldn't come. And had to be carried to bed at the Brown Palace Hotel, where he fell into a drunken sleep and could hardly be roused to go to the auditorium and make his speech.'

"And I said:

" 'How strange! I was here with him that night, covering his appointment for my paper, and he seemed sober when he left the car. I went with him to the Brown Palace, where he talked with us for a while before going into the dining room. When he came out I went with him to the auditorium, where he made a fine speech. Somehow I didn't notice the things you saw. They all escaped me.'

"The conversation languished."

If "honest and truthful men become obscene liars the moment the name of a public man is mentioned," we need not wonder that people of the character of Roxie Stinson and Gaston B. Means allowed their imagination to soar when rehearsed and offered great rewards for their services.

Every word Means testified to before Wheeler he afterwards swore was a lie. His vicious, obscene book, *The Strange Death of President Harding*, the writer, Mrs. Thacker, found to be false and has repudiated in *Liberty* Magazine, November 7, 1931, as a "colossal hoax   a tissue of falsehood from beginning to end."

When Gaston B. Means volunteered his eight thousand word affidavit repudiating his testimony before Wheeler's Committee, I was no longer Attorney-General and could have done nothing to mitigate the sentence he was about to serve as a convicted felon. Whatever his motive, he knew this.

On emerging from the Atlanta penitentiary three years later he found in Mrs. Thacker, wife of a distinguished Presbyterian Evangelist, a sympathetic listener. She had met him while doing religious work in Southern prisons. Means was plausible, eloquent, convincing. He convinced her that he could tell a story of doings in Washington that would be a most important contribution to American history and an invaluable lesson in politics.

He told his story. She believed it and wrote the monstrous book which she has since been compelled by her conscience to denounce as a tissue of falsehood from beginning to end.

The discovery that she had been deceived by Means came to her gradually during the year following the publication of the book. The first thing that appalled her was his failure to furnish the documents he swore that he possessed — documents needed to verify the most important facts presented in the story.

He made excuse after excuse for not producing these papers, and finally promised on his oath to deliver them to her by express the moment he could find the time to dig them out of his twelve trunks packed with records. He showed her the trunks and samples of his files, with which he declared they were filled.

The book went to press but not a line of the promised proofs was ever delivered. She next discovered to her horror and amazement that Gaston B. Means had never crossed the threshold of the White House during the Harding administration. That the record of every human being who had entered, day or night, by front or back door, was on file and Means' name was not on the list!

He had laid sixteen important scenes of the book in the White House. This association, intimate and personal, with Mr. and Mrs. Harding was the foundation on which the entire story rested.

The opening sentence of Chapter I in the book reads:

"Mrs. Harding wants me to come to the White House." This in quotation points. Means was repeating a summons just received from Mrs. Harding.

She next discovered that the only documents which he had furnished her, the three volumes recording his testimony before the Wheeler Committee, were a tissue of falsehoods. She received the rude awakening on discovering a copy of Gaston B. Means' affidavit repudiating this testimony, in which he swore that he helped Wheeler coach Roxie Stinson and frame the whole attack on the Attorney-General.

These discoveries utterly destroyed the validity of the book. The supervising editor of *Liberty* Magazine had been present at the original conference between Means and Mrs. Thacker, and he immediately asked her to write a repudiation of the book and a study of Means' character for his magazine.

It is unnecessary, therefore, to treat at any length the details of the story which makes up this "colossal hoax."

When the Means book appeared I gave out a statement to the press in which I said:

"I may be overoptimistic about the good sense of the American people, but nevertheless I do not believe that a man's reputation can be lastingly made or marred by men like Gaston B. Means. I can understand, however, why the people expect a public defense to every charge or insinuation, for I have myself wondered at the silence of some of President Harding's associates and official family during the repeated attacks made on the fair name of their dead chief.

"It cannot be that they believe these charges. Perhaps their silence is due to the contempt they feel for the ghouls, I hope so.

"The attack upon Mrs. Harding and President Harding, both of whom are dead, is a disgrace to America, but as long as people live and thrive on gossip and falsehood, and as long as unscrupulous, sensational publications spread such falsehoods, the standard of American citizenship will be lowered.

"The book will appeal to those envious souls who love to see men in high places befouled when they cannot be broken, and will put soiled money in the pockets of the author, who is just returned from the penitentiary, where in my official routine of duty I was compelled to send him. He is no doubt in need of money, and he cannot hope to get it from any honest pursuit, for his public career started with a trial for the murder of a woman and ended as a convict.

"Read him and weep — but not for me. He was for a short time one of many hundred subordinates of assistants of mine, and I never talked with him to exceed two minutes in my life, and then in the presence of assistants whom I trusted and who were begging me to give him a chance. I gave him the chance and then sent him to the penitentiary for abusing it. Need I say more?"

To millions of credulous people who believe in the kind of imaginary myths that Gaston B. Means concocts, Jess Smith presents a strange, fascinating figure. They never tire of the fables about him. And for this reason I must treat these stories at some length.

CHAPTER XXI

The True Story of Jess Smith

I WRITE this chapter with the greatest reluctance. I never recall this man without a heartache. I knew him in life as a loyal, lovable friend and good fellow. And I have not yet found it possible in my heart to think evil of him.

What he was to me in loyal friendship he was, only in a lesser degree, to hundreds of men in public life. He had a genius for making friends and keeping them. He lived to serve others.

The news of his death brought scores of letters and telegrams of sympathy and appreciation. They came from every state in the Union and from beyond the sea.

Albert Lasker of the Shipping Board was his friend and wrote me a touching letter on learning of his death.

Will Hays wired me: "I mourn with you and your grief is mine."

Coleman Du Pont of Delaware, and Senator Theodore Burton of Ohio, wired their deepest sympathies.

Wayne B. Wheeler, General Counsel and Manager of the Anti-Saloon League, then at the zenith of his power, wired: "I was greatly shocked at the news of Smith's inexplicable death. Give his loved ones my sympathy."

Another distinguished man wrote:

"I was generally shocked when I heard last night of poor Jess' death. He told me that he had diabetes. I reassured him that it was curable, and required only a little patience and careful dieting. We parted with my injunction not to walk too fast back to his hotel.

"If I can do anything for you in your trouble, my dear fellow, let me know. Hastily, John Hays Hammond."

John Oliver La Gorce, associate editor of the *National Geographic Magazine* and vice-president of the Society, wrote me the following letter:

National Geographic Society
Washington, D. C.

May 31.

Dear General:

I know of no one else to write to in voicing my grief and shock at the passing of dear old Jess — God rest him. You will need all the courage you have developed in a lifetime of service to stand up under this heart wound but I'm sure you can and will.

I really wish there was a little something I could do.

Sincerely,
(signed) J. O. La Gorce.

Perhaps the most interesting and significant message which I received came from a distinguished newspaper correspondent with whom I had crossed swords more than once:

The Goring Hotel,
Belgravia,

London, S. W. I.
12th June — 23.

My dear General Daugherty,

I was inexpressibly shocked by the sad news about Jess which was cabled over here. Why should he, of all men, have done this? He was such a wholesome, optimistic fellow. I always thought of him as a man who enjoyed life fully, and as one who got immense pleasure out of devotion to his friends. I had come to like him with unusual feeling, and to think of myself as a friend of his. When I read the news, my first thought was that if I had been at home and had been in touch with him, I might have learned of what he was thinking and might have been able to argue him out of it. I suppose though that is a vain thought. Next to my sympathy for him, I sympathize with you. I know how much he meant to you with his complete loyalty and devotion and I can understand how much you will miss him.

It is a queer world and the tragedy of it is all mixed up with the pleasures of it.

A. B. Fall
Secretary of the Interior, of Teapot Dome Fame.

His kindness was infinite

From left to right: *President Hoover, Mrs. Harding, Jess Smith, Warren Harding, Harry M. Daugherty.*

I suppose that when Jess Smith, as a quiet citizen of Washington Court House, shared with you your common triumph of putting your friend into the White House, he must have looked forward to life as an exhilarating thing, packed with the pleasures of success and the pleasures of friendship. To think that it has now ended so tragically is very, very saddening.

Sincerely yours,
(signed) Mark Sullivan.

Certainly Mark Sullivan was never a man to associate with crooks on terms of intimate friendship. And the sentence: "I had come to like him with unusual feeling, and to think of myself as his friend," was not written to me as a conventional courtesy.

Whatever my feeling for a dead friend, it has become a duty to myself, my living friends, and my country to tell the facts about Jess Smith as I knew him.

He was a great reader of detective stories and had deathless curiosity about detectives and their work, the kind of interest a fourteen-year-old boy would manifest.

Gaston B. Means, whom he met through W. J. Burns, head of the Bureau of Investigation in the Department of Justice, fascinated him from the first. Means was the type of man I couldn't endure, and Jess, knowing this, never mentioned his name in my presence. I learned afterwards that he spent many hours with Means listening to his thrilling stories.

It was this unfortunate association that gave to Gaston B. Means the power to blacken his friend's name with carefully concocted stories when coached by Senator Wheeler.

Means afterwards swore that these allegations were lies out of whole cloth. But the press had carried them in great headlines and failed to carry the contradictions. Newspapers never like to reverse a stand once taken.

The impression which Senator Wheeler sought to make, and which he succeeded in making in large measure, was that the Government of the United States had become hopelessly corrupt and should be destroyed. That Jess Smith had been the go-between in a conspiracy of crime and corruption of which the Attorney-General was the head and front.

What, if anything, this unfortunate friend of mine ever did that was questionable he carefully concealed from me.

What are, in brief, the true facts of Smith's life and death?

When he was a young man in Washington Court House my brother and I became very fond of him. He was a genial, lovable youngster, and we helped him build his store into a successful business from which he accumulated a comfortable fortune. His intense devotion to the Daughertys was one of the first things in his life.

He had made many friends during the primary and national campaigns, and greatly enlarged the circle in Washington. For the first year and a half he was to me an unfailing source of helpfulness and cheerful companionship.

He kept my accounts and attended to unimportant personal and social correspondence. He contracted and paid all bills incident to my household, as he had kept the political account during the primary and national campaigns.

This account was in the Midland National Bank of Washington Court House, Ohio, of which my brother was president. It was marked "Jess Smith, Extra." Through this account had passed many thousands of dollars of campaign funds. They were perfectly legitimate transactions but involved men and women whose names, and the amount they contributed, could not be divulged without a breach of trust. For example, many Democrats had this year contributed to the Republican campaign fund. The publication of their names would have injured their businesses.

I mention this fact here carefully because this confidential fund became the storm center of a famous controversy.

Smith's social success in Washington, as evidenced by the messages from Coleman Du Pont, Senator Burton, John Hays

Hammond, Will Hays, John Oliver La Gorce, Wayne B. Wheeler, Albert D. Lasker, Mark Sullivan, and hundreds of others was, to say the least, an unusual achievement for a stranger from the sticks, holding no official position in the government.

Jess enjoyed it. He loved the bright lights. He gloried in his association with Mr. and Mrs. Harding at the White House. They liked him and he frequently dined with them. He was received in many socially prominent homes. He had accompanied the President on the trip to Panama and it was one of the brightest memories of his life. He had his picture taken with Harding at every opportunity and treasured these mementos as more precious than all the gold he possessed. And he was a man of independent means.

He had become in many ways indispensable to my personal comfort and I relied absolutely on his honesty and loyalty.

At the end of a year and a half his health broke down. He went to Mt. Carmel Hospital in Columbus, Ohio, in a serious condition. It was found that he was suffering from appendicitis complicated by diabetes.

He remained for several days in a semi-conscious state caused by the diabetes and absorption from the acute infection in the abdomen. After treatment for eleven days, an operation was performed and the appendix removed.

He again relapsed into a semi-conscious condition for four days, rallied, and gradually improved. At the end of a month he was discharged from the hospital, but the wound never healed. He was compelled to wear a truss-like belt until the day of his death.

On May 12, 1922, the day before he was operated on, he drew his will and had it duly witnessed. The will was in twenty-three sections and made bequests to twenty-five different people, disposing of an estate which he valued at about $200,000. This will, afterwards admitted to probate, gave to my brother $25,000, and to me a similar amount, and named us his executors. He left Roxie Stinson a like amount. The remaining $125,000 he bequeathed to relatives and charities.

He was never himself physically or mentally at any time after this operation. The genial good fellow became morose and irritable, and finally it was next to impossible for him to get along with servants. Before this he was noted for his skill in handling all sorts of help.

In the spring of 1923, when the President was planning his trip to Alaska, he surprised and shocked me with the statement that he had been informed that Smith was not conducting himself properly and that for the good of all concerned it would be well to advise him to go home.

"What is he doing?" I asked.

"I am informed he is running with a gay crowd, attending all sorts of parties. And you should know too that he is using the Attorney-General's car until all hours of the night."

"I'm amazed," I answered. "I will look into the matter at once."

The President hesitated a moment and then spoke regretfully:

"I suggest that you tell him it will be impossible for him to go with us on the trip to Alaska. The party is already filled."

I understood what that meant, of course, and faced Jess as quickly as I could find him. He made no effort to fight the decree, though I could see that he was heartbroken. He had counted on this trip to Alaska.

Also I told him point-blank that he would have to leave Washington. We discussed his health and I begged him to go to a hospital for treatment. This he refused to do at first. He agreed finally to go back with me to Ohio, look after some business, and enter a hospital. I remained in Columbus while Smith went on to Washington Court House.

Instead of entering a hospital, as he had promised, he

asked that he might return to our apartment in Washington to see a few friends and wind up a little business he had there.

I agreed. And on our way back to the capital he told me he had straightened out his affairs and arranged with my brother to wind up the details of the sale of his store. Friends on the train remarked to me that he was acting "queer." He was not drinking. After his death I learned that while in Ohio he had bought a pistol — a thing I had never known him to own before.

When we reached Washington I went direct to the White House, in accordance with an arrangement with the President, who, knowing of Smith's intention to remain in Ohio, asked me to stop at the White House for a few days. Jess went to our apartment at the Wardman Park Hotel. I got in touch with Mr. Warren F. Martin, one of my assistants in the Department of Justice, and asked him if he could arrange to stay at the apartment with Jess for the few days he expected to be there, as I was uneasy about his condition.

Martin complied with my request. And on the morning of May 30, Smith shot himself. Martin rushed to his room and found him dead. The bullet had driven through his right temple and lodged in the door jamb.

He immediately called W. J. Burns, who lived in the hotel, and Burns notified the authorities.

On the morning of the 30th, shortly after breakfast, the President and Dr. Boone came to my room in the White House and told me of the suicide. The President was greatly shocked.

To my surprise, I found on reaching my apartment that Jess had destroyed all my house accounts and my personal correspondence. In fact there was hardly anything left pertaining to my personal affairs.

The act could be accounted for only on the ground of a complete mental collapse. These moments of collapse were,

In the presence of Almighty God
and being of sound mind,
I make this my last will.
  I give all I possess.
share and share alike
to Edmund St John,
Finroe St John Thomson,
Roxy R. Stinson, Harry M
Daugherty and M S Daugherty,
I ask that M S Daugherty be
made my Executor   Jess W Smith.
May 28-1923.

of course, a peculiarity of his disease. After his death an open malignant wound left by his operation was discovered.

A new will in Jess' handwriting but not witnessed was found on his desk. It left the entire estate to five persons. The will drawn on May 12, 1922, divided the property among twenty-five people and was witnessed. The court was asked to probate the first will, which was done.

When the estate was settled it did not reach the amount of Smith's estimate. It netted about $125,000. If he had taken graft right and left as my enemies claimed, what had become of the money? The gossips of Washington, of course, accounted for it. They declared he had buried millions in the graveyard at Washington Court House! Nobody has found it as yet.

The will of Jess Smith written on the stationery of the Wardman Park Hotel becomes an important document in this story for several reasons. (Facsimile of will is shown on opposite page.)

Heflin, the blatherskite of the Senate, knowing of the existence of this will in Jess Smith's handwriting and dated two days before he killed himself, had the brazen effrontery to stand up in the Senate and declare under immunity that Jess Smith was murdered in my apartment, and to hint that I was a party to the crime! Gaston B. Means, of course, more than hinted it.

A suicide under any circumstance is shocking. Under such conditions it became a national scandal. Many reasons were advanced and many suspicions aroused.

In these sad hours, the Senate of the United States had ceased to be itself and had become an aggregation of howling dervishes. It was Heflin's day. It was Wheeler's day. And as every dog has his day, they certainly had theirs.

The question whether Jess Smith took money from bootleggers and others became for me a vital issue.

To the hour of his death, I heard absolutely nothing of it, if there ever was any truth in it.

Liquor withdrawal permits are issued only by the Treasury Department. The Department of Justice has nothing to do with it.

The Prohibition Enforcement branch of the Treasury Department also gathers the evidence and presents to the Department of Justice all violations of the Volstead Law.

Orders for the prosecution of such cases are issued by the Attorney-General upon the recommendation of his assistants. At least a dozen men, including district attorneys, would have to be controlled if anything improper in the handling of such cases were attempted.

That Smith approached no one in the Prohibition Enforcement branch of the Treasury Department was shown by a letter addressed to me by Commissioner Haynes, of whom I made inquiry. The Commissioner wrote: "Mr. Smith never talked to me about liquor withdrawal permits in behalf of himself or anyone else." And Mr. Jones, Assistant Commissioner, stated: "Mr. Smith never discussed liquor withdrawal permits with me. I do not find anything to indicate that Smith ever took up the matter of the withdrawal of permits for intoxicating liquor in behalf of anyone with this office."

I was afterwards informed that Mr. Crim, Assistant Attorney-General, had said that he obtained evidence that Smith had been mixed up in questionable deals, confronted him with the truth, and informed him that I would be made acquainted with the facts. And that this was but a few days before Smith committed suicide.

Mr. David Lawrence, the brilliant founder and editor of the *United States Daily*, says in one of his articles:

"That Jess Smith received money from various persons who sought to influence government action is unquestioned. That Harry M. Daugherty knew nothing about it until it was too late is also accepted by his friends as absolute truth.

"Although Jess Smith worshiped Harry Daugherty, he concealed from him what he was really doing in Washington."

The only direct charge connecting me with improper conduct while I was Attorney-General arose in connection with the American Metals case — the case in which Colonel Miller was afterwards indicted and sentenced to the U. S. Penitentiary in Atlanta.

The office of the Alien Property Custodian, of which Colonel Miller was the head, is in no way connected with the Department of Justice.

The American Metals case involved the return of alien property which had been unlawfully taken during the war and subsequently returned to its rightful owners.

It was not possible for me to investigate personally the hundreds of such cases referred by the Alien Property Custodian to the Department of Justice. This particular case was investigated by two able, honest lawyers, with their assistants, in charge of that branch of work in the Department. These two men, Colonel Guy D. Goff and Mr. Adna R. Johnson, decided, in the ordinary course of business, without consulting me, that the property had been unlawfully taken and should be returned to its rightful owners.

In the trials that followed not a single piece of evidence was produced to show that I was in any way responsible for the decision to return the property.

When the criminal feature of the American Metals case became a matter for investigation, Hon. Hiram C. Todd, an outstanding lawyer, was appointed special Assistant Attorney-General and assigned to the case by Attorney-General Harlan F. Stone, my successor in office.

Up to this time no charge had been made against me.

The investigation developed that John T. King, representing the claimants, had received a fee of $400,000 from them, and that part of the fee, paid in Liberty bonds, had found its way to Colonel Miller and a part to Jess Smith.

King testified before the grand jury that he had given the bonds to Smith in return for Smith's help in expediting the handling of the American Metals case by the Alien Property Custodian. He told the grand jury that Smith always cautioned him, "Don't ever tell General Daugherty a word about this."

King insisted that he had a right to accept employment in the Metals case. And undoubtedly he had. He was a man of high standing. He was connected with and represented big interests. There were hundreds of men in Washington engaged in the same business, representing clients before the different departments of the government in a legitimate and proper effort to get cases advanced and disposed of quickly and, if possible, favorably. This has always been done and probably always will be.

But, knowing Smith's close relations with me, King had no right to hire Jess Smith to influence the Alien Property Custodian or anyone in the Department of Justice even to the extent of merely hurrying the case, as he claimed.

Smith never breathed a word to me that he had done the idiotic thing, nor did he ever mention the American Metals case to me or to anyone in the Department so far as I know.

A short time before his death King apologized to me for having drawn Smith into the matter and repeated to me what he had testified before the grand jury.

According to the records, the Liberty bonds in the Metals case were given to Smith by King in September 1921. It was not until August 1924, when the Department of Justice sent an agent to Washington Court House to examine the accounts of the bank, that the bonds were traced to Smith.

He had kept an account in the Midland National Bank known as "Jess Smith, Extra," in which contributions and expenditures of the 1920 campaign had been handled. He also kept a "Personal" account and a "Store" account.

The bank gave the agent of the Department of Justice a certified copy of its records showing every bond received for Smith. The bank, of course, had no means of knowing where Smith got the bonds, and the transaction was handled in the usual way.

When the facts were developed it naturally raised a suspicion of my possible knowledge and put me in an equivocal position.

My brother, as president of the bank, was subpoenaed as a witness before the grand jury. He took with him the ledger sheets of the bank showing the transactions in the several accounts of Jess Smith, his own account, and my account.

I went with him to New York.

He testified that on Smith's last visit to Washington Court House a few days before he committed suicide, he left at the bank $50,000 in Liberty bonds to straighten up his affairs. The bonds were disposed of and his affairs were adjusted as he directed.

We explained to Mr. Todd, the special counsel, what this "Jess Smith, Extra" account comprised. That it was purely a political account and had nothing to do with my government duties or activities. He saw for himself that the ledger sheets contained no names, but only figures, and since he already had the sworn testimony of King that he had given the bonds to Smith, he told us that he did not propose to inject politics into the case and would have no further use for the sheets.

He returned them to us and when my brother and I left New York we took them. Having been informed by Mr. Todd that the ledger sheets were of no value in the case, I burned them with a lot of other papers I had no use for, just as I had done many times before and since.

The burning of the ledger sheets was of no importance, as far as the American Metals case was concerned, for the government had in its possession a certified copy of the bank records showing the bond transactions of Smith, which was the only matter involved. The loss of these sheets was felt only by those who for their own purposes were interested in prying into the transactions of the 1920 campaign.

I was not indicted in the first instance with Colonel Miller.

Subsequently, Emory R. Buckner of New York was appointed District Attorney. He took over the case and succeeded to the work theretofore assigned by Attorney-General Stone to Mr. Todd.

Buckner had me indicted. Contrary to the general impression, it was not for bribery, but under an old statute charging negligence in the performance of duty in the disposition of the American Metals case.

By the time I was called before the grand jury by Mr. Buckner I was fully aware of the plot of political enemies to force me to testify regarding certain contributions and expenditures in the Harding campaign. I made up my mind not to answer a single question regarding these accounts, as such things had nothing to do with the American Metals case.

When questions were asked by the District Attorney before the grand jury that I thought improper, I compelled him to submit them to the court. I then answered every question that the court held to be proper.

Because of this attitude on my part I was indicted by the grand jury, not, as I have said, for bribery, but for alleged negligence in the performance of duty.

On the trial I refused to take the stand and submit to cross-examination as to the ledger sheets, which contained information whose publication would have amounted to a breach of trust on my part.

And I'd refuse again tomorrow were I put to the test, even if I hung for it.

I had been out of office for a long time. Jess Smith was dead and his accounts closed. I did not propose to be dragged before the public on a fishing excursion by those who sought to pry into what had been done in a political campaign. I stood my ground and took my chances. It was the only way I knew how to play the game.

And further, I did not testify at the trial because not a line of testimony had been introduced against me. I had never passed on the merits of the American Metals case, as shown by unimpeached testimony. I had never seen the claimants.

Senator Goff of West Virginia, Assistant to the Attorney-General at the time, was at the head of the force that handled all cases presented to the Department of Justice by the Alien Property Custodian.

I never even heard of the case until long after it had been disposed of and the property returned to its rightful owners. A discharged employee of the Alien Property Custodian's office addressed a letter to President Harding in which he claimed irregularity in the settling of the case. The President sent the letter to me, and, as was customary, I referred it to the man in charge of that branch of the work, Colonel Goff, with the request that he give me a statement of the facts for the information of the President. This he did, but before it could be transmitted the complaining party wrote the President another letter in which he withdrew the charges.

The President, being thus fully advised by Colonel Goff's statement, was satisfied, as I was at the time, of the regularity and propriety of the release of the property, and the incident of the complaint was dismissed by him.

The sworn testimony of Goff, now a United States Senator, shows that he passed on the claim finally and allowed it as Acting Attorney-General in my absence, and that he never discussed the matter with me. Others testified to the same effect, and no one to the contrary.

The only questions passed upon by the Department of

Justice in Alien Property cases are questions of title and citizenship. In this particular case there was no question of money involved as far as the interest of the government was concerned. The fairness of the award of the property to its rightful owners was not contested by the government and never has been. This is clearly developed in an angry letter from Senator Goff to District Attorney Buckner, the day following the District Attorney's impassioned speech to the jury.

I quote the Senator's message verbatim:

> If the press reports of your evil-speaking clamor concerning my connection with the American Metals case are correct, and doubtless they are, since you number among your retainers representatives of the Associated Press, you will permit me to answer that you are a liar and a coward. Your attack is an overt act in a conspiracy composed of deliberately dishonest and vicious character assassins, debased as they are un-American, and you are their spokesman. For weeks your hirelings sneaked, snooted, rooted, whispered, and telephoned in the filthy, slimy gossip of the capital city to gather material for your little strut across the stage in your examination of me as a witness a week ago. The success of your hypocrisy and treachery was reflected in the derision and the ridicule with which your examination was received in a crowded courtroom. You then made honor a jest and the dignity of a judicial office a thing of scorn, as you now well know and as you then appreciated.
>
> You stated in a written motion dated August 14, 1926, dismissing the indictment against Merton and the officers of the Swiss Society, and which is now a record of the United States Court for the Southern District of New York, that as a result of your investigations in Europe and the United States you were convinced that there was no available evidence to substantiate the charges there made against this alien individual and corporate defendants. You specifically said: "I am further of the opinion as the result of my extensive investigations of this case as aforesaid that the facts found therein do not involve or impute any degree of criminality to any of the foreign individual defendants named in the indictment."
>
> Your conclusions then and there, reached after mature consideration, of necessity recognized the validity of the claim.

They coincided with the views I entertained when the claim was allowed. Why are you not now honest and fair enough to admit the truth as you then found it? Is it possible that in this written document, now a record of the United States Court, you did not mean what you said, but your findings were merely the price you paid for the presence of an alien witness not otherwise obtainable? If so the taint and the shame is indelibly yours.

Your cowardice in this proceeding is as insolent as it is notorious. The road of desertion, not resignation, should be left open to you, in the hope that the jurisprudence of this nation may be fumigated and freed from the shrinking delinquency and the miserable demagogism to which your connection with the Department of Justice has reduced it.

(signed) Guy D. Goff.

No conviction was found against me in either trial, and the case was finally dismissed by the court upon the voluntary motion of Mr. Buckner.

Jess Smith, in a misguided moment, had undoubtedly become interested in pressing the claims of the American Metals Company. In this he deceived me. From a legal standpoint he had as much right as King to represent the claimants. But from a moral standpoint, in view of his association with me and on account of my official position, it was a betrayal of my confidence and a deadly thing to do.

Smith's mother died of diabetes, and throughout her long illness Jess nursed her with devotion. One of his relatives said that Jess had then remarked that if he ever had diabetes there would be a shorter way out for him.

This insidious disease plays sad tricks with the human brain. It has caused loss of memory. It has produced homicidal impulses. It has made suicides. It has broken down the moral fiber of character.

I shall always remember my friend before his illness when he was himself, kindly, helpful, loyal, generous.

President Harding's Last Picture

"It is yet too early to see him in a true, full perspective—a
modern Abraham Lincoln whose name and
fame will grow with time."

Calvin Coolidge
"I found him both a practical politician and statesman."

CHAPTER XXII

Harding's Last Will and Testament

THE final day of Harding's preparation for his trip to Alaska is one I shall never forget. Every detail of the hours we spent together on June 19, 1923, is indelibly etched in my memory.

I was not in the best of health. I had returned from Asheville, North Carolina, April 29, greatly strengthened by my rest, only to run into the tragic situation developed by Jess Smith's rapid decline both in body and mind.

I had been compelled to arrange for him to leave Washington. I had returned to Ohio with him and received there daily confirmation of his mental unbalance. We returned to Washington on the twenty-ninth and he killed himself in my apartment on May 30.

In this last conference with the President I found my heart aching over Jess's tragic fate. The poor fellow had dreamed of this trip as the climax of his life.

I recalled the sickening look that overspread his kindly face when told he could not go. He received it as a prisoner receives a death sentence. He gloried in doing the little things that made life sweet and strong for those he loved.

I thought of him that day with a bitter pang of regret and sympathy.

After I had spent three hours of hard work with the President, helping him clear his desk of many matters, he was tired and I was also worn out.

Late in the afternoon he said:

"Now I want to get some law business out of you for nothing."

"Well," I laughed, "that's what you've been doing all day. What is it? Fire away."

"I want you to draw a new will for me."

"All right," I agreed. "Let me see your old one."

He sent for it and while it was being located and delivered we discussed the provisions he wished made in the new one.

I read the old will carefully and began to make the draft of the new document.

One of the things about which he was anxious was the sale of his newspaper. It was a valuable piece of property. But he had been compelled to ignore its existence in the rush of endless work his office involved.

The document proved to be a long one, in which several trusts were set up to carry out its provisions.

As I look back now at this intimate discussion of the last confidences of his life with a man whom I had known and loved for thirty years, and recall the slanders which followed his death, my blood boils.

If Nan Britton or any other woman had ever borne a child to my friend he could not have passed through this solemn hour with me without the frankest discussion of all the facts. He was never a secretive man. He couldn't have concealed such a thing from me if he tried; it would have inevitably come out.

It didn't come out. Because such a thing had never happened.

The name of no woman outside his loved ones for whom he made provision passed his lips.

It would have been the work of but a few minutes for me to draft in my own handwriting a deed of trust that would have made ample provision for Nan Britton and her child, outside the terms of his regular will.

It is easy to say that a man neglects to do such things often until it is too late. Many men do. But Harding could not have done such a thing. He was too gentle, too kind, too sentimental. He never had any such relations with Nan Britton as she claims in the book in which she boasts of her own shame. If he had, he would have provided for the child on this memorable day of his life. He was that kind of a man. For in these friendly hours we talked of the deep things of life and death and eternity.

I resent the imprint of callous cruelty which this slander puts on my friend even more than the slander itself. Any strong man might fall for a woman if tempted, but no man of Harding's character could have found it in his heart to treat her afterwards with studied, beastly neglect. He had a small fortune. Mrs. Harding had an estate of her own also. He had no children. His people were all well-to-do and capable of taking care of themselves. And he loved children. He was never known to pass a child without a smile or a touch of his big, gentle hand.

My experience with Harding in this tender, solemn hour writes the word "Fake" over every page of the book that bears the name of Nan Britton.

Here again we have a whole volume of scandalous tattle about a President of the United States in line current with the tales about Washington, Lincoln, Arthur, Harrison, Cleveland, Roosevelt, and Wilson.

With due apologies, because I am, of necessity, writing of a woman who has invited the attack, I must tell the plain truth about Miss Britton. She challenged every man of honor who ever knew Harding when she published her alleged fall and advertised her own shame in the betrayal of the man she says she loved. A girl who would do this is clearly entitled to no protection from the survival of chivalry in our civilization.

Without hesitation, therefore, I say that I never heard of her, nor heard her name spoken, until the appearance of the book, *The President's Daughter*.

In all our intimate talks Harding never once mentioned her name. I never heard Mrs. Harding mention it. And I am sure that she was never the subject of any discussion or quarrel between them. If they had quarreled over Nan Britton I would have heard of it from one of them. There was scarcely a day when I was in Washington that I did not call at the White House and talk with one or both of them.

Gaston B. Means's book, since repudiated by his writer, appeared after Nan Britton's, and his references to her were made obviously to give credibility to his yarn. He merely enlarges on the tale as she told it, describing imaginary scenes in the White House between Harding, Mrs. Harding, and Nan Britton. Scenes he was supposed to have secretly witnessed, when the fact developed that he was never in the White House!

The only scratch of a pen she possesses from Harding is one of his campaign portraits inscribed to her as follows:

"To Miss Nan Britton with the good wishes of a Marion neighbor and friend. Sincerely, Warren G. Harding."

This was a stock campaign photograph furnished Harding by the National Campaign Committee for the purpose of autographing for friends. He inscribed and signed thousands of them.

She claims to have worked for the Republic Campaign Committee in Chicago and publishes two alleged snapshots (which could have been taken anywhere at any time since) showing her displaying Harding's campaign portraits.

It is possible she worked for the Committee. Hundreds of girls were employed by it. If so, she naturally handled his portraits and may have kept a lot of them as souvenirs.

Again Miss Britton says that Harding never saw his baby, notwithstanding the fact that it was born in 1918 while he was a comparatively unimportant figure in the Senate. No Secret Service men dogged his steps. If he had met this girl again and again during the progress of their affair, surely he could have stepped around the corner to see the child.

This is a curious slip of the writer. It is strange how people who commit crimes so often leave the evidence of their guilt thus uncovered. It is unthinkable that a man of Harding's temperament, if he had taken all the risks of hotel registers in New York, of Pullman rides across half a dozen states, could not create an opportunity to see his baby!

If he had ever been the father of one, no power on earth could have kept him from it. The thing is preposterous on the author's own showing.

But perhaps the most convincing reason for my lack of faith in a line of this book is that in all its 439 closely printed pages there is produced not a single letter of Harding's to Miss Britton. The writer says that he was an habitual writer of love letters and sent her hundreds — many of them forty to sixty pages long! The author of *The President's Daughter* could not produce one of these, for a simple reason. They were never written. They were never received by Miss Britton. One genuine love letter would have been enough to establish her case. But she never has and never can produce it.

The probable origin of the tale becomes clear when we recall the fact that Richard Wightman, the writer of her book, was sued for divorce by his wife for his association with Miss Britton. Finally, her last claim for vindication by the people of America was completely destroyed by the verdict of the jury in the Federal Court at Toledo, Ohio, in November 1931. This was a jurisdiction which she herself chose in which to establish her reputation and the veracity of her story. The verdict of the jury has left her thoroughly discredited and determined her status for all time.

I studied Harding's face with a curious interest. It did not occur to me that he cherished any premonition of a tragic ending of his trip. Yet he seemed mortally tired. No man ever sat in the Presidential chair who felt more keenly its obligations or tried more faithfully to fulfill them to the last detail. And I have known many presidents, six quite intimately. His kindness was infinite. He gave of himself, soul

and body, without stint or thought of giving too much.
He looked at me a moment tenderly and said:

"I'm awfully sorry you're not going with me on this
trip. You put it into my head with your description of the
wonders of Alaska which you once saw with Mrs. Daugherty."

"Yes, I know," I answered. "But it's out of the question."

"I realize that," he nodded. "Mellon is in Paris. Hughes is
on a vacation. And I'm taking three other men out of the
Cabinet with me, who should see Alaska, particularly the
Secretaries of Commerce, the Interior, and Agriculture. Some-
body must keep house for the government while I'm away.
And I've put the job on you."

When it became known that I had been closeted alone with
the President for hours, the White House grounds and
Executive offices immediately swarmed with reporters and
correspondents, and all sorts of rumors began to spread.

I assured the boys that I had only been helping the
President clear up a little unfinished business on his desk
before he started for the West.

They were naturally suspicious of the length and secrecy
of our conference. Crazy rumors were swiftly set in circulation and many of them were printed. One in particular
developed the surmise that Harding was breaking with his old
associates and friends and on his return I would have to leave
the Cabinet. The conference had developed into a violent
quarrel, that presaged a new régime in the White House!

The thing was too contemptible for notice and I let them
rave and imagine vain things. A policy I would rectify if I had
to live that day over again.

Toward the end of our conference I caught on the
President's face a look that distressed me.

In the spring, following a long period of overwork without
a day's real rest, he had suffered an attack of influenza that
put him to bed in a very weakened condition. It was followed

by night attacks of difficult breathing. His recovery had been slow, so slow that I insisted on his dropping everything and taking this trip to Alaska.

He had also suffered from acute indigestion, high blood pressure, and defective action of the kidneys, indicating a possible attack of Bright's disease.

I had thought of this trip with a feeling of relief. If only he would not overexert himself and would stick to the limited program of speaking on which we had agreed.

When he showed the program of his itinerary I threw up my hands in surprise.

I turned to the President and said with all the emphasis I could put into words:

"If you make all of the speeches required of you on this trip at this time of the year, June twentieth to the end of July, it will kill you."

He lifted his hand in mild protest and I added:

"It would kill any man who would attempt it."

We cut the original program to pieces, recast it, and arranged a restful trip back through the Panama Canal to Cuba and New York. I had thought this arrangement definitely settled, yet I had a vague fear that it might be changed as the trip progressed.

The President gave me an affectionate good night; and as I was leaving, he said:

"I'm counting on your meeting me at Seattle and we will drive through the Yosemite Valley together to San Francisco."

"Not me," I promptly objected. "It's too hot. This is a terrific summer. You should not make such a trip. I'll meet you in Seattle and we'll take the boat to San Francisco."

Again I caught the look of weariness in his face.

And my fears more than came true.

Almost from the first day the program of restricted speech-making and conserving of strength was forgotten.

The itinerary developed into an orgy of speech-making. I never realized, until I read the speeches, afterwards published in a memorial volume, what a mad performance the whole thing was.

From June 20 to July 31, he made eighty-five public speeches! An average of more than two a day through the hottest days of one of the hottest summers on record.

In addition to these public addresses he was compelled to talk daily to the army of newspaper men who accompanied him, attend banquets, and shake hands with thousands of people.

The strain was enough to have killed a much younger and more robust man, to say nothing of a man with a weakened heart who had not yet recovered from the influenza and was threatened with Bright's disease.

I left for the Pacific coast toward the end of July to meet him and make my final investigation in the Southern Pacific Railroad case, which had been on the docket for seventeen years, disturbing the peace and security of the Western railway systems and threatening the financial structure of the country.

The people of California treated me royally. I shall never forget the warmth and generosity of their greeting. I found to my surprise I had more friends in California than in any state in the Union. It was the only state I had never visited before. I found these people had long memories. They had not forgotten that the railway injunction which I had secured in Chicago had not only cleared the deserts of abandoned trains and restored law and order, but had saved a hundred million dollars' worth of their fruit that would have rotted.

From the time Harding left Washington, I had been kept informed as to his whereabouts, and when he became ill I received daily bulletins, so that when I reached Seattle I was not surprised to find awaiting me a long distance call from Mr. George Christian, the President's secretary. He suggested that I take a special and get to San Francisco at the earliest possible moment. I asked him about the President's condition and it was just as I had feared. In spite of his illness he had insisted on making his scheduled speeches at Vancouver and Seattle.

I am satisfied that the exertion of these speeches was the direct cause of Harding's complete collapse on his reaching the Palace Hotel in San Francisco.

I am particular in following the details of his last days because of the vile insinuations circulated by Gaston B. Means about the President's tragic end.

On arrival, I immediately called at the Palace and found Harding under the care of the three physicians who accompanied him to Alaska, Sawyer, Boone, and Work, and they had called in two famous doctors, Ray Lyman Wilbur and C. M. Cooper.

I found that everything was being done that could be thought of except that the floor on which he had been placed was crowded with too many people.

Mrs. Harding scolded me for not stopping at their hotel where accommodations had been reserved for me. I shook my head:

"There are too many people tramping over this floor now. I'll not add to the confusion. What he needs is absolute quiet and rest. I'll keep in touch with you every hour and call again soon."

"You'll come in now and see him a minute?"

"No."

"But he's asking about you."

"Tell him I'm here ready to do anything he wishes except disturb him. He mustn't worry about anything.

"The country is all right. Everything is all right at Washington. I have nothing of pressing importance to see him about. If he saw me he would talk and he must not talk. Tell him I will see him in a day or two. Keep everybody away."

I went to the St. Francis Hotel and called at the Palace every few hours to talk with Mrs. Harding.

On the afternoon of August 2, the President was reported better, and I held a reception for the judges and lawyers of the coast. I had an appointment with Mrs. Harding to take dinner with her that evening.

After the reception, very tired, I threw myself on the bed to get a little rest before dressing for dinner.

All reports which I had received from the President's bedside that day showed that he was resting comfortably.

Dr. Boone and a nurse pressed their way softly into my room. I saw in a flash from the expression on their faces that something dreadful had happened.

I held my breath for a moment and asked as quietly as I could:

"How is the President?"

"He has passed away," Dr. Boone slowly replied.

I could say nothing. I had received the hardest blow of my life. For a moment I felt the foundations of the world sink.

I rose and hurried to the Palace to see Mrs. Harding and confer with the other members of the Cabinet present.

Before talking to Mrs. Harding I went to the telegraph office in the hotel and wired Vice-President Coolidge at Northampton, Massachusetts, that the President had died and suggested that he immediately take the oath of office as his successor.

Mrs. Harding had withstood the shock with heroic courage. She was a woman of wonderful grit. I knew that her heart was broken. She was not one who easily revealed her feelings. I had never known her to weep in public. She didn't now, but in the lonely hours which followed in her room I knew that the long pent-up flood would break. Her love for Harding was one of great depth and tenderness.

I asked her to tell me how the end had come. And she did

so with a quiet restraint, more terrible to me than a paroxysm of weeping.

"We all thought that he was better. I had gotten the *Saturday Evening Post* at Seattle containing Mr. Blythe's wonderful article about him entitled, 'A Calm View of a Calm Man.' He had glanced at the story, but as his illness developed the reading was postponed. He seemed so well and so cheerful this evening that I began to read it again to him. I stopped for a moment, thinking that he had fallen asleep, when he looked at me and said:

" 'That's good, read some more.'

"I turned to the page again and as I did he threw his right arm over his head. I saw his face twitch. I leaped to my feet, bent over him. He was dead.

"It all happened in a second.

"I rushed to the hall and cried: 'Call Dr. Boone — get Dr. Boone — quick, please.' "

She paused and spoke in a low, strained voice:

"I'm not going to break down."

"I know you're not, but you must go to your room now, and rest."

Her nurse was in attendance all the time.

The five physicians who attended the President issued a statement saying that he had died from a stroke of apoplexy. That his death came after an apparent recovery from his late illness. But that it might have occurred at any time just as it had in the case of one of his sisters.

The official bulletin issued said:

The President died instantaneously and without warning while conversing with members of his family at 7:30 p.m. Death was apparently due to some brain evolvement, probably an apoplexy. During the day he had been free from discomfort

My dear General.

I wish to thank you most sincerely for your very gracious letter.

My plans are still somewhat indefinite, but I hope to be in Washington by January first, and

that I may then
have the opportunity
of seeing you both
very soon

I wish all the
blessings that the
coming New Year
can hold for you
and yours.

Sincerely yours

Florence Kling Harding

Sunday

and there was every justification for anticipating prompt recovery.

(Signed) C.E. Sawyer, M.D.
Ray Lyman Wilbur, M.D.
C.M. Cooper, M.D.
Hubert Work, M.D.
J.T. Boone, M.D.

There was no mystery of any kind about his death.

As the funeral train traveled across the continent, Mrs.
Harding frequently sent for me. My car was next to hers and
we had many talks. She bore up bravely but I knew the
struggle that went on beneath her restrained exterior. I knew
that she would not survive him many months.

Her lips would quiver as she talked to me with a forced
calm that was pitiful.

"You knew, of course," she sighed, "that he did too much.
It was a strain no human body could endure. I warned him."

"As I did again and again," I broke in, "begged him to take
a rest and not try to see everybody."

"But he was a man," she went on calmly, "who really
never took any care of himself. I couldn't get him to lie down
and take naps to break the strain. He wouldn't lie down in
the daytime and he was always late in turning out his reading
light at night. He thought he could stand anything and
everything. He gave, gave, gave to others and when the final
test came he had no reserves to draw on."

At every stop great crowds of people stood with uncovered
heads. At Cheyenne, as the train came to a stop, a terrific
storm burst, lighting flashed, thunder pealed, and the rain fell
in torrents.

I looked through the windows in amazement. Not a man,
woman, or child sought shelter. They stood in their tracks,
while a band of school children sang "Nearer, My God, to
Thee."

As we swept through the wide reach of Western farms I

saw more than one farmer stop, uncover his head, and stand immobile until the train passed.

They knew instinctively that a man of the people had passed.

Of all the obscene lies told about the Hardings, the one that cut me deepest and that I can never forgive in this world is the infamous story invented by Gaston B. Means on which he founded the book, *The Strange Death of President Harding*.

This unspeakable scoundrel left the readers plainly to infer that Mrs. Harding murdered her husband, an act she was no more capable of performing than she could have taken a knife and cut out the heart of her own babe in her arms. For she loved Harding not only with the strength of her womanhood, she loved him with the infinite tenderness of a mother as well.

Because of the outrage perpetrated on the American people, the injustice done the Hardings, the falsehoods that scoundrels and liars have told for money, I am glad that Mrs. Thacker, who wrote the book, *The Strange Death of President Harding*, had the courage to denounce and repudiate the volume as a tissue of falsehoods from beginning to end.

CHAPTER XXIII

The Coming of Calvin Coolidge

WHEN Mr. Coolidge came to Washington as Vice-President I found him both a practical politician and a statesman, a real man, honest, sincere, unaffected, strong. I loved the Yankee twang in his voice, the mysterious twinkle in his eye, and his clear-cut, vigorous personality.

I had a desire to see more of him, feel the temper of his mind and test his capacities as a political force.

Hitherto the Vice-Presidency had been considered a respectable tomb in which to bury alive a good man whom leaders wished to get rid of, or a bone to throw to a disappointed dog in the race for the Presidency.

There had been sharp clashes between the Executive and the Legislative branches of the government under Wilson. President Harding was desirous of healing this breach at the earliest possible moment, and we discussed the advisability of his personal appearance in the Senate to announce his Cabinet.

As I saw the President and Vice-President seated side by side in the Senate, it suddenly occurred to me, why shouldn't they sit together in the Cabinet and establish a real, vital contact between the Executive and Legislative branches of the government?

Mr. Coolidge, as the presiding officer of the Senate, would be in touch with the feeling on Capitol Hill. He could give to the Cabinet his impressions, the President and Cabinet could give him their views.

In this way the Vice-Presidency might be raised from the dead and made a vital part of our national government.

I made the suggestion to Harding that he invite Coolidge to sit at the other end of the Cabinet table and give us the benefit of his knowledge of legislation as it developed.

The Vice-President accepted the invitation and took his place as a regular attendant at Cabinet meetings.

And Mr. Coolidge more than fulfilled my predictions of usefulness. He was a wonderful listener. And when asked for his opinions gave them with a crisp Yankee vigor that was like a breeze from his native Vermont mountains. He never intruded his views unless asked for them.

When I sent to Mr. Coolidge the wire informing him of Harding's death and suggesting that he immediately take the oath as President, he was sworn in by his fine old father, Colonel John Coolidge, a magistrate and notary public.

Incidentally, when I read this report in the press, I had grave doubts of the legality of this oath.

Shortly afterwards, the opposition press raised the question.

Mr. Coolidge's father was not a little disturbed by the discussion and issued a statement in which he said:

"I am quite sure it was binding and proper. I would never have attempted such a thing if assurances had not been given by Washington officials that it was perfectly legal and all right for me to do it.

"I guess it's all right and holds good," he continued.

"Though I expect it may be administered again in a more formal manner at Washington. At least I hope so."

Mr. Coolidge was very fond of his father and not a little proud of the unique distinction fate had conferred on him in the opportunity to make his own son a President.

I easily read between the lines of Colonel Coolidge's statement that he was uneasy on that particular point, when he said:

"The only fear I had was that it would not be legal for me to administer an oath of such import to my own son. I was qualified to administer an oath to anyone I knew, but whether or not the Presidential oath could be administered by one's father was a question in my mind."

When I returned to Washington from the Marion funeral ceremonies I asked my Solicitor-General, James M. Beck, to examine the law and give me his opinion in a memorandum. He did and declared that he did not believe the oath administered was valid.

President Coolidge had not yet taken possession of the White House, out of deference to Mrs. Harding, who was packing her things preparatory to moving.

I called on the President and told him that in my opinion, as well as the opinion of the Solicitor-General, the oath administered by his father was not a valid one for a President.

He was very much surprised.

I read to him Beck's memorandum and advised that such a situation might cause trouble if some lawyer should raise this question as to one of his official acts.

Under the law only judges of a certain rank could administer this oath.

The new President moved into the White House and I sent for Judge A. A. Hoehling, Justice of the Supreme Court of the District of Columbia. He was in Atlantic City on his vacation.

He came the next day, met the President in the White House at four o'clock in the afternoon and administered the required oath.

I asked Judge Hoehling to say nothing about the matter and no publication of the fact was ever made.

Soon after the new President was settled in office I offered him my resignation as his Attorney-General.

He refused to consider it for a moment, arguing that my withdrawal would weaken his administration and give the impression that Harding's friends no longer supported him. He assured me of his appreciation of my work and would not listen to my plea.

I mentioned another man for his consideration as my successor, Mr. Wallace McCammant of Oregon, a warm friend of his. But Coolidge urged me to remain.

And so I made another blunder . . . I stayed!

Mr. Coolidge and I became close friends and I mapped out the schedule for his nomination at the next Republican Convention.

Watson of Indiana could give him trouble. He was beginning to feel his way into the campaign. I met Senator Butler of Massachusetts and Mr. Stearns, the President's close friend, in a conference at the Willard, and they were worried over Watson's attitude.

I seized the telephone and asked Watson, who had been my friend for years, to come down to the hotel.

Without ceremony I began:

"Your suspected candidacy against the President is embarrassing us all. I wish you would make a speech in the Senate and announce that you are for the President to succeed himself."

Watson frowned and then laughed.

"You go right after things, don't you?"

"That's the only way to do. Will you make the speech?"

"Yes," he answered squarely.

When I went out to the elevator on leaving the conference I found him in the lobby talking to a crowd of newspaper men. He had announced at once that he was not a candidate for the Presidency but was heartily in favor of Coolidge.

There was now no opposition and the field was clear. Word reached the President as to Watson's position and he thanked me cordially. Nothing occurred to mar our relations in any way until the Red leader of the Senate sprang his resolution for an investigation of my conduct as Attorney-General.

And in the beginning of this fight Coolidge stood by me sturdily — stood by me in fact until two months before the

Republican National Convention met and the clamor for my removal had become irresistible.

The pressure on the President was terrific.

My enemies laid siege to the White House. They kept Coolidge from his sleep. They waylaid him if he went for a walk. Men who had posed as my friends hurried to the President and told him that the only way to stop the crusade against the Party was to ask for my resignation.

The Red howlers in the Senate and their associates sent word to the White House that if I were turned out of the office of Attorney-General, they would swing their forces to the support of his Administration and vote for his program of constructive legislation. A thing they never intended to do. And they never did.

The Investigating Committee of the Senate under the direction of Wheeler, Brookhart, and Ashurst, ignoring the other members of the committee, made demands upon the Department of Justice for everything imaginable, reasonable and unreasonable. I instructed the entire personnel of the department to respond promptly and accurately. And they did. Reports and files were dispatched to the committee. But they were put aside untouched. The committee did not want dependable information. A racketeering expedition was on foot.

And then out of the past came ghosts to see Coolidge — ghosts who had scores to settle.

Two distinguished Senators of my own party called on Mr. Coolidge and asked for my head. Lodge of Massachusetts and George Wharton Pepper of Pennsylvania. When men lead in an attack, unjust and unreasonable, on a public official, it is always a safe bet that their patriotism has been stirred to action by a personal grudge of some kind.

In this case I had no difficulty in locating the trouble. Senator Lodge had become highly incensed against me because I had asked for the resignation of a friend of his in

Boston who was rattling around in the office of the United States District Attorney. He was utterly incompetent. The office was in hopeless confusion. And I refused to listen to Lodge's plea for personal friendship. I demanded of the President the removal of this incompetent officer. As a result the Senator from Massachusetts, who had secured his appointment, went after my scalp.

He was accompanied by Pepper of Pennsylvania, a man whom I had mortally offended by turning him down as a candidate for Solicitor-General in favor of James M. Beck.

In an unexpected turn of the political wheel, Pepper was now in the United States Senate and found himself in a position to get his revenge, and he did so without hesitation. Yet after he had gone to the White House and attacked me behind my back, he had a twinge of conscience that day and wrote me a typical letter:

UNITED STATES SENATE
Washington

February 20, 1924.

Dear Mr. Attorney-General:

I have just done as hard a thing as I have ever been called upon to do, and I want to play fair with you by telling you of it. As one of two Senators delegated for the purpose I went to the White House and told the President that, in the opinion of practically all the Republicans in this body, he ought to intimate to you that your resignation would be for the good of the party.

In speaking to him I expressed the opinion that it is not a question of justice or injustice — but a case in which you are on the wrong side of an issue in the mind of the public — and that when a man gets into that position, as was the case with Newberry, the rightness of his position is immaterial; nobody can save him — and he must go.

You have been considerate to me and to Mrs. Pepper. You have gained and will retain our friendship — if you care to have it. You have helped me and my state politically; and my contacts with your Department have proved its efficiency.

But I have felt that in this thing I must act impersonally; and something in me makes me want to tell you so. If you resign and face your accusers as a free man — free, I mean, from the complication of placing the President and the Party upon trial — you will, it seems to me, put yourself in the best position to refute whatever is charged against you. To resign and to insist on a hearing seems to me the part that a man of your spirit ought to play in the terrible drama which is now being enacted.

Yours sincerely,
(signed) George Wharton Pepper.

To The Hon. H. M. Daugherty,
  Attorney-General.

I answered immediately in a letter that received wide publicity and much editorial comment:

February 21, 1924.

Hon. George Wharton Pepper
United States Senate
Washington, D.C.

My dear Senator:

Please accept my thanks for your very kind note of yesterday. Your complimentary reference to my administration of the Department of Justice is, at this time, most highly appreciated. I note with amazement your suggestion that my interests are not to be decided on the basis of "justice or injustice," even though my honor, reputation and all that I hold dear in this world are at stake. Your expressions of personal regard are most gratifying and keenly appreciated, and I am sure that nothing will ever happen to change our friendly relations.

Coming now to the subject matter of your letter, I am interested in your statement that I am on the wrong side of an issue in the mind of the public. I assume you have in mind the resolution of Senator Wheeler and his speech on the floor of the Senate. You have then concluded that I am on the wrong side of an issue, without hearing, without evidence, and accepted as final the baseless, scandalous and defamatory charges of my political adversaries.

You further imply that the public has also concluded that I am on the wrong side of an issue without evidence, on ex-parte statements, and baseless charges of those same adversaries. You must realize, as I do, that these charges against me, made on the eve of a Presidential election, are made with other motives than that of injuring me. My destruction is but the accomplishment of one phase of the program which will be immediately followed by other and more drastic demands by these same adversaries.

My elimination, voluntarily or otherwise, will be a confession of the truth of all the baseless charges of our adversaries, and will justify them in claiming that we have thereby admitted their truth, and such admission will accomplish the ultimate end and purpose most gratifying to such adversaries.

I will never be a party to such a program.

You say that my fate does not involve a question of "justice or injustice." My dear Senator, my personal interests sink into insignificance when compared with the magnitude of the issues now involved. Is the preservation of the orderly processes of the law, and the preservation of constitutional rights, of no importance? Shall reputations be destroyed and public officials driven from office by clamor, insinuation and falsehood?

The basest criminal standing before the bar of justice has a right to trial by his peers. Am I to be denied a right granted to even the basest criminal?

If I am on the wrong side of the issue to which you refer, and it has already been concluded against me by the Senate, to which forum I have no access, without evidence of the truth or falsity of the charges against me; and if the public has likewise, as you claim, without evidence, concluded that I am on the wrong side of such issue, then nothing remains for me to do except to plead my cause before the bar of public opinion. And in order to do so, accept some of the numerous invitations to make addresses throughout the country and present before that great tribunal all of the facts bearing upon these matters. That tribunal, my dear Senator, by which we will all ultimately be tried — the one before whose verdict we must all bow with respectful humility.

Very sincerely yours,
(signed) H. M. Daugherty,
Attorney-General.

In the leading editorial of the *New York Times* the next day Pepper's proposal was held up to scorn. In referring to my reply the editor said:

The principles laid down in Mr. Daugherty's letter have an application running far beyond his office or his personality.

If the administration, if Congress, is to be intimidated in the discharge of its duty by fear of being on the wrong side, there is an end of responsible government.

This is no way to get good legislation. The timid majority which rushes away from what it thinks the wrong side, will speedily be forgotten.

The public men whom the people will in the end delight to honor are those who stand by what they believe to be right and just, and are willing to say with Cato that they even prefer the wrong side, if it squares with their innermost convictions and their sense of official duties.

The next assault on me reached its climax in a man of bigger brain and personality, and dealt me a vicious blow.

Senator Borah went to Mr. Coolidge and urged that he ask for my resignation. I was, of course, not surprised at this, remembering the weakness of human nature. I had helped kill his resolution for the recognition of Soviet Russia as a matter of principle. He had taken my act to heart as a personal attack. Nothing was further from my mind. I have always hated Soviet Russia. Borah knew this.

The thing I could not forgive in this assault was that he used his power as the most eloquent leader of the Senate to even a personal score. An act unworthy of a man capable of great leadership.

Hearing that Borah had gone to see the President I went to the White House on Sunday afternoon, talked with Mr. Coolidge, and asked him to send for the Senator. This he did. I went back to my apartment and returned about eight o'clock that evening. I wanted the President and Borah, who had arrived in the meantime, to have time to discuss the matter before I got there.

I said to the Senator:

"Let's lay all our cards on the table. The President is the one man who should know the facts."

For two hours we discussed the situation in all its phases. Borah was immovable in his position that I should resign.

"Not under fire!" I firmly declared. "Unless I am asked to do so by the President. It's his Cabinet after all, not the Senate's."

"I have never questioned your personal integrity," Borah countered. "But you have some bad men around you."

"Name one!" I challenged.

He couldn't, and I went on:

"The President boldly declared in a recent speech in New York that he could not be driven by public clamor to do an injustice to any man by a hue and cry and the mingling of innocent and guilty."

With feeling Borah flatly stated:

"The country's against you!"

"Because deceived by liars — "

"The press is against you," he added.

"The press has been deceived and I have never been heard in my own defense."

"Then put it another way," he said with final decision. "It makes no difference. The whole thing has been planned on the Hill. It can't be stopped. They have decreed that you must go."

By this time I was angry. I walked over to him and said:

"Well, if the whole thing has been framed, you may go back to the Senate and tell them to build their scaffold before the presiding officer's desk and I will walk upon it to-morrow at twelve o'clock. But I will never resign under fire unless the President himself requests it."

Mr. Coolidge had said very little. He was much distressed. I was sorry but it could not be helped.

When Senator Borah left, I turned to the President:

"If the time comes that you wish my resignation, just put

it in writing and give me your reasons. It should be a matter of record."

He walked with me to the door of his study, and as I said "Good night," he did a thing I shall never forget. It surprised me greatly.

He slipped an arm around me, looked into my eyes through a mist, and said:

"I'll never strike you a blow."

"I'll fight this out," I responded, "and I will win just as I won in the impeachment proceedings. I shall not ask you to do anything for me. But if I were to submit to this clamor and resign it would be a cowardly thing and all the charges against me would be accepted as true."

I left the White House gratified over the result of the encounter with Borah, and confident that the President would see me through the fight raging in the Senate. The Billingsgate with which it now echoed was unparalleled in our history.

Another reform needed in the Senate after it has been made a representative body is to deprive its members of the right to slander, vilify, and denounce an outside enemy on the floor of the Senate Chamber and not be called to account for it. This law of immunity is a coward's refuge. And no man who takes advantage of it to lie about a public official is worthy of its honors.

At a time like this, when a member of the President's Cabinet is being attacked, he should have the privilege of the floor of the Senate to make immediate reply to his slanderers. If he cannot do so, then he should quit. But under our present custom and laws no such privilege is granted.

There suddenly came a demand from the Senatorial Investigating Committee for access to the entire files of the Department of Justice.

Thousands of these files must be secret and confidential. I felt that it would be contrary to the best interests of the government and to my oath of office to accede to their demands.

I prepared a reply to the Committee in which I set forth my position. I took it to the White House, and advised the President that this was an effort to break down his administration.

When I read the letter to the President he objected to my saying that he had given his approval to my stand in the matter. I told him that if the paragraph was not in accordance with his wishes, I would leave it out, but the refusal and stipulation of terms would remain and be sent to the Committee within fifteen minutes. He suggested that he would like to think the matter over until the next day.

I said to him:

"Mr. President, I am accustomed to giving this Committee prompt service. They are not inclined to wait and I am not inclined to ask them to wait. I will eliminate the paragraph to which you object and send the letter to the Senate immediately." This I did.

I think now as I thought then that Wheeler and Brookhart were extremely anxious to secure and destroy the secret records of their visit to Soviet Russia.

The next morning as I neared the Department of Justice a Secret Service man riding with me called my attention to the White House car. He smiled about it and I remarked to him:

"This probably means something serious."

I went to my office on the seventh floor and one of my secretaries informed me that Mr. Slemp, secretary to President Coolidge, was waiting to see me. I told him to tell Slemp to bring it in. I was confident that continued pressure had finally shaken the President.

Slemp entered and handed me a letter.

"They got to the President at last?" I asked.

"Can't say anything under the circumstances," the secretary fenced. "I'm just bringing you the letter."

I opened and read it.

He had taken advantage of a technical point in my struggle with the Wheeler Committee to ask my resignation, and had assumed the amazing stand that an accused official cannot perform the duties of office and at the same time defend himself.

I saw at once the impossible position in which this letter would place the President. And on its publication the press was not slow to see it.

I said to Slemp:

"Please ask the President to withdraw this letter and send me a brief note asking for my resignation. This document will turn up to embarrass him in the future.

"Tell him I shall render him my best services to the last. That from this hour I will not transact a single piece of government business. But for his own protection and that of the government, I should hold title to the office in my name until my successor is selected. Give him my regards, please. I have no feeling against him."

I said this sincerely, notwithstanding the fact that he had struck me a blow that almost killed.

I have never believed that he intended to do so willingly. No man could have uttered the courageous words used by President Coolidge in his New York speech Feb. 12, 1924, and then retreated from that position, unless through an unprecedented pressure brought to bear upon him by Senatorial racketeers and others.

I waited until the next morning in order to give the President time to reconsider the form of his letter. I was committed to his support for the nomination and proposed to keep my promise, notwithstanding his broken promise to me. The letter was not changed. And before a Cabinet meeting on March 28, I submitted my formal resignation, accompanied by a second letter which I addressed to him as a private citizen. Their full text will be found in the Appendix.

Among other things I said in my letter of protest:

"Your suggestion that an attack upon a Cabinet officer disqualifies him for further official service is a dangerous doctrine. All the pretended charges against me are false. But whether true or false, if a member of the Cabinet is to be incapacitated or disqualified by the preferment of charges against him, no matter how malicious and groundless, and he is compelled to give up his responsible position and sacrifice his honor for the time being because of such attacks, no man in any official position is safe and the most honorable, upright, and efficient public servant could be swept from office and stable government destroyed by clamor."

I think Mr. Coolidge regretted his action at an early date.

He sent in the name of Charles W. Warren of Michigan, an able and competent man in every way, for the office of Attorney-General as my successor. And the gentlemen in the Senate who had determined now to usurp the functions of the Executive promptly rejected his choice and threw the nomination back into his face.

He sent in the name of Harlan F. Stone of New York, who was bitterly opposed, but finally confirmed.

After an attack in the Senate on Andrew W. Mellon, his Secretary of the Treasury, just two weeks after my resignation, Mr. Coolidge surprised Congress by a sharp rebuke of the brazen attempt of Capitol Hill to run the business of the White House.

The *New York Herald Tribune* backed him strongly:

"President Coolidge was fully justified in rebuking the Senate for the present orgy of government by investigation. Such government, attempted by the legislative branch, quickly disorganizes the public business. It becomes destructive and lawless."

The *New York Times* observed:

"President Coolidge has again been compelled to protest to

the Senate against insidious attempts to break down the constitutional rights of the Executive.

"As was pointed out at the time when Attorney-General Daugherty was forced to resign, the pretensions of the Senate, if unchecked, would place every member of the Cabinet in peril of his official life."

To permit the resignation of Secretary Denby was a tragic blunder on the part of the Administration. An innocent man was crucified in answer to the clamor of fools. And his forced retirement hastened his death if it did not directly cause it.

At the last Cabinet meeting he spoke to me affectionately: "Don't you resign. Fight it out. I could not very well help myself. You can."

But when the President of the United States asks a member of his Cabinet to resign there is no appeal.

A renewed effort was made by the Senatorial Committee to secure the files of the Department of Justice, yet no successor of mine has ever submitted to such demands. They stood their ground thereafter.

No formal report was ever made by the Senatorial Committee on my case. The purpose was achieved with my retirement. I have no complaint to make. I have no apology to make. When a man does his duty as he sees it, without taking orders from anybody, he need make no apology. But in asking for my resignation the President left a shadow on my name. He created the impression that he had found something wrong with the Department of Justice and the Attorney-General. This is not true. And to my dying day I shall expect Mr. Coolidge to make an explanation of his action.

Two weeks later, by his vigorous message, he brought the Senate to heel and the country sustained him. My tragedy was that he did not take the bit in his teeth and send this message earlier. If he had, in spite of slander, lies, and filthy gossip, the country would have sustained him then.

February 14, 1924.

My dear Mr. Attorney General:

Your favor has just been received, transmitting
the report of the activities of the War Transactions
Section of the Department of Justice, from July 1, 1922
to February 1, 1924. It reveals a tremendous amount of
work on the part of your Department, involving the
investigation of thousands of claims amounting to more
than $1,750,000,000 of the contract value. I note with
satisfaction that you have collected $4,500,000, and have
settlements pending which would aggregate about the same
amount.

The advisory council express their satisfaction
with the progress of the work, and the cooperation between
themselves and the Court of Claims.

This work has been much more extensive than
anything which I had anticipated. The report is clear
and explicit. I wish you would express to your staff my
appreciation for the work which they have done under your
direction.

Very truly yours,

Hon. Harry M. Daugherty,
Attorney General

If Harding Had Lived and Could Speak

IF WARREN HARDING had lived and completed the full eight years of the office to which he would have been called, he would rank in history as one of our great Presidents.

James M. Beck says of him:

"I question whether any President ever discharged his duty in a more unselfish spirit. His were the same qualities that enabled Lincoln to carry through his great effort to preserve the Union."

The record of achievement in the two years and four months of his administration compares more than favorably with the first two and a half years of any President the country ever had.

Calvin Coolidge clearly sums up this record:

"When he began his term our domestic situation was chaotic. Credit was over-extended. Commodity prices had fallen. Unemployment was extensive. Agriculture was prostrate. The national debt was enormous. War taxes prevailed. Government expenses were heavy. All kinds of business were in distress, foreign relations were precarious. We had rejected the treaty of Versailles, but we had not made peace. We were engaged in building the greatest navy in the world. The islands in the Pacific Ocean were a source of friction. Europe looked on us with suspicion.

"To deal with these problems President Harding summoned the Congress and kept it in session for nearly two years.

"The credit stringency was relieved.

"Our markets were protected by the enactment of a new tariff law.

"Labor was protected by restricting immigration.

"A budget system was established and rigid economy adopted.

"To discharge our obligations to ex-service men the Veterans' Bureau was organized.

"A new internal revenue law reduced taxes hundreds of millions of dollars annually.

"Supplies, war materials and Treasury assets were turned into cash to pay expenses and reduce debt.

"The shipping business and the railroad administration were put in the way of liquidation.

"Peace treaties were negotiated with those with whom we had been at war.

"A long-standing difference with Colombia was generously compromised.

"Diplomatic relations were resumed with Mexico.

"A Commission was appointed under the authority of Congress, to investigate a settlement of our foreign debts under which an agreement was speedily made with Great Britain.

"In spite of a universally genuine desire for peace, the world was engaging in a competitive race in armaments which was a source of expense and suspicion. To relieve humanity of this increasing menace President Harding called the historic Washington Conference on the limitation of armaments. A preliminary treaty was drafted for the present and future settlement of differences among the many international interests in the Pacific Ocean. The British and Japanese Alliance was terminated. The five great maritime powers then entered into a solemn covenant limiting most of the different types of warships in respect to number, tonnage and armaments.

"When that treaty was signed it marked an epoch in history.

"Under these benign influences, trade revived, and a better international understanding prevailed."

Contrast the record of these achievements with the first two and half years of one of our greatest Presidents — the immortal Abraham Lincoln.

The first period of Lincoln's administration was futile by comparison. The war was a failure. Defeat after defeat all but crushed the heart out of the North.

At the end of his first two and half years Lincoln was the most unpopular man who had ever occupied the Presidential chair. Now he belongs to the ages.

Charles Evans Hughes beautifully says of Harding:

"He was a man of the people, indulging no consciousness of superiority, incapable of arrogance. Nothing human was alien to him and he had the divine gift of sympathy. He wrought mightily for the prosperity of the Nation and for the peace of the world, but he clothed the exercise of power with the beautiful garments of gentleness.

"He gave his life for his country. No one can do more than that. He exhausted himself in service, a martyr in fidelity to the interests of the people for whom he labored with a passionate devotion."

If Harding had lived and could speak, not one of the three infamous books of slander could have been written about him. Only the silence of his death made them possible.

If Harding had lived we would not have had, in my judgment, the boom times of Coolidge, nor the depression of Hoover.

Harding had already gone on record by showing that big business was not going to be permitted to run amuck, and the Anti-Trust prosecutions had the master minds carefully watching their steps. But with his death, high finance seemed to feel that the brakes were off, and the orgy which followed led to the inevitable smash.

If Harding had lived there would have been no attempt to take this country into the League of Nations and all the troubles of the outside world by the back-door route. He wasn't a chum of any international banker and he wasn't an *efficiency expert* who would ignore the deep-seated desire of the American people to mix in the quarrels of the rest of the world as little as possible. He was just a plain, honest American who meant what he said when he urged his policy of getting the country back to normalcy. There must be few who would not welcome a return to the solid, good times of his administration after the boom and collapse under his successors.

And last of all, if Harding had lived, the Wheelers and Reds, the Roxies and Nans, and the Gaston Means', the Samuel Hopkins Adams', would not have stolen the stage. It is true, he came from a region where granite was not native. But he had some of it in his make-up and he would have stood by the friends who loyally and faithfully stood by him.

The age of the loose lip would never have been, and fear would never have been enthroned in the seats of the mighty.

If Harding had lived!

It is yet too early to see him in true, full perspective — a modern Abraham Lincoln whose name and fame will grow with time.

Appendix

THE FABLE OF THE "SMOKE-FILLED ROOM
AT THE BLACKSTONE HOTEL"

"WHY have more crazy stories been told about Harding's nomination than of any other man ever elected President?"

The question was asked me by a well-known muckraker in quest of scandal.

I lifted my shoulders slightly at his evident thirst for malodorous gossip but answered good-naturedly:

"I've often wondered myself. I think there are certainly two reasons for the growth of these tales. The unexpected and overwhelming vote by which he was elected — a seven million plurality that took our breath — followed but three years later by his untimely death.

"In his genial personality and appealing human traits he was in his day perhaps the most popular man who has ever held the office of President — "

"You think so?" my questioner drawled.

"At the time of his death," I went on, "he was not only liked by the rank and file of his triumphant party and its leaders as well, he was liked by his Democratic opponents.

"His renomination and election was a foregone conclusion. There was nowhere an opponent who would dare contest his position — "

"Mr. Hoover, perhaps?"

"He was a candidate, of course — had been since he decided to cast his first vote as an American citizen. But no leader in the councils of the party at this time took his ambition seriously. Had Harding lived, it would have amounted to nothing."

"You mean to say that at the time of his death there was not a cloud on the horizon of Harding's future?"

"Not the size of a man's hand!"

"Surely Fall — "

"Fall's resignation from the cabinet was in no way connected with the scandals which developed after Harding's death. And whatever the guilt or folly of his first Secretary of the Interior, no sane man in America ever connected the President with them.

"Fall resigned to accept a mission to Europe to organize a merger of the oil interests of the world, exactly as Hays resigned to accept a position from the Motion Picture Producers.

"Forbes' betrayal of his trust was a bitter personal grief to Harding but had no effect on the standing of the President of the United States, either with the people at large or his party. All skies were clear when he was stricken in San Francisco in the fatal summer of 1923. His renomination and triumphant reëlection were as sure as anything could be on earth."

The muckraker hurried to another task. I had proven a disappointment.

Perhaps the most interesting of all the fables about the nomination is one that Harding was selected by a powerful clique of the U.S. Senate who had hatched a plot to usurp the Government, Executive, Legislative, and Judicial.

This, at first sight, is a plausible tale. For several years the Senate had been trying to encroach on the powers of the President and the Supreme Court. A Senatorial legend had grown into a law in this august body that they, and they alone, constituted the real government of the United States.

They had the power to confirm or reject every nomination of the Executive. They had the power to approve or reject every treaty with a foreign Government. They could strangle every act of legislation. And a purpose to reconstitute the personnel of the Supreme

Court had been boldly proclaimed by one of their leaders.

During the Wilson administration their aggressions became on several occasions a national scandal.

The Senate of the U.S. probably murdered Woodrow Wilson.

This, I think, will be the final verdict of history. A conspiracy of Senators to name one of their number a puppet to execute their will might, therefore, be a possibility, in the light of the twelve preceding years.

The trouble with the thing is, it didn't work. And it couldn't work.

As manager of Harding's campaign for the Presidency I tried in vain to secure a compact body of his colleagues in the Senate to stand back of him. They wouldn't. They couldn't. They didn't.

And for simple reasons. They were all rivals of Harding. They regarded him as an amateur who had just arrived. They rated him as a man of inferior ability. Every leader among them dreamed that he might get the prize for himself. Therefore the Senate never backed Harding.

The U.S. Senate has never backed anybody for President. Every Senator is too busy looking in the mirror and adjusting his own hair to bother about another candidate.

A direct outgrowth of the Fable of the Senatorial Clique is the amazing yarn that has gained wide currency to the effect that Harding was chosen by a powerful group of United States Senators who met in the smoke-filled room of Colonel George Harvey at the Blackstone Hotel an hour before he was nominated.

Here is the substance of this astounding story as told in *The Saturday Evening Post* by Mr. Willis Fletcher Johnson.

One hour before the 10th and final ballot was cast in the Chicago Convention Mr. George Harvey called a meeting of the "inner Soviet Council" of the U.S. Senate in his room to decide on the next President.

This group of invincibles was made up of Brandegee, Lodge, Smoot, Watson, McCormick, Wadsworth, and Calder. They canvassed many names and found all wanting. Harvey gravely announced: "We must name somebody. We're here for that purpose. Neither Wood, Lowden, nor Johnson, the leaders, have a chance. They've fought each other to a standstill. How about Warren G. Harding of Ohio?"

"An idea!"

"Before the Convention on every ballot — "

"With a substantial number of votes."

"Is there any obstacle or handicap in his case?"

The verdict was unanimous:

"None!"

"Well, let's see how his name impresses the delegates."

"I'll go out and sound the various delegations," Senator Smoot volunteered.

He went and sounded them all! In a few minutes, mind you. A job that could not have been accomplished by a superman in less than twenty-four hours' hard work.

However, he *immediately* reported that New York was quite ready to vote for Harding. This remarkable performace with Senator James W. Wadsworth of New York sitting in the Solemn Council. Why didn't they consult Wadsworth? He was supposed to carry the New York delegation in his pocket. Was this a mistake? Had the Senator no knowledge of the mind of his delegation, that Smoot must go to their headquarters and find out where they stood? If Wadsworth controlled no votes, certainly no other Senator present could make such claim. This was a remarkable confession of impotence on the part of the August Assembly. And if they were there to decide on a candidate why consult mere delegates?

Mr. Smoot also reported in a few more minutes that most

the New Englanders from their six states were ready to vote for Harding.

"Was there any objection anywhere?" the Chairman asked. "None."

"Send in his name!" the Sanhedrim shouted in chorus.

This, mind you, was but one hour before the closing of the 10th and last ballot.

On the preceding 9th ballot, Harding had received 374 votes, overwhelming both Wood and Lowden, and leading the field. The state of New York had already cast 66 votes for him. And Smoot sounded them out to find how they felt toward him!

Harding in reality was nominated on the 9th ballot. We had the delegates sewed up and could have named him then, had we not delayed for a good reason.

Yet we are gravely informed that this Sanhedrim of Solemn Senators decided to "send in his name to the Convention!" Send in the name of a man who had already leaped into the lead on the ballot before and whose manager, with the delegates pledged, and names in his pocket, only awaited the roll call to put Harding over in an overwhelming triumph!

But we must hold our breath a little longer. The Sanhedrim must have assurances from Harding himself before they would "send in his name to the Convention!"

And now comes the dramatic climax. They summon the poor man whom they had selected for the Presidency to appear before them and purge himself of all error and all taint.

"One moment, gentlemen," cries Col. Harvey, "let us first speak with Senator Harding himself."

They call Harding.

The time is short. The Convention is in session. Within an hour the 10th ballot will be recorded. They are sitting in a smoke-filled room at the Blackstone Hotel.

Harding suddenly appears before the August Assembly who hold his fate in their hands. His manager has already informed him that his 374 votes on the ninth ballot would grow to 700 on the next roll call. He only needed 501 in all.

Still this man, already the victor, humbly appears before his masters, suddenly, in the twinkling of an eye.

I must quote the exact language of the author of this miraculous story. It's too good to lose even the dot of an eye.

"Senator Harding," Harvey gravely informs the assembly, "we are about to present your name to the Convention."

The next President of the U.S. bowed.

"But first, Senator Harding," said Harvey with impressive solemnity, "I wish you to assure these gentlemen and myself, upon your sacred honor and before your God, that you know of no reason, arising out of anything in your past life, why you should not stand with confidence before the American people as a candidate for the highest office within their gift?"

Harding was profoundly moved.

God knows he should have been!

"He was silent for a moment," goes on the tale. "And then he said:

" 'Gentlemen, I should like to be alone for a little while with my God.' "

The Lord was right outside and Harding promised to be back in a minute!

"He went into the next room and closed the door. For nearly fifteen minutes he remained there, and then returned still deeply moved, yet calm and confident.

" 'Gentlemen,' he said firmly, 'there is no such reason!' "

Harding retired. And the Sanhedrim went into executive session.

"Senators!" Colonel Harvey gravely announced:

"There is no popular explosion for Harding. There is little spontaneity. We will nominate him because there is nothing against him. The weather is warm. The delegates are tired. We all want to go home. I had a hunch at a dinner party more than a year ago that this man would be your nominee for the Presidency, wrote his name on a piece of paper and sealed it in an envelope. The matter is settled. Send in the name of Warren Gamaliel Harding!"

Mr. Johnson informs us *positively* that *within an hour* after that decision he was nominated by the Convention for the Presidency of the United States!

The meeting of the Sanhedrim of Solemn Senators therefore adjourned at 5:23 on Saturday afternoon, for Harding was nominated at 6:23.

Observe carefully the date and the hour of this remarkable chronicle. Of all the asinine stories ever concocted this is the limit.

There were doubtless many meetings in Mr. Harvey's room. He was a genial host. And no doubt many fine cigars contributed to the smoke.

A group of worthy Senators may have thought they were sending Harding's name in to the Convention. As a matter of fact they had been informed, by some one who knew, that Harding would be nominated on the next ballot, and looking through a fog of smoke saw themselves as the Convention. Such miracles have happened before. And they will be repeated again.

I was Harding's campaign manager. I knew with practical certainty how many votes he would receive on every ballot before it was cast. I never saw or spoke to Mr. Harvey during the Convention. I never heard of such a meeting until long after the nomination.

The meeting was a myth.

The Senators assembled couldn't have changed fifty votes if they had tried.

The only Senator I consulted on the day of the nomination was Penrose of Pennsylvania, with whom I talked over the long distance telephone, and he placed in my hands the entire vote of Pennsylvania to be cast for Harding when I saw fit to use it. And I did on the 10th ballot.

The nomination of Colonel Harvey as Ambassador to the Court of St. James doubtless gave rise to this fable.

He was appointed Ambassador, *not* for anything he did at Chicago. He received the reward for his merciless attacks on President Wilson which resulted in breaking the backbone of the Democratic Party long before the Convention had assembled.

The simple truth as related in this volume of how Harding was placed in the race and nominated at Chicago is far more dramatic than any of the fables.

LETTER OF U.S. SPECIAL COUNSEL, PROSECUTING A.B. FALL, EXONERATING ATTORNEY-GENERAL HARRY M. DAUGHERTY

ATLEE POMERENE
1857 Union Trust Building
Cleveland, Ohio

July 22, 1931.

Honorable Paul Howland
Engineers Building,
Cleveland, Ohio.

DEAR MR. HOWLAND:

I have your favor of the 18th inst. relative to the charges current to the effect that former Attorney-General Harry M. Daugherty was involved in the Naval Petroleum Reserve leases and contracts, which have been the subject of litigation under joint resolution passed by Congress of the United States.

You say in your letter:

"I hope that your investigation and knowledge on this subject will warrant you in advising me that the evidence in the entire oil fraud litigation does not involve Harry M.

Daugherty as Attorney-General of the United States, or as an individual, in the slightest degree."

In reply I beg to say that on or about May 8, 1921, the Secretary of the Navy, Mr. Edwin Denby, wrote a letter to former Attorney-General Harry M. Daugherty, calling his attention to certain mineral claims outstanding on small portions of Reserve No. 1. These claims were held by the previous Secretary of the Interior, John Barton Payne, to be without any legal merit and he so reported to President Wilson. Secretary Denby asked the Attorney-General in his letter for his view as to the legality of these claims and sent a copy of this letter to Secretary Fall. After receiving it, Secretary Fall, on May 11, 1921, wrote Attorney-General Daugherty in substance that he was not contending that these claims had any legal validity, but claimed that there were certain equities in favor of the claimants and suggested that it was a question solely for the discretion of the President and that any opinion from the Attorney-General as to their legality would seem unnecessary. We never found any reply to Mr. Fall's letter.

This correspondence occurred prior to the making of the leases and contracts which were the subject of attack.

I believe that in some of the hearings some reference was made to the effect that the subject of the oil leases was discussed in a Cabinet meeting. This was denied by Mr. Daugherty and later the papers reported the former Secretary of State, Honorable Charles Evans Hughes, now Chief Justice, as having said in substance that these leases and contracts were never discussed in a Cabinet meeting, and if referred to at all it was only incidentally.

Mr. Daugherty testified, in one of the cases, that his opinion as to the legality of these leases and contracts was never asked, either in the Cabinet meetings or elsewhere; that if his opinion had been asked he would have required the question to be submitted to him in writing. This, he said, was never done and he never gave an opinion, orally or in writing, concerning their legality. Mr. Daugherty's statement in this behalf is corroborated by the following facts:

The Teapot Dome Lease was dated April 7, 1922. The contract with the Pan-American Petroleum and Transport Company providing for the building of the 1,500,000 barrels of tankage at Hawaii, filling it with fuel oil, and the payment therefor by an exchange of crude royalty oil, was dated April 25, 1922. This contract gave the Pan-American Petroleum and Transport Company a preferential right to a lease to all oil lands owned by the government in Reserve No. 1, aggregating something more than 30,000 acres. Later, on December 11, 1922, a further contract was made with the Pan-American Petroleum and Transport Company for the building of additional storage, 2,700,000 barrels, the same to be filled with fuel oil, and all to be paid for by an exchange of crude royalty oil, belonging to the government. On December 1, 1922, a lease was made to the Pan-American Petroleum Company of all government land in Reserve No. 1 in accordance with the preferential right contained in the contract of April 25, 1922, and without any competition whatever.

There were only three bids for the contract of April 25, 1922. One, the Standard Oil Company, which provided only for the exchange of fuel oil for crude royalty oil to fill the tanks and contained no provision for the construction of tankage. Another, a bid by Associated Oil Company, which provided for the required tankage and the filling of it with fuel oil to be paid for by crude royalty oil, but expressly provided that it was subject to the approval of Congress. A third bid by the Pan-American Petroleum and Transport Company contained two proposals, "A" and "B." Proposal "A" was in strict accordance with the specifications. Proposal "B" was for a less number of barrels of crude oil, but provided that the bid was made as a whole and if it was accepted by the government it would carry with it a preferential right to a lease of the entire holdings of the government in Reserve No. 1.

The government officials, including Director of Mines H. Foster Bain, were advised by the General Counsel, representing the Standard Oil Company, that such a proposal would be illegal. Mr. Weil, representing the Associated Oil Company, also expressed very grave doubt as to the legality of the proposed contracts. There was therefore only one regular bid for the tankage and fuel oil to be paid for by crude royalty oil. That bid was proposal "A" of the Pan-American Petroleum and Transport Company. Proposal "B" containing the preferential right to a lease on the whole of the reserve was accepted by Fall and Denby. No opportunity was given to any other bidders to secure a preferential right to such lease, and in fact the other bidders did not know that such a preferential right would figure in the leasing until the bids were opened.

With this information and knowledge before him H. Foster Bain, the Director of the Bureau of Mines, then in San Francisco, wrote a letter on May 12, 1922, to Albert B. Fall, at Three Rivers, New Mexico, in which he expressed surprise at the technical attitude adopted by the Standard Oil Company and General Petroleum Company with respect to these leases, called Fall's attention to the fact that Mr. Sutro, counsel for the Standard Oil Company, and Mr. Weil, counsel for the General Petroleum Company, were doubtful as to the right of the Department to make the exchange contract, meaning thereby an exchange of crude royalty oil for the tankage and the fuel oil, and added this:

"There is, however, another phase of it. None of us want Mr. Denby to get into trouble and I take it we will want to do anything we can to make it easy for him.****

"Out of all this has come the suggestion repeatedly that the opinion of the Attorney-General be obtained as to the legality of the contract. I realize the objections to asking such an opinion, but I have thought it proper to let you know the difficulties that are being raised here so you might consider the matter and decide as to whether you might not properly ask the Attorney-General to put in writing what I have understood was his informal and verbal expression of opinion favorable to the action the Department had taken. I am not certain that Mr. Doheny cares, but Mr. Cotter (Mr. Doheny's personal counsel) will see him to-morrow and if it does seem to them important I am giving Mr. Cotter this letter to show you so that you may know what I have found out here."

The testimony shows that this letter was delivered by Cotter to Doheny, read by him, and he in substance said he did not care anything about it as he had the opinion of his own attorneys as to the validity of the transaction. This letter was apparently never delivered to Fall.

Director Bain also testified that Fall knew of the Sutro opinion, which was dated January 27, 1922, to the effect that the government had no authority to build the storage tanks, fill them with fuel oil, and pay for same by an exchange of crude royalty oil. Director Bain also testified that Fall felt "there was no necessity of getting the opinion of the Attorney-General."

The question as to the legal authority of the government to enter into a contract to build tankage, fill it with fuel oil, and pay for the tankage and fuel oil by an exchange of crude royalty oil held by the government, was involved in both the Pan-American Petroleum and Transport Company case and the Teapot Dome case. The opinions of Sutro and others as to the illegality of such a contract were before the Supreme Court in the Mammoth Oil Company or Teapot Dome case.

Mr. Justice Butler, in the case of Mammoth Oil Company v. United States, 275 U.S. 46, says:

"In January, 1922, Fall was informed that counsel for certain oil companies had held that the use of royalty oil to pay for fuel depots was not authorized by law. He expressed fear that, because of the 'question as to the legality of bartering of royalty oil for storage, people would not bid for this contract and lease in California.' But he refused to submit the question to the Attorney-General; and, as a reason for not taking such legal advice, said that 'the chances were not at least even, or at least there was some chance that an adverse opinion would be given and if the Attorney-General signed such an opinion he (Fall) would be stopped from doing anything.' "

The testimony just referred to, and the opinion of Mr. Justice Butler, make it clear that Mr. Daugherty's opinion was not asked as to the legality of such contracts and leases.

The Solicitor of the Interior Department, Edwin S. Booth, also testified that he was never consulted as to their legality.

There is no evidence in the record of any of the oil leases or contracts.

I hold no brief for Mr. Daugherty. Your letter of July 18 is written by you as his attorney. It merits a frank answer. I give it as above written.

> Very sincerely,
> (signed) Atlee Pomerene.

LETTERS BETWEEN PRESIDENT COOLIDGE AND ATTORNEY-GENERAL DAUGHERTY ON HIS RESIGNATION

THE WHITE HOUSE
Washington

Mar. 27, 1924

My dear Mr. Attorney-General:

Since my conference with you, I have examined the proposed reply you suggest making to the demand that you furnish the Committee investigating the Department of Justice with the files from that Department, relating to litigation and to the Bureau of Investigation. You represent to me and to the Committee in your letter that it would not be compatible with the public interest to comply with the demand, and wish to conclude your letter with a statement that I approve that position. Certainly I approve the well-established principle that departments should not give out information or documents, for such a course would be detrimental to the public interests, and this principle is always peculiarly applicable to your Department, which has such an intimate relation to the administration of justice. But you will readily perceive that I am unable to form an independent judgment in this instance without a long and intricate investigation of voluminous papers, which I cannot personally make, and so I should be compelled to follow the usual practice in such cases and rely upon your advice as Attorney-General and head of the Department of Justice.

But you will see at once that the Committee is investigating your personal conduct, and hence you have become an interested party, and the Committee wants these papers because of a claim that they disclose your personal conduct of the Department. Assuming that the request of the Committee is appropriately limited to the designated files, still the question will always be the same. In view of the fact that the inquiry relates to your personal conduct, you are not in a position to give to me or the Committee what would be disinterested advice as to the public interest.

You have a personal interest in this investigation which is being made of the conduct of yourself and your office, which may be in conflict with your official interests as Attorney-General.

I am not questioning your fairness or integrity. I am merely reciting the fact that you are placed in two positions, one your personal interest, the other your office of Attorney-General, which may be in conflict. How can I satisfy a request for action in matters of this nature on the ground that you, as Attorney-General, advise against it, when you as the individual against whom the inquiry is directed necessarily have a personal interest in it? I do not see how you can be acting for yourself in your own defense in this matter, and at the same time and on the same question acting as my adviser as Attorney-General.

These two positions are incompatible, and cannot be reconciled. I am sure you will see that it is necessary for me to have the advice of a disinterested Attorney-General, in order that I may discharge the duties of my office in this and other matters.

I feel certain that you will know how deeply I regret that the situation has arisen. It only illustrates the difficulties which are certain to recur with ever-increasing embarrassment, and your inability to perform satisfactorily the duties of Attorney-General under the present conditions.

You will readily understand that it is not now my intention to prejudge the issues which remain to be developed in this investigation. I recognize that you are entitled to a full and fair hearing. But as there is no way by which you can divest yourself of the interest you have personally in the investigation, I can see no way but for you to retire as Attorney-General, and I am therefore compelled to request your resignation.

(signed) Calvin Coolidge.

RESIGNATION OF ATTORNEY-GENERAL, WITH HIS LETTER TO PRESIDENT COOLIDGE

March 28, 1924.

My dear Mr. President:

I hereby acknowledge receipt of your letter of March 27, by the hand of your secretary, requesting my resignation as Attorney-General of the United States.

Solely out of deference to your request and in compliance

therewith, I tender my resignation. While you do not state when you desire my resignation to become effective, I most respectfully request that it become effective forthwith. Yours very truly,

(signed) H.M. Daugherty,
Attorney-General.

The ex-Attorney-General then wrote:

My dear Mr. President: Under separate cover I have just handed you my formal resignation as Attorney-General of the United States, to take effect forthwith. Now that I am no longer a member of your cabinet, I feel constrained, as a private citizen, in all kindness, to call certain matters to your attention.

Your request, Mr. President, for my resignation, is based on grounds that seem to me untenable. As you will perhaps remember, I did not intend to seek your advice with regard to compliance with the demands of the Senate committee for indiscriminate delivery of the confidential files of the Department of Justice, or parts thereof. As I explained to you, my duty was clear, for I had frequently been called upon to determine this question. My answer was ready, as I informed you, and I furnished you a copy thereof.

My sole purpose in taking the matter up with you was to let you know the position I was compelled to take in the interest of the public business and for the protection of the government, that you might be in a position to advise other departments, if similar requests were made, what course they should pursue.

Your suggestion that I cannot function as Attorney-General and defend myself against the charges at the same time, I believe, is hardly warranted by the facts. You know I have employed counsel, at my own expense, to take the responsibility of representing me at the hearings before the Senate committee, in order that I could devote my time to the public business, which I have been doing continuously.

Those employed in the department have given no time belonging to the government to this so-called investigation, except to furnish data required by the various congressional committees. The business of the department is at its peak in efficiency and accomplishment, and I am prepared to demonstrate this fact before any tribunal if opportunity is offered.

Your suggestion that an attack upon a cabinet officer disqualifies him for further official service is a dangerous doctrine. Mr. President, all the pretended charges against me are false. But, whether true or false, if a member of the Cabinet is to be incapacitated or disqualified by the preferment of charges against him, no matter how malicious and groundless, and he is compelled to give up his responsible position and sacrifice his honor for the time being because of such attacks, no man in any official position is safe, and the most honorable, upright, and efficient public servants could be swept from office and stable government destroyed by clamor.

I have often advised you that my elimination is part of the program now being carried on. The origin of the persistent and vindictive attempt to discredit me as Attorney-General is well known. It principally proceeds from two sources: the powerful individuals and organizations, who resent my successful action, in conformity with my sworn duty to save this country from violence and anarchy during an industrial crisis far more serious than the general public has ever known; second, from those equally powerful individuals and organizations guilty of graft upon the government during the World War while the youth of our land was making the supreme sacrifice for the nation.

I have to the best of my ability discharged my sworn duty

to prosecute all such individuals and organizations, but the task has been beset with peculiar difficulties by reason of the fact that the official record in most of these cases was made up by men supposedly representing the government in these transactions who were either knowingly or stupidly parties to the crime.

This partnership of the rioter and the war profiteer has ceaselessly sought to break down the faith of the American people in me and the Department of Justice.

In the high court of impeachment their attempt to fasten guilt upon me collapsed in disgrace to its originators, and they did not dare to appeal again to the consitutional court.

In the low courts of scandal, gossip, rumor, and innuendo, to which appeal is now made, it will have no better success with the people of this country who read and think and believe in justice and the square deal, but coupled with threats of similar treatment of other public men, it has impressed politicians who think everything of personal and party expediency, and nothing of the principle involved, with the necessity of offering me as a sacrifice to propitiate the vengeful interests which seek my destruction.

I cannot escape the conviction, Mr. President, that your request for my resignation is also most untimely. It comes at a time when the truth is banishing falsehood from the public mind, even though I have not as yet had an opportunity to place upon the witness stand before the Senate committee a single witness in my defense, or in explanation or rebuttal of the whispered and gossipy charge against me.

No better evidence of the failure to substantiate charges of wrongful action on my part could be offered than the character of the proceedings by the Senate committee engaged in conducting the present inquiry. If my accusers had believed me guilty, they would have been scrupulously careful to select as members of the tribunal men of judicial character with open minds, in order that an unprejudiced verdict might be rendered. The choice, as majority members of this committee, of men, some of whom have openly, bitterly and falsely assailed me under Senatorial immunity, and who have also assailed my administration of the Department of Justice; the designation of a member of this court as prosecutor who is the responsible author of the resolution against me; the refusal to apply to the proceedings any rule of evidence to grant me the customary immediate right of cross-examination and early opportunity of rebuttal; and, above all, the character of the witnesses, including blackmailers, bootleggers, confessed corruptionists, and discharged and discredited government employees, not one of whom has given testimony that would be admitted as evidence in the most loosely conducted court of the land; all this proves to fair-minded men that in the absence of competent and creditable testimony, the elements in control of this committee seek to convict by immaterial and malicious gossip retailed by irresponsible witnesses. In such a tribunal, by such methods, and out of the mouths of such witnesses, an honest man could be convicted of any crime.

I am aware, Mr. President, that the suggestion has been made to you that my retirement from the Cabinet would serve the ends of party expediency. Had I believed this, I would have retired when this contention was first raised.

Twice since you became President, and when I could have done so without criticism, I have offered to retire from your Cabinet, and you have in each instance requested me to remain, because, as you were kind enough to say, of your satisfaction with the splendid accomplishments of the Department of Justice under my administration.

After this recent attack and while under fire, I stood my ground because I believed that cowardice and surrender of principle are never expedient and that every sacrifice of justice to clamor is followed by demand for still greater sacrifices.

From the beginning, this attack upon me has in fact been an attack upon the administration and the Republican Party, which my assailants are seeking to discredit for partisan purposes. Since the assault upon me began, the purpose to attack every administration official of prominence, including the President himself, has been publicly revealed.

The American people confront a crisis in national affairs equal in gravity to any we have faced in all our history. Is this to remain a government of law and order, of constitutional procedure, with its guarantees of individual rights, and its safeguards for equal justice to the highest and the humblest, or is it to become a government by slander, by terrorism and by fear?

In the battle for my rights as an official and a citizen, the rights of every citizen of this republic are involved, for who of all our millions of people knows but that he may be the next to become the object of unjust accusations obtained by lawless inquisition?

In conclusion, Mr. President, please accept my thanks for your statement that you do not question my fairness or integrity and believe me, Yours very truly,

(signed) H.M. Daugherty.

JUDGE WILKERSON'S ORDER OF PRELIMINARY INJUNCTION IN THE RAILWAY STRIKE

It is ordered, adjudged and decreed, as follows, viz.

(1) That said defendants, and each of them, and each and all of their officers, attorneys, servants, agents, associates, members, employees, and all persons acting in aid of or in conjunction with them, be temporarily restrained and enjoined from —

(a) In any manner interfering with, hindering or obstructing said railway companies, or any of them, their officers, agents, servants or employees in the operation of their respective railroads and systems of transportation or the performance of their public duties and obligations in the transportation of passengers and property in interstate commerce and the carriage of the mails, and from in any manner interfering with, hindering or obstructing the officers, agents, servants or employees of said railway companies, or any of them, engaged in the construction, inspection, repair, operation or use of trains, locomotives, cars, or other equipment of said railway companies, or any of them, and from preventing or attempting to prevent any person or persons from freely entering into or continuing in the employment of said railway companies, or any of them, for the construction, inspection, repair, operation or use of locomotives, cars, rolling stock, or other equipment;

(b) In any manner conspiring, combining, confederating, agreeing and arranging with each other or with any other person or persons, organizations or associations to injure or interfere with or hinder said railway companies, or any of them, in the conduct of their lawful business of transportation of passengers and property in interstate commerce and the carriage of the mails; or to injure, interfere with, hinder or annoy any officer or employee of said railway companies, or any of them, in connection with the performance of their duties as such officers or employees, or while going to or returning from the premises of said railway companies in connection with their said employment, or at any time or place, by displays of force or numbers, the making of threats, intimidation, acts of violence, opprobrious epithets, jeers, suggestions of danger, taunts, entreaties, or other unlawful acts or conduct, or to injure, interfere with, hinder, or annoy by any such acts any persons or person desirous of, contemplating or intending to enter into such employment;

(c) Loitering or being unnecessarily in the vicinity of the points and places of ingress or egress of the employees of said railway companies, or any of them, to and from such premises in connection with their said employment for the purpose of doing any of the things herein prohibited; or aiding, abetting, directing or encouraging any person or persons, organization, or association, by letters, telegrams, telephone, word of mouth, or otherwise, to do any of the acts heretofore described in this and preceding paragraphs; trespassing, entering or going upon the premises of the said railway companies, or any of them, at any place or in the vicinity of any place where the employees of said companies, or any of them, are engaged in constructing, inspecting, overhauling, or repairing locomotives, cars, or other equipment, or where such employees customarily perform such duties or at any other place on the premises of said railway companies, or any of them, except where the public generally are invited to come to transact business with said railway companies as common carriers of passengers and property in interstate commerce;

(d) Inducing or attempting to induce with intent to further said conspiracy by the use of threats, violent or abusive language, opprobrious epithets, physical violence or threats thereof, intimidation, displays of force or numbers, jeers, entreaties, argument, persuasion, reward, or otherwise, any person or persons to abandon the employment of said railway companies, or any of them. or to refrain from entering such employment;

(e) Engaging, directing or procuring others to engage in the practice commonly known as picketing, that is to say, assembling or causing to be assembled numbers of the members of said Federated Shop Crafts, or others in sympathy with them, in the vicinity of where the employees of said railway companies, or any of them, are required to work and perform their duties, or at or near the places of ingress or egress, or along the ways traveled by said employees thereto or therefrom, and by threats, persuasion, jeers, violent or abusive language, violence or threats of violence, taunts, entreaties or argument, or by any similar acts preventing or attempting to prevent any of the employees of said railway companies, or any of them, from entering upon or continuing in their duties as such employees, or so preventing or attempting to prevent, any other person or persons from entering or continuing in the employment of said railway companies, or any of them; and aiding, abetting, ordering, assisting, directing, or encouraging in any way any person or persons in the commission of any of said acts;

(f) Congregating or maintaining, or directing, aiding, or encouraging the congregating or maintaining upon, at or near any of the yards, shops, depots, terminals, tracks, waylands, roadbeds, or premises of said railway companies, or any of them, of any guards, pickets, or persons to perform any act of guarding, picketing, or patrolling any such yards, shops, depots, terminals or other premises of said railway companies, or any of them; or in any manner threatening or intimidating, by suggestions of danger or personal violence towards any servant or employee of said railway companies, or any of them, or towards persons contemplating the entering of their employment; or aiding, encouraging, directing, or causing any other person or persons so to do;

(g) Doing or causing, or in any manner conspiring, combining, directing, commanding or encouraging the doing or causing the doing by any person or persons of any injury or bodily harm to any of the servants, agents or employees of said railway companies, or any of them; going singly or collectively to the home, abode, or place of residence of any employee of the said railway companies, or any of them, for the purpose of intimidating, threatening, or coercing such employee or member of his family, or in any manner by violence or threats of violence, intimidation, opprobrious epithets, persuasion, or other acts of like character, directed towards any said employee or member of his family, for the purpose of inducing or attempting to induce such employee to refuse to perform his duties as an employee of said railway companies, or any of them; or so attempting to prevent any person or persons from entering the employ of any of said railway companies, or aiding, encouraging, directing, commanding or causing any person or persons so to do;

(h) In any manner directly or indirectly hindering, obstructing, or impeding the operation of any train or trains of said railway companies, or any of them, in the movement and transportation of passengers and property in interstate commerce or in the carriage of the United States mails, or in the performance of any other duty as common carriers, or aiding, abetting, causing, encouraging or directing any person or persons, association or organization to do or cause to be done any of the matters or things aforesaid;

(i) In any manner, with intent to further said conspiracy, by letters, printed or other circulars, telegrams, telephones, word of mouth, oral persuasion, or communication, or through interviews published in newspapers, or other similar acts, encouraging, directing or commanding any person, whether a member of any or either of said labor organizations or associations defendants herein, to abandon the employment of said railway companies, or any of them, or to refrain from entering the service of said railway companies, or any of them;

(2) The said defendants J. F. McGrath, James W. Kline, and J. A. Franklin, and each of them, as officers as aforesaid and as individuals, be restrained and enjoined from —

(a) Issuing any instructions, or making any requests, public statements or communications heretofore enjoined and restrained in this decree to any defendant herein, or to any officer or member of any said labor organizations constituting the said Federated Shop Crafts, or to any officer or member of any system federation thereof, with intent to further said conspiracy, for the purpose of inducing or calculated to induce any such officer or member, or any other persons whomsoever, to do or say anything intended or calculated to cause any employee of said railway companies, or any of them, to abandon the employment thereof, or any persons to refrain from entering the employment thereof to aid in the movement and transportation of passengers and property in interstate commerce and the carriage of the mails;

(b) Using, or causing to be used, or consenting to the use of any of the funds or moneys of said labor organizations in aid of or to promote or encourage the doing of any of the matters or things hereinbefore restrained and enjoined.

But nothing herein contained shall be construed to prohibit the use of the funds or moneys of any of said labor organizations for any lawful purpose, and nothing contained in this order shall be construed to prohibit the expression of an opinion or argument not intended to aid or encourage the doing of any of the acts hereinbefore enjoined, or not calculated to maintain or prolong a conspiracy to restrain interstate commerce or the transportation of the mails.

Enter:

JAMES H. WILKERSON,
United States District Judge.

10 o'clock A.M.
October 5, 1922.

JUDGES APPOINTED ON RECOMMENDATION OF HARRY M. DAUGHERTY, ATTORNEY-GENERAL

William Howard Taft, Chief Justice, U.S. Supreme Court.
George Sutherland, Associate Justice, U.S. Supreme Court.
Pierce Butler, Associate Justice, U.S. Supreme Court.
Edward Sanford, Associate Justice, U.S. Supreme Court.

Marion De Vries, President Judge, Ct. of Customs & Patent Appeals.

Oscar E. Bland, Associate Judge Ct. of Customs & Patent Appeals.

Chas. S. Hatfield, Associate Judge, Ct. of Customs & Patent Appeals.

Julius M. Mayer, U.S. Circuit Judge, 2nd Circuit.

Edmund Waddill, Jr., U.S. Circuit Judge, 4th Circuit.

John C. Rose, U.S. Circuit Judge, 4th Circuit.

Robert E. Lewis, U.S. Circuit Judge, 8th Circuit.

Wm. S. Kenyon, U.S. Circuit Judge, 8th Circuit.

Frank H. Rudkin, U.S. Circuit Judge, 8th Circuit.

John Foster Symes, U.S. District Judge, Colorado.

F. C. Jacobs, U.S. District Judge, Arizona.

Wm R. Barrett, U.S. District Judge, Georgia, Southern.

Lake Jones, U.S. District Judge, Florida, Southern.

James H. Wilkerson, U.S. District Judge, Illinois, Northern.

Adam C. Cliffe, U.S. District Judge, Illinois, Northern.

Walter C. Lindley, U.S. District Judge, Illinois, Eastern.

George C. Scott, U.S. District Judge, Iowa, Northern.

Charles H. Moorman, U.S. District Judge, Kentucky, Western.

John A. Peters, U.S. District Judge, Maine.

Frank Kerrigan, U.S. District Judge, Calif., Northern.

J.S. Partridge, U.S. District Judge, Calif., Southern.

W. P. James, U.S. District Judge, Calif., Southern.

Paul J. McCormick, U.S. District, Calif., Southern.

Morris A. Soper, U.S. District Judge, Maryland.

James A. Lowell, U.S. District Judge, Mass.

E. H. Brewster, U.S. District Judge, Mass.

Charles C. Simons, U.S. District Judge, Michigan, Eastern.

George F. Morris, U.S. District Judge, N.H.

Wm. N. Runya, U.S. District Judge, New Jersey.

Orie L. Phillips, U.S. District Judge, New Mexico.

Andrew Miller, U.S. District Judge, North Dakota.

Paul Jones, U.S. District Judge, Ohio Northern.

Smith Hickenlooper, U.S. District Judge, Ohio Southern.
Robert M. Gibson, U.S. District Judge, Pa., Western.
F. P. Schoonmaker, U.S. District Judge, Pa., Western.
Chas. L. McKeehan, U.S. District Judge, Pa., Eastern.
Ernest F. Cochran, U.S. District Judge, South Carolina, Eastern.
J. W. Ross, U.S. District Judge, Tenn., Western.
Xenophon Hicks, U.S. District Judge, Tenn., Eastern and Middle.
John J. Gore, U.S. District Judge, Tenn., Middle.
Wm. H. Atwell, U.S. District Judge, Texas, Northern.
D. Lawrence Groner, U.S. District Judge, Va., Eastern.
J. Stanley Webster, U.S. District Judge, Washington, Eastern.
Wm. Eli Baker, U.S. District Judge, W. Va., Northern.
Geo. W. McClintic, U.S. District Judge, W. Va., Southern.
Claude Z. Luse, U.S. District Judge, Wis., Western.
Thos. Blake Kennedy, U.S. District Judge, Wyo.

Thos. M. Reed, District Judge, Div. 1, Alaska.
G. J. Lomen, District Judge, Div. 2, Alaska.
Elmer E. Ritchie, District Judge, Div. 3, Alaska.
Cecil H. Clegg, District Judge, Div. 4, Alaska.
John F. McGee, District Judge, Minnesota.
Wm. A. Cant, District Judge, Minnesota.
Chas. B. Davis, District Judge, Missouri, Eastern.
Albert L. Reeves, District Judge, Missouri, Western.
Chas. N. Pray, District Judge, Montana.
John D. Wallingford, District Judge, Canal Zone.
Emil C. Peters, Chief Justice, Supreme Court, Hawaii
Alex Lindsay, Jr., Associate Justice, Supreme Ct., Hawaii.
Antonio M. Perry, Chief Justice, Supreme Ct., Hawaii.
Frank Audrade, Circuit Ct., First Circuit, Hawaii.
Ray J. O'Brien, Circuit Ct., First Circuit, Hawaii.
James J. Banks, Circuit Ct., First Circuit, Hawaii.
John R. Desha, Circuit Ct., First Circuit, Hawaii.

Daniel H. Case, Cir. Ct., 2nd Cir. Hawaii.
Jas. Wesley Thompson, Cir. Ct., 3rd Cir. Hawaii.
Homer L. Ross, Cir. Ct., 4th Cir. Hawaii.
Wm. C. Achi, Jr., Cir. Ct., 5th Cir. Hawaii.
John T. De Bolt, U.S. District Judge, Hawaii.
Wm. Rawlins, U.S. District Judge, Hawaii.
Emilio del Toro, Chief Justice, Supreme Ct., Porto Rico.
Arthur F. Odlin, U.S. District Judge, Porto Rico.

Adolph A. Hoehling, Associate Justice, Supreme Ct., D.C.
Charles V. Meehan, Judge of the Municipal Ct., D.C.
Robert H. Terrell, Judge of Municipal Ct., D.C.
George C. Aukam, Judge of Municipal Ct., D.C.
Mary O'Toole, Judge of Municipal Ct., D.C.
Gus. A. Schuldt, Judge of Police Court, D.C.
Francis A. Winslow, District Judge, N.Y. Southern.
Henry W. Goddard, District Judge, N.Y. Southern.
William Bondy, District Judge, N.Y. Southern.
Marcus B. Campbell, District Judge, N.Y. Eastern.
Robert A. Inch, District Judge, N.Y. Eastern.
Franklin E. Kenamer, District Judge, N. Okla.